# Promoting
# Literacy
# Development

# 50 Research-Based Strategies for K–8 Learners

# Promoting Literacy Development

Patricia A. Antonacci
Catherine M. O'Callaghan
*Iona College*

Los Angeles | London | New Delhi
Singapore | Washington DC

Los Angeles | London | New Delhi
Singapore | Washington DC

FOR INFORMATION:

SAGE Publications, Inc.
2455 Teller Road
Thousand Oaks, California 91320
E-mail: order@sagepub.com

SAGE Publications Ltd.
1 Oliver's Yard
55 City Road
London EC1Y 1SP
United Kingdom

SAGE Publications India Pvt. Ltd.
B 1/I 1 Mohan Cooperative Industrial Area
Mathura Road, New Delhi 110 044
India

SAGE Publications Asia-Pacific Pte. Ltd.
33 Pekin Street #02-01
Far East Square
Singapore 048763

Executive Editor:  Diane McDaniel
Editorial Assistant:  Theresa Accomazzo
Production Editor:  Brittany Bauhaus
Permissions Editor:  Adele Hutchinson
Copy Editor:  Megan Speer
Typesetter:  C&M Digitals (P) Ltd.
Proofreader:  Laura Webb
Indexer:  Rick Hurd
Cover Designer:  Bryan Fishman
Marketing Manager:  Katharine Winter

*Cover photos credits:*
Main image: ©iStockphoto.com/bonniej
Side image #1: Comstock/Comstock Images/Thinkstock
Side image #2: Jupiterimages/Goodshoot/Thinkstock
Side image #3: ©iStockphoto.com/aldomurilloaldomurillo
Side image #4: Jupiterimages/Goodshoot/Thinkstock

Printed in the United States of America

Library of Congress Cataloging-in-Publication Data

Antonacci, Patricia.

Promoting literacy development : 50 research-based strategies for K–8 learners / Patricia A. Antonacci, Catherine M. O'Callaghan.

p. cm.
Includes bibliographical references and index.

ISBN 978-1-4129-8708-0 (pbk.)

1. Language arts (Elementary) 2. Language arts (Middle school) I. O'Callaghan, Catherine M. II. Title.

LB1576.A58 2012
372.6—dc22
2010050949

This book is printed on acid-free paper.

11 12 13 14 15 10 9 8 7 6 5 4 3 2 1

# Contents

## Section VI. Essential Strategies for Teaching Comprehension of Informational Text    149

## 26   Visualize It!    154

## 27   Discussion Circles    158

## 28   Scaffolding Academic Reading    163

# Preface

## THE PURPOSE OF OUR BOOK

Our purpose for writing this book is to assist teachers in developing literacy skills in young students. When planning and designing *Promoting Literacy Development: 50 Research-Based Strategies for K–8 Learners,* we were quite optimistic about being able to develop an easy-to-use handbook of instructional strategies for classroom teachers. Our goal directed us to select a set of research-based literacy strategies that address the national standards in the English language arts and to organize them in an easy-to-use method for the busy teacher.

For this purpose, we have consulted research on teaching literacy as well as the statements made by policymakers that inform the English language arts curriculum to identify those core areas in literacy development required for teaching young readers and writers. Thus, 50 research-based strategies are organized around the following 10 areas for teaching and learning literacy:

I. Phonemic Awareness

II. Phonics

III. Reading Fluency

IV. Vocabulary

V. Story Comprehension

VI. Comprehension of Informational Text

VII. Questioning for Understanding

VIII. Discussion for Understanding

IX. Narrative Writing

X. Writing Across the Curriculum

The writing of this text was encouraged by the classroom teachers' need for an easy-to-use handbook that contains best strategies for teaching literacy. Therefore, we purposefully designed a handbook of 50 research-based instructional strategies based on 10 critical areas of literacy development for planning instruction. The 50 instructional strategies are clearly written and presented in a step-by-step method. Further, understanding that not all students learn at the same rate or in the same way, we have included suggestions for differentiating instruction for English language learners as well as for students with special needs.

## AUDIENCE

*Promoting Literacy Development: 50 Research-Based Strategies for K–8 Learners* may be used by pre-service teachers as a supplementary handbook to their core literacy textbook, or it may serve as a valuable resource for the in-service teachers engaged in professional development workshops. In any case, classroom teachers in kindergarten through grade 8 will consider it a user-friendly resource for planning instruction for the English language arts as well as for reading and writing across the curriculum. Reading teachers will find this collection of strategies extremely functional for teaching students who receive support services for literacy instruction. Literacy coaches and instructional leaders in elementary and middle school may employ this text as a valuable source for designing professional development for classroom teachers.

## ORGANIZATIONAL FEATURES OF THE TEXT

Our intention in writing *Promoting Literacy Development: 50 Research-Based Strategies for K–8 Learners* was to fashion a well-organized handbook for busy classroom teachers. Therefore, the organization of the handbook was designed to include instructional strategies that are concise but clearly written, to offer a brief but useful summary of background knowledge, and to utilize the critical areas of literacy development for planning and organizing literacy instruction.

*Organizing literacy instruction:* We have identified 10 areas for teaching literacy development. Each of the 10 areas is organized around a section that provides a comprehensive discussion of the research and practice related to that literacy area, followed by a strategy for assessing the area and a guide for using Response to Intervention for the area. Further, within each section, there are 5 research-based strategies that are aligned with the core area of literacy instruction. Thus, a total of 50 instructional strategies are organized around these 10 core areas that have been identified by best practice and supported by research reviewed by the National Reading Panel (National Institute of Child Health and Human Development, 2000) and the No Child Left Behind Act of 2001.

*Fifty instructional strategies:* Five research-based literacy instructional strategies are organized around 10 critical areas targeted for developing proficient readers and writers in kindergarten through grade 8.

*Step-by-step procedure:* To ensure a well-organized approach to the implementation of each strategy, a step-by-step procedure is provided. The teachers follow a planned and structured approach to teaching from the start to its finish, through clear and concise steps.

*Format of instructional strategies:* For each instructional strategy, a full description is provided that follows the same format in each of the 50 strategies. Included in each instructional strategy are the following: (a) a brief overview of the strategy, (b) suggestions for when to use the strategy within the literacy block, (c) tips on modifying the strategy for use with different grade levels, (d) a step-by-step procedure for implementing the strategy, (e) an application of the strategy using children's literature for a specific grade level, (f) an approach to differentiating the strategy for teaching English language learners, (g) an approach to differentiating the strategy for teaching students with special needs, and (h) a list of references.

## PEDAGOGICAL FEATURES OF THE TEXT

*Ten core areas for literacy instruction:* To support literacy instruction, we have carefully selected the critical elements for effective classroom literacy instruction. Ten core areas for literacy development selected for the handbook have received substantial support from research and professional associations, as well as from "best practices" identified by classroom teachers, literacy coaches, and instructional leaders. Each of the 10 core areas receives an ample discussion within the appropriate section of the handbook.

*Research-based literacy strategies:* Selected for instruction are core areas for literacy development and strategies that have received support from the research. A discussion of the theory and research related to the core literacy area and related strategies are presented within each section of the handbook. Additionally, for each strategy a brief overview is provided that includes a rationale for using the selected strategy and ensures an effective instructional approach for that literacy area.

*Using the strategy:* When is the strategy to be used? Can it be modified for different grade levels? Suggestions are made for using the strategy within the literacy block. For example, some strategies are more effective before, during, or after engaging students in reading or writing, while others work well throughout the literacy event. Further, tips are offered for modifying the instructional strategy for different grade levels.

*Clear descriptions of each instructional strategy*: Included within the text are clear and well-developed descriptions of the 50 instructional strategies. Each strategy contains a brief summary of background information with information on when to use the strategy and how to modify the instruction for different grade levels. Teachers will benefit from the step-by-step description of implementing the strategy by receiving appropriate information on what they and the students are required to do. Each step is concise and easy to follow. To further support the description of the procedure, there is an application of the strategy for classroom use and suggestions for modifying instruction for English language learners and students with special needs.

*Strategy applications with children's literature:* To demonstrate how to implement each strategy, an application using outstanding children's literature with a range of grade levels across the 50 strategies is provided.

*Graphics:* Throughout the text, many graphics are used to provide visuals for teachers and students. For example, teachers are offered some figures that clarify literacy concepts that are discussed, strategies for classroom-based assessments provide rubrics and tables to assist the teacher in observing and scoring students' literacy performances, and many strategies include graphic organizers to support student learning.

*Integration of technology:* Suggestions are made for the appropriate use of technology with selected instructional strategies.

*Differentiating instruction for English language learners:* There is a wide range of diversity among students at all grade levels. Among students from diverse backgrounds are English language learners. The International Reading Association and other professional organizations have made clear policy statements regarding appropriate reading instruction for children who are learning English. For each instructional strategy, suggestions for differentiating teaching for English language learners are provided.

*Differentiating instruction for students with special needs:* Students with special needs frequently are disabled readers and writers. Teachers need to modify the literacy strategies when working with students with special learning needs. Each of the 50 instructional strategies provides one or more ways to use the strategy with students who are struggling readers and writers.

*Strategies for assessing literacy performances:* For each of the 10 critical areas of literacy development, an assessment strategy is provided. Classroom-based assessments are offered for each of the 10 literacy areas that may be used by the teacher to determine students' performances in these areas.

*Guides for using Response to Intervention (RTI):* Teachers are becoming more responsive to those students who need help in specific literacy areas. For each of the 10 literacy areas, a guide for using RTI is provided.

*Professional resources:* For each of the 10 critical areas for teaching literacy, professional resources are provided. These include selected books and handbooks of additional strategies in those particular areas for literacy development.

## REFERENCES

National Institute of Child Health and Human Development. (2000). *Report of the National Reading Panel. Teaching children to read: An evidence-based assessment of the scientific research literature on reading and its implications for reading instruction* (NIH Publication No. 00-4769). Washington, DC: U.S. Government Printing Office.

# Acknowledgments

It is with deep appreciation that we express our sincere thanks to the competent team at Sage Publications. Our special thanks to Diane McDaniel, acquisitions editor, who once again has shown outstanding leadership by providing insightful suggestions, ongoing support, and perceptive feedback and, with her gentle encouragement, has motivated and sustained us throughout the project. Thank you, Diane! We offer sincere gratitude to our editorial assistants—Ashley Conlin, who began the process, and Theresa Accomazzo, who completed it—for providing us with immediate answers to all our questions and facilitating the process of this publication. To the team of editors at Sage—Brittany Bauhaus, production editor; Adele Hutchinson, permissions editor; and Megan Speer, copy editor—who have taught us so much about writing and the writing process, we thank you.

The valuable comments and practical suggestions offered by our reviewers were indeed useful during our revision process. Our special thanks to

Linda K. Allen, *Texas Tech University*

Jennifer P. Bailey, *University of West Florida*

Carolyn Backus, *Marietta College*

Kathy H. Barclay, *Western Illinois University*

Esther Berkowitz, *St. Joseph's College*

Deborah Farrer, *California University of Pennsylvania*

Irene Lang Kleiman, *Miami University*

Mary Kay Moskal, *St. Mary's College of California*

Tammy Schimmel, *University of Tampa*

Beth Walizer, *Fort Hays State University*

To our own students, our in-service teachers who have used the literacy strategies in their classrooms, and our pre-service teachers who tried them out in their fieldwork and have provided wonderful feedback, we continue to be indebted. Finally, to you, our readers, who will use the information, techniques, and strategies within your classrooms, we offer a special *thank you*.

# Setting Standards in the English Language Arts

Although we present these standards as a list, we want to emphasize that they are not distinct and separable; they are, in fact, interrelated and should be considered as a whole.

## IRA/NCTE STANDARDS FOR THE ENGLISH LANGUAGE ARTS

1. Students read a wide range of print and nonprint texts to build an understanding of texts, of themselves, and of the cultures of the United States and the world; to acquire new information; to respond to the needs and demands of society and the workplace; and for personal fulfillment. Among these texts are fiction and nonfiction, classic, and contemporary works.

2. Students read a wide range of literature from many periods in many genres to build an understanding of the many dimensions (e.g., philosophical, ethical, aesthetic) of human experience.

3. Students apply a wide range of strategies to comprehend, interpret, evaluate, and appreciate texts. They draw on their prior experience, their interactions with other readers and writers, their knowledge of word meaning and of other texts, their word identification strategies, and their understanding of textual features (e.g., sound-letter correspondence, sentence structure, context, graphics).

4. Students adjust their use of spoken, written, and visual language (e.g., conventions, style, vocabulary) to communicate effectively with a variety of audiences and for different purposes.

5. Students employ a wide range of strategies as they write and use different writing process elements appropriately to communicate with different audiences for a variety of purposes.

6. Students apply knowledge of language structure, language conventions (e.g., spelling and punctuation), media techniques, figurative language, and genre to create, critique, and discuss print and nonprint texts.

7. Students conduct research on issues and interests by generating ideas and questions, and by posing problems. They gather, evaluate, and synthesize data from

a variety of sources (e.g., print and nonprint texts, artifacts, people) to communicate their discoveries in ways that suit their purpose and audience.

8. Students use a variety of technological and informational resources (e.g., libraries, databases, computer networks, video) to gather and synthesize information and to create and communicate knowledge.

9. Students develop an understanding of and respect for diversity in language use, patterns, and dialects across cultures, ethnic groups, geographic regions, and social roles.

10. Students whose first language is not English make use of their first language to develop competency in the English language arts and to develop understanding of content across the curriculum.

11. Students participate as knowledgeable, reflective, creative, and critical members of a variety of literacy communities.

12. Students use spoken, written, and visual language to accomplish their own purposes (e.g., for learning, enjoyment, persuasion, and the exchange of information).

---

# Introduction

For teachers in primary, elementary, and middle schools, teaching children to read and write is a dominant concern. Their commitment to students' literacy is visible throughout the schools in the children's artifacts hanging on the walls, the teachers' posters, classroom libraries, and literacy instruction taking place in classrooms throughout the day.

A teacher's dedication to students' achievement in literacy instruction is built on a foundation of teaching and learning. We wish to present a handbook that assists in-service teachers by extending their professional knowledge base and supports pre-service teachers as they begin to create a foundation for teaching reading and writing to young children. Within the introduction, we have addressed the significant constituents that are regarded by the professional community for becoming effective teachers of literacy. These are the factors used in designing *Promoting Literacy Development: 50 Research-Based Strategies for K–8 Learners*.

*Research-based instruction:* Why do effective teachers use research-based instruction? Teaching approaches that are informed by research demonstrate a positive impact on student learning. Selecting such research-based instructional strategies is, therefore, likely to lead to greater gains in student achievement than selecting those with little or no support from scientific studies. We have provided the background from research for each of the 10 literacy areas and a summary of research to support the effectiveness for each of the 50 instructional strategies presented. Just as we are aware of the importance of selecting the appropriate instructional approaches, *what* we teach children is just as important. Standards-based instruction provides the basis for *what* we teach young children as they journey to become proficient readers and writers.

*Standards-based instruction:* National and state standards, developed by policy groups and informed by research, tell us what students need to know. Teachers frequently use standards as a way to measure student performance by determining the levels at which students have met the standard for a specific skill or concept in reading or writing. Additionally, such student performances or outcomes based on standards are used by many to determine their own teaching effectiveness. Each of the instructional strategies addresses the national standards jointly developed for the English language arts by the International Reading Association and the National Council for the Teachers of English.

*Differentiated instruction:* Our classrooms are diverse with a growing student population of English language learners as well as students with special learning needs. Many English language learners' reading levels fall below those of students whose first language is English. Students with special learning needs most frequently have difficulty learning to read and write. The No Child Left Behind Act of 2001 targets the literacy achievement of all students, especially those who are struggling to read, and teachers are charged with closing the achievement gap for all student populations. The goal stipulates that 100% of the nation's students reach the level of proficiency in reading and the language arts, with all teachers sharing in this responsibility. How does the classroom teacher assist diverse students achieving a level of proficiency in reading and the language arts? Using research-based instructional strategies that work for all students but are modified to meet the needs of English language learners and students with special needs will help in closing this widening achievement gap. Thus, differentiating instruction for English language learners as well as students with special needs is no longer considered an option. Rather, it is a requirement within all classrooms where teachers are committed to producing higher literacy levels for all students.

*Classroom-based assessment:* When teachers are engaged in classroom-based assessment to determine their students' literacy performances, the results may become more valuable in assisting children in becoming better readers and writers. "Assessing children's literate learning requires attending not only to what they know and do but also at least as much to the context in which they know and do" (Johnston & Costello, 2010, p. 65). Classroom assessment is aligned with what students do within the classroom in becoming literate; it allows for authentic learning, occurring within a context that is familiar to the teacher as well as the student. The teacher may reflect on teaching and learning, using the results to ask, "What approach or strategy did I use that worked or did not for each of the students?" Further, the teacher is more apt to use the assessment results of students' performances in literacy to improve their learning. The teacher focuses on those students' performances that did not reach the target level and applies an appropriate intervention strategy.

*Response to Intervention (RTI):* RTI is a new approach to assessment and instruction of students at risk (Johnston, 2010). Prior to the 2004 reauthorization of the Individuals with Disabilities Education Act, schools identified students with learning disabilities based on the discrepancy approach, which labeled learners when their IQs did not match achievement levels (Scanlon & Sweeney, 2010). As Marie Clay noted in 1987, often students labeled as "learning disabled" were struggling due to the inadequacies of their instruction rather than a cognitive deficit. In RTI, the assumption is that the curriculum needs to be adjusted to meet students' needs rather than the belief that something is wrong with the learner.

The process of RTI begins with universal screening to compare students' performance with established literacy benchmarks (Mesmer & Mesmer, 2010). Working collaboratively, teachers and literacy specialists select students for scientifically based interventions. The most common RTI model uses three tiers of intervention with careful progress monitoring across all interventions (Fuchs & Fuchs, 2006; Johnston, 2010). Tier I occurs at the classroom level with increased instructional support provided by the classroom teacher in small reading groups. Students who still do not meet the benchmarks after receiving Tier I intervention are selected for further support. Tier II intervention is usually provided by a teacher with specialized knowledge in systematic, explicit instructional support with small reading groups. Students at risk should continue to receive Tier I support while they are targeted for Tier II intervention (Dorn & Henderson, 2010). If data analysis determines that a few Tier II students are showing limited or no growth, they are targeted for more intensive individual instruction in Tier III with a skilled instructor. After such intensive, targeted support, Tier III students who continue to demonstrate little or no growth in literacy are considered for classification as learning disabled (Scanlon & Sweeney, 2010).

The key to successful RTI programs is the quality of instruction provided by the teacher (Scanlon, Anderson, & Sweeney, 2010). Unfortunately, many school districts are buying scripted intervention programs when dynamic assessment and responsive instruction can be provided only by a trained teacher (Dorn & Henderson, 2010). A knowledgeable teacher understands that responsive teaching entails "on-the-spot" decision making regarding students' needs and explicit, systematic instructional support (Scanlon, Anderson, & Sweeney, 2010). This text adheres to the model of dynamic assessment and responsive teaching by providing instructors with rubrics at the end of each section that may be used for progress monitoring. After careful data analysis, teachers may choose to use the recommended RTI strategy in each section for further intervention; however, it should be noted that all interventions should be adapted to meet the specific needs of striving readers.

## REFERENCES

Clay, M. (1987). Learning to be learning disabled. *New Zealand Journal of Educational Studies, 22,* 155–173.

Dorn, L., & Henderson, S. (2010). A comprehensive assessment system as a Response to Intervention process. In P. Johnston (Ed.), *RTI in literacy: Responsive and comprehensive* (pp. 1–6). Newark, DE: International Reading Association.

Fuchs, D., & Fuchs, L. (2006). Introduction to Response to Intervention: What, why, and how valid is it? *Reading Research Quarterly, 41,* 94–99.

Johnston, P. (2010). A framework for Response to Intervention (RTI) in literacy. In P. Johnston (Ed.), *RTI in literacy: Responsive and comprehensive* (pp. 1–6). Newark, DE: International Reading Association.

Johnston, P., & Costello, P. (2010). Principles of literacy assessment. In M. Cappello & B. Moss (Eds.), *Contemporary readings in literacy education* (pp. 57–68). Thousand Oaks, CA: Sage.

Mesmer, E., & Mesmer, H. (2010). Response to Intervention: What teachers of reading need to know. *The Reading Teacher, 62,* 280–290.

Scanlon, D., Anderson, K., & Sweeney, J. (2010). *Early intervention for reading difficulties: The interactive strategies approach.* New York: Guilford.

Scanlon, D., & Sweeney, J. (2010). Response to Intervention: An overview: New hope for struggling learners. In P. Johnston (Ed.), *RTI in literacy: Responsive and comprehensive* (pp. 13–23). Newark, DE: International Reading Association.

# SECTION I

# Essential Strategies for Teaching Phonemic Awareness

**W**hat is phonemic awareness and how does it impact reading? Many early childhood and primary grade teachers wrestle with these questions on a daily basis. This section presents the research on phonemic awareness and best practices for training students to identify sounds.

## A BRIEF OVERVIEW OF PHONEMIC AWARENESS

*Phonemic awareness* is the ability to focus on and manipulate phonemes in the *spoken* word (Ehri, Nunes, Willows, & Schuster, 2001). Phonemes are the smallest units in the spoken language, with English containing approximately 41 phonemes (Ehri & Nunes, 2002). Young students often have difficulties letting go of the letters and just concentrating on the sounds in the spoken word. Yet research indicates that phonemic awareness and letter knowledge are key predictors to students' success in learning to read (National Reading Panel, 2000). In fact, predictive studies show that when children enter kindergarten with the ability to manipulate phonemes and identify letters, they progress at a faster pace in learning to read (Ehri & Roberts, 2006).

An ongoing discussion in the field of literacy is whether phonemic awareness is a conceptual understanding about language or whether it is a skill. According to Phillips and Torgesen (2006), it is both an understanding and a skill. For example, in order to identify the phonemes in [cat], students must understand that there are sounds at the beginning, middle, and end that can be manipulated. Students must also be able to complete phonemic awareness tasks such as the following:

- Phoneme *isolation:* Isolate phonemes; for example, "Tell me the first sound in *cat.*"
- Phoneme *identity:* Recognize common sounds in different words; for example, "Tell me the same sound in *rug, rat,* and *roll.*"

1

- Phoneme *categorization:* Identify the word with the odd sound in a sequence; for example, "Which word does not belong in *sat, sag, rug?*"

- Phoneme *blending:* Combine separate sounds to form a word; for example, [b-a-t] for *bat.*

- Phoneme *segmentation:* Break out the word into separate sounds; for example, "What are the sounds in *bag?*" (Ehri et al., 2001)

There is also a developmental progression for young children in tackling these phonemic awareness tasks. Research indicates that identifying beginning and ending sounds is much easier than recognizing medial phonemes (Inverizzi, 2003). This finding points to the need for explicit, systematic instruction in phonemic awareness that is integrated within a literacy program (National Reading Panel, 2000).

## INSTRUCTION IN PHONEMIC AWARENESS

Many students enter preschool or kindergarten having already obtained knowledge of letters and sounds through language play or exposure. However, for those who need these concepts and skills, explicit, systematic instruction in phonemic awareness will be necessary (Phillips & Torgesen, 2006). It is critical to know that older striving readers and English language learners also benefit from phonemic awareness training. Research shows that when English language learners are provided explicit phonemic awareness instruction, they are able to catch up with native speakers' progress on word identification and spelling (Geva & Siegel, 2000).

The key to success is data-driven instruction that uses assessment to determine students' level of phonological awareness. Phonological awareness is the broader construct for knowing speech sounds, rhyming, and alliteration and includes phonemic awareness (Inverizzi, 2003). When teachers use data to inform instruction, targeted sessions are implemented on specific needs such as phoneme blending or categorization. It is also important to note that data may determine that some students do not require instruction in phonemic awareness as they already possess the concept and skill. According to the National Reading Panel (2000), effective phonemic awareness instruction occurs in small groups and is combined with letter identification to aid transfer of skills to reading. This chapter presents several strategies that use guidelines formed from research on best practice to instruct students in identifying and manipulating sounds.

## GUIDELINES FOR TEACHING PHONEMIC AWARENESS

During the past several years, a body of research indicates that early, systematic, explicit phonemic awareness instruction can successfully jump-start emergent and early readers' reading performance (McGee & Ukrainetz, 2009). The following guidelines provide the framework for phonemic awareness instruction:

1. Analysis of phonemic awareness assessment data should drive instruction, as only a small percentage of students need explicit instruction (Ehri & Roberts, 2006).

2. Phonemic awareness instruction should be a positive, enriching experience that allows students to engage in language play (Yopp, 1992).

3. Effective phonemic awareness instruction provides for individual differences in abilities and uses leveled scaffolding to facilitate growth (McGee & Ukrainetz, 2009).

4. Developmentally appropriate phonemic awareness instruction uses chants, poetry, songs, and rhymes to engage students' curiosity about language and to develop metalinguistic awareness (Yopp & Yopp, 2000).

5. Effective phonemic awareness instruction explicitly labels sounds and demonstrates the process of blending-segmenting of sounds (Ehri et al., 2001).

## A Strategy for Assessing Phonemic Awareness

Research indicates that phonemic awareness tasks are the best predictors of students' success with reading acquisition (Yopp, 1995). Due to its critical nature, it is imperative that teachers assess students' phonemic awareness skills in order to differentiate instruction or to provide intervention if necessary (Ehri et al., 2001). The purpose of assessing phonemic awareness may be to screen for targeted instruction or to conduct progress monitoring. The Phonemic Awareness Checklist shown in Figure I.1 may be used for either formative or summative assessment. However, teachers need to analyze and reflect on the data to denote patterns among students. For example, if students are struggling with a particular subskill, such as blending and segmenting phonemes, teachers may need to reteach the skill before selecting students for small-group instruction.

## A Guide for Using Response to Intervention for Phonemic Awareness

After analyzing the data from the Phonemic Awareness Checklist (Figure I.1), students at the developing or beginning levels may be selected for intervention. The instructor groups students with similar needs, such as blending or segmenting phonemes, and uses the Sound Sorts activity to target specific sounds. Instructors may choose to begin with picture sorts if students are in the beginning stage. Learners that were evaluated as "developing" may begin with sound sorts without picture clues. In this section, "Essential Strategies for Teaching Phonemic Awareness," five instructional strategies are presented to facilitate phonological awareness. The strategies, which are based on data analysis of student needs, are presented as guides for teachers to use.

## Professional Resources

Adams, M., Foorman, B., Lundgerg, I., & Beeler, T. (1997). *Phonemic awareness in young children: A classroom curriculum.* Baltimore, MD: Brookes.

Blevins, W. (1999). *Phonemic awareness activities for early reading success.* New York: Scholastic.

Florida Center for Reading Research. (2009). *Florida Center for Reading Research.* Retrieved from http://www.fcrr.org

Justice, L., & Sofka, A. (2010). *Engaging children with print: Building early skills through read-alouds.* New York: Guilford.

Scott, V. (2009). *Phonemic awareness: Ready-to-use lessons, activities, and games.* Thousand Oaks, CA: Corwin.

| Figure I.1 | | | |
|---|---|---|---|

### PHONEMIC AWARENESS CHECKLIST

**Directions:** Observe the student perform a phonemic awareness task focused on the appropriate sub-component. Based on observational data from a minimum of three sessions, evaluate the student's performance as *Beginning, Developing,* or *Proficient.*

| PA Skill | Beginning | Developing | Proficient |
|---|---|---|---|
| Recognizing Rhymes | Student *rarely* identifies words as rhyming. (1 point) | Student *sometimes* identifies words as rhyming. (2 points) | Student *always* identifies words as rhyming. (3 points) |
| Generating Rhymes | Student *rarely* generates rhyming words. (1 point) | Student *sometimes* generates rhyming words. (2 points) | Student *always* generates rhyming words (3 points) |
| Identifying Phonemes | Student *rarely* identifies targeted phoneme. (1 point) | Student *sometimes* identifies targeted phoneme. (2 points) | Student *always* identifies targeted phoneme. (3 points) |
| Manipulating Phonemes | Student *rarely* manipulates phonemes in initial/media/final position. (1 point) | Student *sometimes* manipulates phonemes in initial/media/final position. (2 points) | Student *always* manipulates phonemes in initial/media/final position. (3 points) |
| Blending Phonemes | Student *rarely* blends segmented sounds to make whole word. (1 point) | Student *sometimes* blends segmented sounds to make whole word. (2 points) | Student *always* blends segmented sounds to make whole word. (3 points) |
| Segmenting Phonemes | Student *rarely* segments words into individual phonemes. (1 point) | Student *sometimes* segments words into individual phonemes. (2 points) | Student *always* segments words into individual phonemes. (3 points) |

*Proficient = 18–13 points*

*Developing = 12–7 points*

*Beginning = 6–1 points*

## REFERENCES

Ehri, L., & Nunes, S. (2002). The role of phonemic awareness in learning to read. In A. E. Farstrup & S. J. Samuels (Eds.), *What research has to say about reading instruction* (pp. 110–140). Newark, DE: International Reading Association.

Ehri, L., Nunes, S., Willows, D., & Schuster, B. (2001). Phonemic awareness instruction helps children learn to read: Evidence from the National Reading Panel's meta-analysis. *Reading Research Quarterly, 36,* 250–287.

Ehri, L., & Roberts, T. (2006). The roots of learning to read and write: Acquisition of letters and phonemic awareness. In D. Dickinson & S. Neuman (Eds.), *Handbook of early literacy research* (Vol. 2, pp. 113–130). New York: Guilford.

Geva, E., & Siegel, L. (2000). Orthographic cognitive factors in the concurrent development of basic reading skills in two languages. *Reading & Writing: An Interdisciplinary Journal, 12,* 1–30.

Inverizzi, M. (2003). Concepts, sounds, and the ABCs: A diet for the very young reader. In D. Barone & L. M. Morrow (Eds.), *Literacy and young children: Research-based practices* (pp. 140–156). New York: Guilford.

McGee, L., & Ukrainetz, T. (2009). Using scaffolding to teach phonemic awareness in preschool and kindergarten. *The Reading Teacher, 62,* 599–603.

National Reading Panel. (2000). *Teaching children to read.* Washington, DC: National Institute of Health and Human Development.

Phillips, B., & Torgesen, J. (2006). Phonemic awareness and reading: Beyond the growth of initial reading accuracy. *Handbook of early literacy research* (Vol. 2, pp. 101–113). New York: Guilford.

Yopp, H. K. (1992). Developing phonemic awareness in young children. *The Reading Teacher, 45,* 696–703.

Yopp, H. K. (1995). A test for assessing phonemic awareness in young children. *The Reading Teacher, 49,* 20–30.

Yopp, H. K., & Yopp, R. H. (2000). Supporting phonemic awareness development in the classroom. *The Reading Teacher, 54,* 130–143.

# Strategy

# 1

# Rhyme Generation

## SPEAKING BRIEFLY: AN OVERVIEW OF THE LITERACY STRATEGY

*Rhyme Generation* is an instructional strategy that develops explicit phonemic awareness skills. During this activity, students are engaged in isolating, blending, and manipulating sounds on several levels. Students first identify the rhyme within an authentic context, such as a poem or song. Playing with language enables students to practice making words through rhyme generation.

The primary purpose for implementing the rhyme generation activity is to encourage students to develop critical phonemic awareness skills such as manipulation of the onset and rime. The onset is the beginning sound/letter, such as /b/ in **b**at. The rime is the stem of the word, such as [**at**] in b**at**. Identification of rhymes is a foundational phonemic awareness skill that many students pick up through language play (Ehri & Roberts, 2006). Rhyme generation typically occurs during the morning message or shared reading time. However, it can be implemented during intervention sessions with students of varying ages who need additional instruction in phonemic awareness.

*Source:* International Reading Association and National Council of Teachers of English (1996).

> ### IRA/NCTE Standards for English Language Arts
>
> 2. Students read a wide range of literature from many periods in many genres to build an understanding of the many dimensions (e.g., philosophical, ethical, aesthetic) of human experience.
>
> 6. Students apply knowledge of language structure, language conventions (e.g., spelling and punctuation), media techniques, figurative language, and genre to create, critique, and discuss print and nonprint texts.

## USING RHYME GENERATION

*When to use the strategy:* Rhyme generation may be used during any segment of the literacy block, depending on student needs. For example, teachers may choose to demonstrate the activity during morning message and then coach students in the phonemic awareness skill during guided reading. Students may also engage in the activity during literacy center time or as an intervention task.

*Strategy modifications for grade levels:* The strategy may be modified for older students by using multisyllabic word families.

## IMPLEMENTING THE RHYME GENERATION STRATEGY: STEP BY STEP

1.  **Introduce rhyme generation to students.** Teachers present the concept of "rhyme" and ask students to define it and give examples.

2.  **Present rhymes in context.** Teachers conduct a shared reading of a poem or song and ask students to identify the rhymes.

3.  **Demonstrate how to manipulate onset and rime.** Teachers use the identified rhymes to color-code the onset and rime on chart paper. Using a word ladder graphic, teachers demonstrate how to generate new rimes from previous words. They list initial consonants and demonstrate how to manipulate the onset to create a new rhyme. For example, the word [**fat**] may be changed to [**sat**] by selecting a new onset.

4.  **Record rhymes generated from original poem or song.** Teachers display selected sentences from the song or poem used to introduce the activity on sentence strips. Students apply the skill by creating their own sentence that generates a new rhyme for the context.

5.  **Facilitate students' application of rhyme generation.** Teachers develop students' skill in manipulating onsets and rimes by encouraging rhyme generation with their names. During literacy stations or intervention, students use their own names to generate rhymes on a word ladder. After exhausting the list for their own names, they may create a new list of rhymes with classmates' names.

## APPLYING THE RHYME GENERATION STRATEGY: KINDERGARTEN LESSON ON RHYME GENERATION

The kindergarten teacher shows students a picture of Buckingham Palace in London and asks students if they know what it is and who lives there. After discussing the picture, the teacher presents the poem "Buckingham Palace" (Milne, 2004) on chart paper and asks students to define what makes a poem special. After introducing the concept of rhymes, the teacher conducts a read-aloud of the poem. After the read-aloud, the teacher invites students to identify the rhymes by highlighting them with colored markers. Using the word ladder graphic organizer shown in Figure 1.1, the teacher directs students to do the following:

*   Make a new word by changing the initial sounds in [came/same].

*   Use the rhymes to generate more words.

*   Create a new sentence for the poem using the generated rhymes.

After they have completed their sentences, students read their new rhyming sentences. The teacher records their generated rhymes on chart paper for students to reread during literacy station time.

| Figure 1.1 | Rhyming Words Ladder |

| RHYMING WORDS LADDER ||
|---|---|
| came | bike |
| | |
| | |
| | |
| | |
| | |

*Source:* International Reading Association and National Council of Teachers of English (1996).

### IRA/NCTE Standards for English Language Arts

10. Students whose first language is not English make use of their first language to develop competency in the English language arts and to develop understanding of content across the curriculum.

## DIFFERENTIATING INSTRUCTION FOR ENGLISH LANGUAGE LEARNERS

Research indicates that English language learners benefit from explicit phonemic awareness training (Geva & Siegel, 2000). In order to provide explicit instruction, teachers may need to scaffold English language learners' understanding of rhyme. English language learners might need a picture sort activity to grasp the concept of "rhyme" before the Rhyme Generation lesson. In this activity, teachers guide students in sorting pictures into rhyming categories such as "*box* with *fox*." Teachers may also use a picture sort activity to gather additional data on students' phonemic awareness skills and their grasp of oral vocabulary.

## DIFFERENTIATING INSTRUCTION FOR STUDENTS WITH SPECIAL NEEDS

Students with special needs may need additional support in manipulating the onset and rime to generate new words. One method for differentiating this activity is to use multisensory materials to enable them to acquire this phonemic awareness skill. Using magnetic letters with raised bumps helps students with special needs create new rhymes from a poem or song. The magnetic letters enable them to visualize the new words they are creating as they transfer skills to reading.

## References

Ehri, L., & Roberts, T. (2006). The roots of learning to read and write: Acquisition of letters and phonemic awareness. In D. Dickinson & S. Neuman (Eds.), *Handbook of early literacy research* (Vol. 2, pp. 113–130). New York: Guilford.

Geva, E., & Siegel, L. (2000). Orthographic cognitive factors in the concurrent development of basic reading skills in two languages. *Reading & Writing: An Interdisciplinary Journal, 12,* 1–30.

International Reading Association and National Council of Teachers of English. (1996). *Standards for the English language arts.* Newark, DE: International Reading Association and Urbana, IL: National Council of Teachers of English.

## Children's Literature Cited

Milne, A. A. (2004). *The complete poems for Christopher Robin.* London: Folio Society.

# Strategy
# 2
# Multisensory Mapping

## SPEAKING BRIEFLY: AN OVERVIEW OF THE LITERACY STRATEGY

*Multisensory Mapping* uses all modalities (auditory, visual, kinesthetic-tactile) to facilitate retention and processing of sounds. Research confirms that the most common barrier to acquisition of emergent reading skills is the inability to process phonologically (Snow, Burns, & Griffin, 1998). Multisensory techniques such as tracing, illustrating, and chanting of sounds enable young learners to process sounds in multiple ways.

As students play and manipulate sounds through the senses, they begin to grasp the alphabetic principle. Research indicates that emergent and striving readers experience rapid growth in performance when they receive intensive, explicit training in phonemic awareness (Torgesen & Bryant, 1993). Multisensory Mapping may be used as an intervention strategy for dyslexic or striving readers. It should be implemented as a supplementary activity to provide students with multiple opportunities to process sounds, rather than as an introduction to phonemic awareness.

*Source:* International Reading Association and National Council of Teachers of English (1996).

---

### IRA/NCTE Standards for English Language Arts

1. Students apply knowledge of language structure, language conventions (e.g., spelling and punctuation), media techniques, figurative language, and genre to create, critique, and discuss print and nonprint texts.

11. Students participate as knowledgeable, reflective, creative, and critical members of a variety of literacy communities.

---

## USING MULTISENSORY MAPPING

*When to use the strategy:* Multisensory Mapping may be presented as a literacy station activity after it has been demonstrated for the students. Teachers may also choose to implement this strategy in a tutorial session with a striving reader who requires additional support to retain and manipulate sounds.

*Strategy modifications for grade levels:* The strategy may be modified for older students by using technology such as digital cameras or computer software to match letters and sounds.

## IMPLEMENTING THE MULTISENSORY MAPPING STRATEGY: STEP BY STEP

1. **Present the target sound in context.** Teachers and students join in a poem or song as keywords are highlighted. After singing the song or chanting the poem, the teacher leads students in a choral reading.

2. **Select target sounds.** Teachers select target sounds such as *"c"* or *"t"* from keywords in the song or poem and identify them for students.

3. **Match letter and sound.** Teachers call on individual students to match the target sound with a picture in a sound sort activity. After the sound sort activity, students write the letter that represents the sound in the air, chanting the sound at the same time.

4. **Trace the letter.** Teachers invite individual students to use cornmeal to trace the letter as they recite the sound. Immediately after tracing the letter, students generate words that begin or end with the target sound.

5. **Review target sounds and letters.** Teachers distribute pictures and letter cards with raised bumps or sandpaper. Students work with partners to repeat the process as a review. Previous sounds and letters should be added to the review.

## APPLYING THE MULTISENSORY MAPPING STRATEGY: FIRST-GRADE LESSON ON MULTISENSORY MAPPING

Students gather on the rug as the teacher leads them in a read-aloud of the nursery rhyme "Jack Be Nimble" (Adams, Foorman, Lundberg, & Beeler, 1998). The teacher demonstrates movements to accompany the read-aloud so that students use whole-body learning to map the rhymes. After color-coding rhyming pairs in the poem, the teacher provides each student with a packet. The packet contains a set of multisensory rhyming pair cards. Using the Multisensory Mapping of Sounds guide shown in Figure 2.1, the teacher directs students to work with their reading partners on the following:

- Match the rhyming pair cards with their pictures (**box, fox**).
- Use the magnetic letters to create the words and trace them.
- Chant the sounds as you trace the letters (**box, fox**).
- Create new words on your Rhyming Pair Word Study sheet that match (**box, fox**).

As students complete their packets, they review the original nursery rhyme "Jack Be Nimble" on the chart. Partners try out new lines for the rhyme with their generated rhymes and add them to the chart. When all students have completed their task, the teacher gathers them on the rug again to read the new rhyming lines generated by the class.

| Figure 2.1 | Multisensory Mapping of Sounds |
|---|---|

| Picture Card | Word | Rhyming Word |
|---|---|---|
| | Fox | Box |
| | Frog | Hog |
| | Knot | Hot |

*Source:* International Reading Association and National Council of Teachers of English (1996).

### IRA/NCTE Standards for English Language Arts

10. Students whose first language is not English make use of their first language to develop competency in the English language arts and to develop understanding of content across the curriculum.

## DIFFERENTIATING INSTRUCTION FOR ENGLISH LANGUAGE LEARNERS

Technology provides the English language learner with multisensory experiences (Hodge, 1998). As second-language learners see the printed word on the text, type in their rhyme, and listen to accompanying songs or stories, they are provided with multiple exposures to sounds. Interactive word-building activities such as "Construct a Word" on the Read/Write/Think website (www.readwritethink.org) enable second-language learners to generate words that match the rhyme. This website provides feedback on each response and also tallies scores. The teacher can provide further remediation with a follow-up podcast of rhyming pairs with an accompanying word sheet so English language learners can practice repeated readings.

## DIFFERENTIATING INSTRUCTION FOR STUDENTS WITH SPECIAL NEEDS

Similarly to English language learners, students with special needs also benefit from repeated exposure to multisensory mapping of sounds (Daly, Chafouleas, & Skinner, 2005). One intervention method for students with special needs is to use the song "Old MacDonald Had a Farm" (Yopp, 1992) to generate rhymes and wordplay. After listening to a podcast of the song, striving readers use their multisensory rhyming pairs to create a flip book. The flip book has pictures of the rhyming animals with color-coded text. Students with special needs swap their flip books with one another for continued practice in wordplay and rhyming.

## REFERENCES

Adams, J. M., Foorman, R. B., Lundberg, I., & Beeler, T. (1998). *Phonemic awareness in young children.* Baltimore, MD: Paul H. Brooks.

Daly, E., Chafouleas, S., & Skinner, C. (2005). *Interventions for reading problems: Designing and evaluating effective strategies.* New York: Guilford.

Hodge, M. (1998). Teaching foreign language to at-risk learners: A challenge for the new millennium. *Inquiry, 2,* 68–78.

International Reading Association and National Council of Teachers of English. (1996). *Standards for the English language arts.* Newark, DE: International Reading Association and Urbana, IL: National Council of Teachers of English.

Snow, C., Burns, M., & Griffin, P. (1998). *Preventing reading difficulties in young children.* Washington, DC: National Academy Press.

Torgesen, J. K., & Bryant, B. R. (1993). Individual difference variables that predict response to training in phonological awareness. *Journal of Experimental Child Psychology, 63,* 1–21.

Yopp, H. K. (1992). Developing phonemic awareness in young children. *The Reading Teacher, 45,* 696–703.

# Strategy
# 3
# Picture Card Snap

## SPEAKING BRIEFLY: AN OVERVIEW OF THE LITERACY STRATEGY

*Picture Card Snap* provides emergent and early readers with scaffolded practice in identifying and categorizing sounds. Young children often struggle with phonemic awareness activities since we are asking them to treat speech sounds as objects to be manipulated (Yopp, 1992). However, research indicates that with specific training in identifying and manipulating sounds, young readers make significant progress in reading and sound spelling at a much earlier age (McGee & Ukrainetz, 2009).

Picture Card Snap provides emergent and early readers with specific, repeated practice in matching initial, medial, or final sounds to pictures. An integral component of the instructional strategy is the levels of scaffolding that are provided to the young readers as they attempt to complete the card game. As teachers use assessment data to layer their prompts during this activity, young readers receive differentiated feedback to improve their performance. Picture Card Snap should be used as a small-group activity or for intervention tutorials. Once students have participated in the scaffolded activity, the card game may be used as a literacy center activity during the literacy block.

*Source:* International Reading Association and National Council of Teachers of English (1996).

---

### IRA/NCTE Standards for English Language Arts

6. Students apply knowledge of language structure, language conventions (e.g., spelling and punctuation), media techniques, figurative language, and genre to create, critique, and discuss print and nonprint texts.

11. Students participate as knowledgeable, reflective, creative, and critical members of a variety of literacy communities.

---

## USING PICTURE CARD SNAP

*When to use the strategy:* Picture Card Snap uses the group setting to encourage students to play with speech sounds. It is imperative that teachers encourage and positively reinforce young readers' attempts to identify and categorize speech sounds during this picture card activity.

*Strategy modifications for grade levels:* The card activity can be differentiated for challenge level by asking students to match the target sound in all positions (initial, medial, final) or by including several sound card matches.

## IMPLEMENTING THE PICTURE CARD SNAP STRATEGY: STEP BY STEP

1. **Analyze assessment data.** During the planning process, teachers examine assessment data to determine the speech sound to be the focus of the card activity (initial, medial, or final). Teachers also analyze the data to gauge the levels of scaffolding needed by individual students.

2. **Prepare picture cards.** Teachers select pictures to represent target sounds and "odd-man out" pictures to complete the pack of cards.

3. **Model identification of sound.** Teachers explicitly model the target sound. For example, if the target sound is initial [b], teachers will prompt, "I will look for pictures that begin with the sound of [bbb] as in *boy*," elaborating the sound for emphasis.

4. **Match sounds and pictures.** Teachers model taking turns to draw a card from the face-down pile and place it on the face-up pile. When a newly drawn card has the same targeted beginning, medial, or final sound as the top card in the face-up pile, the first child to identify and match the sound says "SNAP!" and takes the whole pile of cards.

5. **Review target sounds.** After students have completed the card activity, teachers facilitate a review of the sound matches by asking individuals to report their matches.

## APPLYING THE PICTURE CARD SNAP STRATEGY: KINDERGARTEN INTERVENTION ACTIVITY

After analyzing assessment data from the prior week's lessons, the teacher selects a group of three students who did not achieve benchmark on isolating and manipulating initial sounds. The teacher creates a Picture Card Snap card pack (see Figure 3.1) based on assessment data, then gathers the small intervention group and provides the following scaffolding:

- *Let's identify the sound at the beginning of [moon]. [Mmm] is the first sound we hear in [moon]. Let's all say it together: [mmm].*

- *Can you think of other words that have the same initial sound as [moon]?* Teacher takes several oral responses. Then the teacher asks students to find the picture from a group of three that begins with the same sound, [m].

- The teacher then models for the group how to play the card game Picture Card Snap. As individual students select picture cards, the teacher identifies the picture. Students repeat the name of the picture and emphasize the initial sound they hear before attempting to match the card.

When students complete the card activity, the teacher reviews each sound match by asking group members to call out their sounds. After the review, students orally generate more examples of words that include the target sound.

**Figure 3.1** Picture Card Snap!

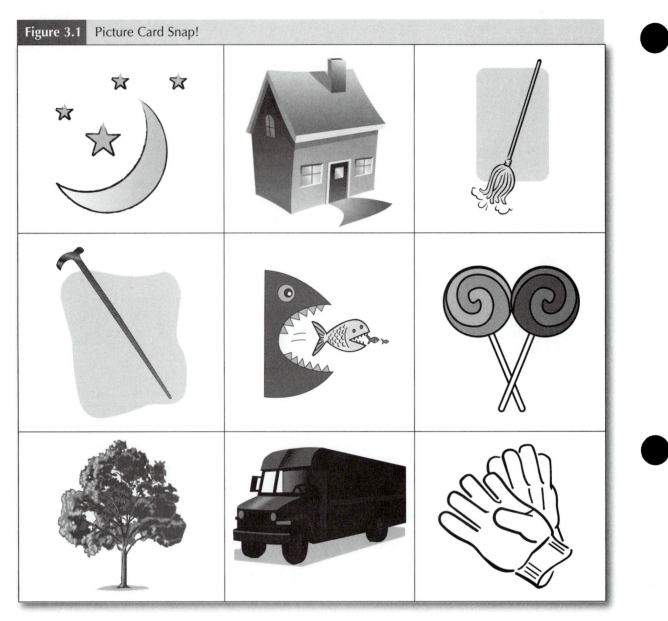

*Source:* International Reading Association and National Council of Teachers of English (1996).

### IRA/NCTE Standards for English Language Arts

10. Students whose first language is not English make use of their first language to develop competency in the English language arts and to develop understanding of content across the curriculum.

## DIFFERENTIATING INSTRUCTION FOR ENGLISH LANGUAGE LEARNERS

English language learners may find it especially difficult to identify and categorize initial, medial, and final sounds. One method for scaffolding Picture Card Snap for second-language learners is to include sound boxes as an addendum to the card activity (McCarthy, 2008). As English language learners select a picture card, teachers ask them to use the sound boxes to identify the number of sounds in the word. For example, as the student selects the picture of a cat, the teacher prompts, *"Let's see how many sounds are in that word. C-a-t. How many sounds did you hear?"* Teachers guide students in placing a token for each sound in the box. Teachers then provide the following prompt, *"Now we're going to focus on the sound in the first box. Let's see if we can find a picture card that also begins with /ccc/."* This simple addendum provides second-language learners with a specific visual prompt to identify and categorize sounds.

## DIFFERENTIATING INSTRUCTION FOR STUDENTS WITH SPECIAL NEEDS

Research confirms that when students with special needs are provided explicit, systematic instruction in phonemic awareness, they make significant gains in reading achievement (Snow, Burns, & Griffin, 1998). Students with special needs respond to multisensory instruction, as it facilitates the processing and retrieval of sounds (Daly, Chafouleas, & Skinner, 2005). One method for differentiating Picture Card Snap for students with special needs is to provide cued signals for sounds. For example, teachers may call students' attention to how their mouths form the sounds or direct them to place their hands in front of their mouths for voiced sounds. When students are given kinesthetic-tactile associations for sounds, it facilitates the processing and mapping of speech.

## REFERENCES

Daly, E., Chafouleas, S., & Skinner, C. (2005). *Interventions for reading problems: Designing and evaluating effective strategies.* New York: Guilford.

International Reading Association and National Council of Teachers of English. (1996). *Standards for the English language arts.* Newark, DE: International Reading Association and Urbana, IL: National Council of Teachers of English.

McCarthy, P. (2008). Using sound boxes systematically to develop phonemic awareness. *The Reading Teacher, 62,* 346–349.

McGee, L., & Ukrainetz, T. (2009). Using scaffolding to teach phonemic awareness in preschool and kindergarten. *The Reading Teacher, 62,* 599–603.

Snow, C., Burns, M., & Griffin, P. (1998). *Preventing reading difficulties in young children.* Washington, DC: National Academy Press.

Yopp, H. K. (1992). Developing phonemic awareness in young children. *The Reading Teacher, 45,* 696–703.

# Strategy
# 4
# Sound Sorts

*Sound Sorts* is an instructional strategy that facilitates students' attention to phonemes. As emergent and early readers focus on and think about sounds, they are developing metalinguistic awareness (Yopp & Yopp, 2000). Metalinguistic awareness is the ability to see language as an object to study (Yopp, 1992). Some students experience difficulties with phonemic awareness instruction because they are unable to see speech sounds as objects that can be manipulated. Sound sort activities provide students with opportunities to step back and focus on the sounds they hear in words.

The primary purpose for implementing the Sound Sorts activity is to facilitate readers' ability to perceive that speech is made up of a series of sounds (Yopp, 1992). Activities that involve blending and segmenting of sounds facilitate emergent and early readers' decoding and encoding skills (Manyak, 2008). As students focus on initial, medial, or ending sounds and categorize them, they improve their ability to identify and manipulate sounds (Griffith & Olson, 1992).

*Source:* International Reading Association and National Council of Teachers of English (1996).

### IRA/NCTE Standards for English Language Arts

2. Students read a wide range of literature from many periods in many genres to build an understanding of the many dimensions (e.g., philosophical, ethical, aesthetic) of human experience.

6. Students apply knowledge of language structure, language conventions (e.g., spelling and punctuation), media techniques, figurative language, and genre to create, critique, and discuss print and nonprint texts.

## USING SOUND SORTS

*When to use the strategy:* Sound Sorts is primarily used for guided reading groups or intervention tutorial sessions. It may be used as a whole class activity to model the task if students are given partners. It is critical that teachers use their assessment data to change the focus of the sound sort activity depending on student needs.

*Strategy modifications for grade levels:* The card activity can be differentiated for older students by using multisyllabic word families for the sound sorts.

## IMPLEMENTING THE SOUND SORTS STRATEGY: STEP BY STEP

1. **Present the target sound.** Teachers present the target sound in a chant to the tune of "Happy Birthday." Students join in as the teacher chants, "Where is the sound? Where is the sound? Can you find it?" Teachers explain that students will be identifying and sorting sounds.

2. **Model the target sound sort.** Teachers present the focus of the target sound sort. For example, the teacher says [**bat, net, fit**]. All have the same ending sound, /t/.

3. **Demonstrate how to sort sounds.** Teachers use picture cards to demonstrate how to sort sounds. Students are selected to come up and align the pictures that all end in /t/. Teachers ask students to explain why the odd picture did not fit in the category.

4. **Pair students to perform task.** Students are paired up and given bags with picture cards. Teachers provide students with the target sound in either initial/medial/ending position to sort. Students note their rationale for categorizing pictures.

5. **Review students' performance.** Teachers ask students to report out their sound sorts and explain their categories. After reviewing the sound sorts, teachers ask students to generate other words that would fit the category. These words are written on chart paper for students to read aloud as a summary of the lesson.

## APPLYING THE SOUND SORTS STRATEGY:
## FIRST-GRADE LESSON ON SOUND SORTS

The teacher calls students to the rug for a shared reading of *There's a Wocket in My Pocket* (Geisel, 1974). After the shared reading, the teacher writes the following words from the book on chart paper: **wocket, pocket, _____**. Next, the teacher asks students to generate more nonsense words that fit the pattern, such as *packet, sacket, macket*. Students chant all the words on the chart paper. After the choral reading, the teacher asks students to identify the ending sound that all the words have in common, /Tt/. The teacher then demonstrates a sound sort with the picture cards cat/bat/net/bus. Students are then placed in pairs to begin sorting their own packet of cards. Using the ending sound sort shown in Figure 4.1, the teacher directs students to do the following:

- Say the name of the picture and talk about the ending sound.

- Match the pictures that have the same ending sounds.

- Explain to your partner why the odd picture card does not fit.

After they have completed their sound sort activity, students review their categories. The teacher also leads students' generation of new words that fit the sound categories they formed.

| Figure 4.1 | Ending Sound Sort |
|---|---|

| | |
|---|---|
| | cat |
| | bus |
| | bat |
| | net |

*Source:* International Reading Association and National Council of Teachers of English (1996).

### IRA/NCTE Standards for English Language Arts

10. Students whose first language is not English make use of their first language to develop competency in the English language arts and to develop understanding of content across the curriculum.

## DIFFERENTIATING INSTRUCTION FOR ENGLISH LANGUAGE LEARNERS

The Sound Sorts strategy enables English language learners to focus their attention on the target sound. Research indicates that second-language learners benefit from explicit, systematic phonemic awareness instruction such as sound sorts (Geva & Siegel, 2000). One method for differentiating Sound Sorts for English language learners is to create individual practice packets based on assessment data. For example, teachers may create picture cards focusing on the medial short [o] sound. Next, English language learners listen to a podcast created by the teacher that labels each picture and provides prompts to categorize the sounds. The cards also contain numbers on the back to provide self-correction. As second-language learners become more adept at categorizing target sounds, they can be weaned off the podcasts.

## DIFFERENTIATING INSTRUCTION FOR STUDENTS WITH SPECIAL NEEDS

The most common barrier to early reading success is the inability to process language phonologically (Ehri & Nunes, 2002). Students with special needs are especially at risk for reading failure if they did not receive phonemic awareness instruction. One way to differentiate the Sound Sorts activity for students with special needs is to provide tactile letter cards to facilitate processing of sounds. For example, before learners sort picture cards with the ending /Tt/ sound, teachers provide them with the letter card containing raised bumps or they write the letter in cornmeal. The process of tracing the letter and chanting its sound will facilitate the sorting task.

## REFERENCES

Ehri, L., & Nunes, S. (2002). The role of phonemic awareness in learning to read. In A. E. Farstrup & S. J. Samuels (Eds.), *What research has to say about reading instruction* (pp. 110–140). Newark, DE: International Reading Association.

Geva, E., & Siegel, L. (2000). Orthographic cognitive factors in the concurrent development of basic reading skills in two languages. *Reading & Writing: An Interdisciplinary Journal, 12,* 1–30.

Griffith, P., & Olson, M. (1992). Phonemic awareness helps beginning readers break the code. *The Reading Teacher, 45,* 516–522.

International Reading Association and National Council of Teachers of English. (1996). *Standards for the English language arts.* Newark, DE: International Reading Association and Urbana, IL: National Council of Teachers of English.

Manyak, P. C. (2008). Phonemes in use: Multiple activities for a critical process. *The Reading Teacher, 61,* 659–662.

Yopp, H. K. (1992). Developing phonemic awareness in young children. *The Reading Teacher, 45,* 696–703.

Yopp, H. K., & Yopp, R. H. (2000). Supporting phonemic awareness development in the classroom. *The Reading Teacher, 54,* 130–143.

## CHILDREN'S LITERATURE CITED

Geisel, T. (Dr. Seuss). (1974). *There's a wocket in my pocket.* New York: Random House.

# Strategy
# 5

# Treasure Chest

## SPEAKING BRIEFLY: AN OVERVIEW OF THE LITERACY STRATEGY

*Treasure Chest* is an instructional strategy that focuses on the skills of segmenting and blending sounds. According to the National Reading Panel (2000), instruction that explicitly focuses on one or two skills in phonological awareness is most effective. When students engage in segmenting and blending sounds, they are preparing for the decoding and encoding of words (Ehri, Nunes, Willows, & Schuster, 2001).

The objective of the Treasure Chest activity is to provide emergent or early readers with repeated practice in segmenting and blending phonemes. This activity is best suited for a literacy center or tutorial session. However, it can also be used as an independent work packet to be used at home with parents.

*Source:* International Reading Association and National Council of Teachers of English (1996).

| IRA/NCTE Standards for English Language Arts |
| --- |
| 11. Students participate as knowledgeable, reflective, creative, and critical members of a variety of literacy communities. |
| 12. Students use spoken, written, and visual languages to accomplish their own purpose (e.g., for learning, enjoyment, persuasion, and the exchange of information). |

## USING TREASURE CHEST

*When to use the strategy:* Treasure Chest is used after teachers have modeled and scaffolded the segmentation and blending of sounds. Its primary purpose is to provide students with multiple opportunities to engage in sound play as they count phonemes and then reconstruct them into words through oral blending.

*Strategy modifications for grade levels:* The card activity can be differentiated for primary grade students by implementing it as a whole class lesson.

## IMPLEMENTING THE TREASURE CHEST STRATEGY: STEP BY STEP

1. **Place students in pairs.** Teachers use assessment data to pair students with a buddy to work on the packet.

2. **Model how to implement activity.** Teachers display the Treasure Chest sheet and instruct students how to proceed with picture cards and penny coins.

3. **Identify picture cards.** Teachers name each picture card in the packet before students begin to work to prevent confusion.

4. **Work in pairs to segment sounds.** Students select a picture card from the deck, and one partner says the name of the picture and places a penny to represent every sound in each box on the Treasure Chest.

5. **Blend phonemes into words.** The other student orally blends the sounds and quickly states the word. After blending the phonemes, the student collects the penny counters.

6. **Repeat process with new picture cards.** Students use a new deck of picture cards to swap roles. The process is repeated with first orally segmenting and then blending phonemes.

## APPLYING THE TREASURE CHEST STRATEGY: FIRST-GRADE LITERACY INTERVENTION ACTIVITY

The first-grade teacher begins by assigning two students to the Phonemic Awareness Literacy Station. The teacher shows the Treasure Chest packet of materials to the students and asks them to choose roles for segmenting and blending sounds. Using the Treasure Chest graphic organizer and picture cards shown in Figure 5.1, the teacher directs students to do the following:

- Say the name of the picture and stretch out the sounds /f/i/sh/.

- Place a penny counter for each sound in the Treasure Chest boxes [three for fish].

- Blend the sounds to quickly say the word to gather the coins in the Treasure Chest.

When students have completed the activity with the first deck of cards, they switch roles to repeat the process with a new set of picture cards.

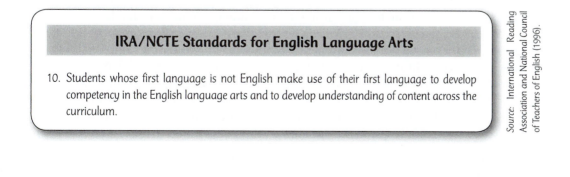

### IRA/NCTE Standards for English Language Arts

10. Students whose first language is not English make use of their first language to develop competency in the English language arts and to develop understanding of content across the curriculum.

*Source:* International Reading Association and National Council of Teachers of English (1996).

| Figure 5.1 | Treasure Chest Graphic Organizer |

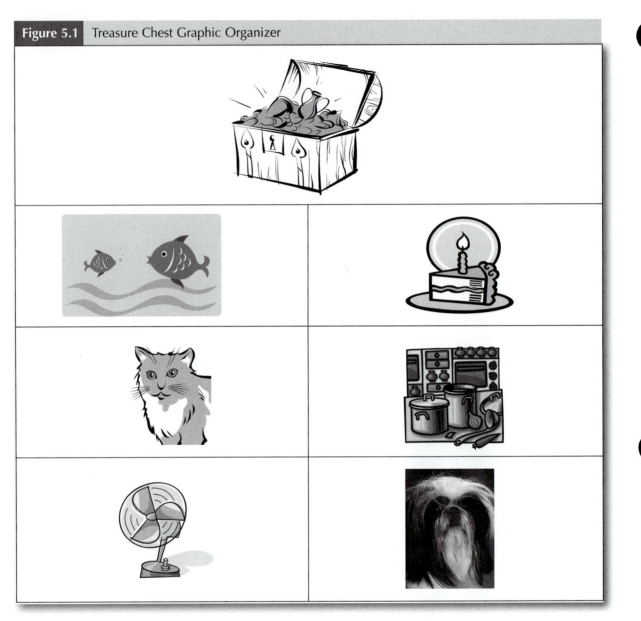

## DIFFERENTIATING INSTRUCTION FOR ENGLISH LANGUAGE LEARNERS

Early, explicit instruction in segmenting and blending phonemes enables readers to develop the prerequisite decoding skills in learning how to read (Pressley, 2006). English language learners need targeted, repetitive practice in separating and blending of sounds. One way to differentiate the Treasure Chest activity for English language learners is to provide students with a podcast identifying the names of the picture cards. The speaker on the podcast would also segment and blend the sounds for the English language learner. As they listen to the podcast at home or in school, students would use the picture cards to work alongside the speaker on the podcast and therefore receive additional support.

## DIFFERENTIATING INSTRUCTION FOR STUDENTS WITH SPECIAL NEEDS

The ability to separate and blend sounds is a critical phonemic awareness skill (Gambrell, Morrow, & Pressley, 2007). Striving readers may receive additional practice in this skill by transforming the Treasure Chest activity into a guessing game. Working with a reading partner, students select a picture card and then give clues to their partner regarding the object. The partner has to respond by segmenting the sounds. For example, if the picture was of a fish, the student might say, "It lives in the sea." The reading partner would respond, "/f/i/sh/."

## REFERENCES

Ehri, L., Nunes, S., Willows, D., & Schuster, B. (2001). Phonemic awareness instruction helps children learn to read: Evidence from the National Reading Panel's meta-analysis. *Reading Research Quarterly, 36,* 250–287.

Gambrell, L., Morrow, L., & Pressley, M. (2007). *Best practices in literacy instruction* (3rd ed.). New York: Guilford.

International Reading Association and National Council of Teachers of English. (1996). *Standards for the English language arts.* Newark, DE: International Reading Association and Urbana, IL: National Council of Teachers of English.

National Reading Panel. (2000). *Teaching children to read.* Washington, DC: National Institute of Child Health and Human Development.

Pressley, M. (2006). *Reading instruction that works: The case for balanced teaching.* New York: Guilford.

# SECTION II

# Essential Strategies for Teaching Phonics

For several decades now, educators have debated the method for teaching young readers how to "break the code." This chapter presents the research on best practices for teaching phonics as well as the strategies for independent learning.

## A Brief Overview of Phonics

The ultimate goal of reading instruction is that the reader attains fluency and comprehends text. Educators have hotly debated the best method for attaining such a goal throughout the history of public schooling in America (Chall, 1987). The National Reading Panel (2000) entered the fray with their finding that research indicated that systematic, explicit instruction was the defining factor for "breaking the code," rather than any specific method.

Systematic, explicit instruction in letter-sound relationships defines best practices in phonics instruction (Pressley, 2006). Recent research indicates that in order to gain fluency, students need instruction that integrates strategies for fluency as well as word identification (Rasinsky, Rupley, & Nichols, 2008). When young readers are given opportunities to apply their word identification strategies within context of use, their reading rate and comprehension improve (Staudt, 2009). In order to gain automaticity, or the rapid recognition of words, readers need to be actively engaged in "breaking the code" by attending to the orthographic features of letters and sounds (Norman & Calfee, 2004). As readers engage with identification of letters and sounds, they can be assessed at various stages of word identification such as the following:

- *Logographic reading:* Reader uses visual cues, such as the golden arches of McDonald's, to identify words rather than using letter-sound correspondence.

- *Alphabetic reading:* Readers use their limited knowledge of letters and sounds to recognize words and begin to understand that there are rules for decoding.

- *Decoding by analogy:* Experienced readers begin to "chunk" parts of words such as prefixes, suffixes, and root words to identify multisyllabic words.

- *Multisyllabic words:* At this stage, students begin to use more than one word identification strategy to tackle more difficult words.

- *Morphemic analysis:* Proficient readers are able to decode words that are not in their listening vocabulary by attending to their meaningful parts, such as prefixes or suffixes. (Ehri, 1991; Gunning, 2001; Pressley, 2006)

In order to progress through these stages, emergent readers need phonemic awareness, or the ability to identify and manipulate sounds (Ehri & Roberts, 2006). As they begin to use their knowledge of letters and sounds to identify words, readers need to develop strategies for independent reading in order to progress to decoding of multisyllabic words (Cunningham, 2007). Instruction that is systematic and explicit also provides readers with opportunities to implement strategies for independence along the developmental continuum of skills for word identification.

## INSTRUCTION IN WORD IDENTIFICATION

Research indicates that proficient readers have self-efficacy, or the belief that their efforts can help them reach goals (McTigue, Washburn, & Liew, 2009). Striving readers, however, often skip over words they do not recognize because they lack word identification strategies to tackle them (Snow, Burns, & Griffin, 1998). When readers are explicitly taught strategies to identify words and then given opportunities to implement them with instructional support, their performance and confidence improve (Adams, 2003).

What are the word identification strategies that readers need to develop? Developing readers need sequential decoding abilities, or the skills to take apart a word in order to identify individual letters or sounds (Cunningham & Cunningham, 2002). As readers develop more exposure to text, they need strategies that help them identify rimes and decode by word patterns and analogy (Pressley, 2006). This chapter presents several instructional strategies that use guidelines formed from research on best practice to instruct students in word identification.

## GUIDELINES FOR TEACHING PHONICS SKILLS

The National Reading Panel (2000) determined that systematic, explicit instruction in phonics impacted reading performance. The following guidelines provide the framework for phonics instruction:

1. Effective phonics instruction helps young readers analyze and blend individual sounds while teaching the use of chunking word parts to decode (Pressley, 2006).

2. Application of word identification skills in context of use leads to automaticity (Staudt, 2009).

3. Using best practices in phonics instruction allows for teaching readers strategies for word identification that emphasize metacognition and flexibility of thought (Taylor & Pearson, 2002).

4. Active engagement by students in word sorts or making words activities fosters individual accountability and application of phonetic skills (Adams, 2003).

5. Effective phonics instruction includes ongoing assessment to facilitate targeted instruction (Mesmer & Griffith, 2005).

## A STRATEGY FOR ASSESSING PHONICS SKILLS

Research indicates that effective phonics instruction focuses on active engagement with decoding and metacognitive awareness (Taylor & Pearson, 2002). In order to provide targeted instruction that ensures students' movement toward fluency, teachers need to conduct progress monitoring (Antonacci & O'Callaghan, 2004). The purpose of assessing students' development of the alphabetic principle and decoding skills is to use assessment data to inform instruction. The Metalinguistic Phonics Inventory shown in Figure II.1 may be used for either formative or summative assessment. Teachers may also scan the assessment data to create a digital portfolio of students' progress throughout the year (Balajthy, 2007).

| Figure II.1 | Metalinguistic Phonics Inventory |

**Directions:** *Ask students to identify the following letters and say their sounds. If student correctly identifies the letter/sound, mark [+]. If student is unable to identify the letter/sound, mark [–].*

| Letter | Assessment | Note |
|---|---|---|
| Cc | | |
| Gg | | |
| Kk | | |
| Rr | | |
| Bb | | |
| Ss | | |
| **Decoding** | | |

**Directions:** *Ask students to decode the following words. If student correctly decodes the word, mark [+]. If student is unable to identify word, mark [–].*

| | | |
|---|---|---|
| skip | | |
| mat | | |
| dust | | |
| cool | | |

*(Continued)*

(Continued)

| | | |
|---|---|---|
| tip | | |
| bean | | |

**Metalinguistic Prompt:** *Select a word that took several attempts to decode. Ask the student, "How did you figure out that word?"*

| Encoding |
|---|

**Directions:** *Ask students to encode the following words. If student correctly writes the word, mark [+]. If student is unable to write the word, mark [–].*

| | | |
|---|---|---|
| ship | | |
| meet | | |
| top | | |
| thank | | |
| flag | | |
| bee | | |

**Metalinguistic Prompt:** *Select a word that took several attempts to encode. Ask the student, "How did you figure out how to spell that word?"*

**Scoring Guide**
**Directions:** Assign a score of [1] for each [+] assessment. If you recorded a [–] mark, assign a score of [0].
Proficient: 18–16 points
Target: 15–13 points
Developing: 12–10 points
At Risk: 9–0 points

# A Guide for Using Response to Intervention for Phonics

The Metalinguistic Phonics Inventory (see Figure II.1) will provide teachers with progress-monitoring data regarding students' ability to decode and encode words. Students assessed at the developing or at-risk level may be selected for further intervention. Using data from the assessment, if students need help with decoding, the Constructing Words Activity will help striving readers identifying letters/sounds and blending. Students requiring further intervention for encoding of sounds may do a modified dictation activity. Using trays filled with cornmeal, striving readers encode letters, words, and sentences based on the teacher's prompt. Instructors choose letters/sounds and word families for dictation based on data analysis. In this section, "Essential Strategies for Teaching Phonics," five instructional strategies are presented for use in developing word identification skills. The strategies are presented as guides for teachers to use based on their ongoing assessment data.

# Professional Resources

Bear, D., Invernizzi, M., Templeton, S., & Johnston, F. (2007). *Words their way: Word study for phonics, vocabulary, and spelling instruction* (4th ed.). New York: Prentice Hall.

Helman, L., Bear, D., Invernizzi, M., & Templeton, S. (2008). *Words their way: Emergent sorts for Spanish-speaking English learners.* New York: Prentice Hall.

Pinnell, G. S., & Fountas, I. (1998). *Word matters: Teaching phonics and spelling in the reading/writing classroom.* Portsmouth, NH: Heinemann.

Rasinski, T., & Padak, N. (2007). *From phonics to fluency: Effective teaching of decoding and reading fluency in the elementary school* (2nd ed.). New York: Allyn & Bacon.

# REFERENCES

Adams, M. (2003). Alphabetic anxiety and explicit, systematic phonics instruction: A cognitive science approach. In S. Neuman & D. K. Dickinson (Eds.), *Handbook of early literacy research* (pp. 66–81). New York: Guilford.

Antonacci, P., & O'Callaghan, C. (2004). *Portraits of literacy development: Instruction and assessment in a well-balanced literacy program, K–3.* Upper Saddle River, NJ: Merrill Prentice Hall.

Balajthy, E. (2007). Technology and current reading/literacy assessment strategies. *The Reading Teacher, 61,* 240–247.

Chall, J. (1987). Two vocabularies for reading: Recognition and meaning. In M. McKeown & M. Curtis (Eds.), *The nature of vocabulary acquisition* (pp. 7–15). Mahway, NJ: Lawrence Erlbaum.

Cunningham, P. M. (2007). Best practices in teaching phonological awareness and phonics. In L. B. Gambrell, L. M. Morrow, & M. Pressley (Eds.), *Best practices in literacy instruction* (3rd ed., pp. 159–178). New York: Guilford.

Cunningham, P. M., & Cunningham, J. W. (2002). What we know about how to teach phonics. In A. Farstrup & S. J. Samuels (Eds.), *What research has to say about reading instruction* (pp. 87–110). Newark, DE: International Reading Association.

Ehri, L. (1991). Development of the ability to read words. In R. Barr, M. L. Kamil, P. B. Mosenthal, & P. D. Pearson (Eds.), *Handbook of reading research* (Vol. 2, pp. 383–417*).* New York: Longman.

Ehri, L., & Roberts, T. (2006). The roots of learning to read and write: Acquisition of letters and phonemic awareness. In D. Dickinson & S. Neuman (Eds.), *Handbook of early literacy research* (Vol. 2, pp. 113–130). New York: Guilford.

Gunning, T. (2001). *Building words: A resource manual for teaching word analysis and spelling strategies.* Boston: Allyn & Bacon.

Mesmer, H., & Griffith, P. L. (2005). Everybody's selling it: But just what is explicit, systematic phonics instruction? *The Reading Teacher, 59,* 366–377.

McTigue, E., Washburn, E., & Liew, J. (2009). Academic resilience and reading: Building successful readers. *The Reading Teacher, 62,* 422–432.

National Reading Panel. (2000). *Teaching children to read.* Washington, DC: National Institute of Health and Human Development.

Norman, K. A., & Calfee, R. (2004). Tile test: A hands-on approach for assessing phonics in early grades. *The Reading Teacher, 58,* 42–53.

Pressley, M. (2006). *Reading instruction that works: The case for balanced teaching.* New York: Guilford.

Rasinsky, T., Rupley, W., & Nichols, W. (2008). Two essential ingredients: Phonics and fluency getting to know each other. *The Reading Teacher, 62,* 257–261.

Snow, C., Burns, M., & Griffin, P. (1998). *Preventing reading difficulties in young children.* Washington, DC: National Academy Press.

Staudt, D. H. (2009). Intensive word study and repeated reading improves reading skills for two students with learning disabilities. *The Reading Teacher, 63,* 142–151.

Taylor, B., & Pearson, P. D. (2002). *Teaching reading: Effective schools, accomplished teachers.* Mahway, NJ: Lawrence Erlbaum.

# Strategy

# 6

# Phonics in Context

## SPEAKING BRIEFLY: AN OVERVIEW OF THE LITERACY STRATEGY

*Phonics in Context* is an instructional strategy that facilitates the development of a strategic approach to word identification (Dahl & Scharer, 2000). As students tackle unknown words, they apply word identification skills to decode. In a process-oriented approach to phonics instruction, students are encouraged to be metacognitive and reflect on how to improve their attempts at word identification (Taylor & Pearson, 2002).

The primary purpose for embedding phonics instruction within context of use is to focus the reading on comprehending the text (Roberts & Meiring, 2006). Phonics in Context is designed for teacher modeling through a read-aloud. However, it can be implemented as a shared reading for further scaffolding and intervention.

*Source:* International Reading Association and National Council of Teachers of English (1996).

### IRA/NCTE Standards for English Language Arts

2. Students read a wide range of literature from many periods in many genres to build an understanding of the many dimensions (e.g., philosophical, ethical, aesthetic) of human experience.

6. Students apply knowledge of language structure, language conventions (e.g., spelling and punctuation), media techniques, figurative language, and genre to create, critique, and discuss print and nonprint texts.

## USING PHONICS IN CONTEXT

*When to use the strategy:* This strategy may be used during the modeling component of the literacy block or shared reading. The success of Phonics in Context as a strategy for word identification is dependent on the selection of text.

*Strategy modifications for grade levels:* This strategy is easily adapted for different grade levels through the selection of text. Teachers must carefully choose texts that represent quality children's literature and also feature the targeted phonetic elements dependent on assessment data.

## IMPLEMENTING THE PHONICS IN CONTEXT STRATEGY: STEP BY STEP

1. **Introduce *letter* and *sound* to students.** Teachers present the targeted letter and sound to students. Students use "sky writing" to trace the letter and echo the sound.

2. **Introduce text.** Teachers conduct a picture walk to introduce the text and encourage students to make predictions.

3. **Set purpose for reading.** Teachers facilitate the development of a focus question for reading. Students are also asked to listen for the targeted letter/sound.

4. **Stop at critical points in the text.** During reading, teachers stop at selected points in the story to ask students to make predictions and respond to the text.

5. **Record words with the targeted letter/sound.** Teachers ask students to list words from the story that contain the targeted letter/sound. Words are listed on chart paper, with students framing the targeted letter/sound.

6. **Application of targeted letter/sound.** Teachers facilitate a structured language experience story using the targeted letter/sound. Students generate the first two sentences of the class story with the teacher as scribe. Students then work in pairs to finish the story using words identified from the story with the targeted letter/sound.

## APPLYING THE PHONICS IN CONTEXT STRATEGY: KINDERGARTEN LESSON ON LETTER Bb

Students gather on the rug as the teacher displays the text *Brown Bear, Brown Bear, What Do You See?* (Martin, 2008). The teacher leads students in a discussion of the cover, and they discuss prior knowledge about bears. After a picture walk, students make predictions about the animals the bear might see in the story. Using chart paper, the teacher introduces the letter [Bb] and its sound with the following steps:

- Identifies the sound for [Bb] and asks students to generate other examples.

- Uses the read-aloud to call student attention to words beginning with [Bb].

- Creates a structured language experience story with words students have generated with initial [Bb].

After beginning the structured language experience story, students are placed in dyads to complete their own versions. Students illustrate their stories and place them in the classroom library for their peers to read and enjoy.

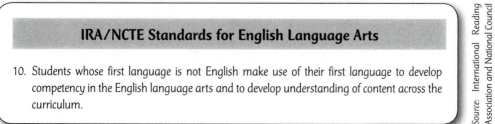

**IRA/NCTE Standards for English Language Arts**

10. Students whose first language is not English make use of their first language to develop competency in the English language arts and to develop understanding of content across the curriculum.

*Source:* International Reading Association and National Council of Teachers of English (1996).

## Differentiating Instruction for English Language Learners

Ongoing assessment of word identification skills is critically important for English language learners. Research indicates that even second-language learners with foundational skills in phonics may falter in attaining word identification strategies if they are not monitored (Rogers & Helman, 2009). One method for ensuring progress monitoring with English language learners is through a follow-up word sort. After the introduction of the targeted letter/sound through the read-aloud, the teacher gathers second-language learners for a word sort activity. Students are given packs of cards to categorize. As students complete the activity, the teacher records their processing of phonetic elements to use for targeted instruction.

## Differentiating Instruction for Students With Special Needs

Similarly to second-language learners, students with special needs need to actively engage with word identification in order to attain phonics skills (Zucker & Invernizzi, 2008). One method for differentiating this activity is to use technology to create e-sorts of words with the targeted letter/sound. Teachers use the SMART Board to select words to be categorized. Students with special needs may work in dyads or with support from the teacher to digitally identify words that contain the targeted letter/sound. Students with special needs use the word sorts to generate additional words on the SMART Board and save them to be printed for their individual word walls.

## References

Dahl, K. L., & Scharer, P. L. (2000). Phonics teaching and learning in whole language classrooms: New evidence from research. *The Reading Teacher, 53,* 584–594.

International Reading Association and National Council of Teachers of English. (1996). *Standards for the English language arts.* Newark, DE: International Reading Association and Urbana, IL: National Council of Teachers of English.

Roberts, T., & Meiring, A. (2006). Teaching phonics in the context of children's literature or spelling: Influences on first-grade reading, spelling, and writing and fourth-grade comprehension. *Journal of Educational Psychology, 98,* 690–713.

Rogers, C., & Helman, L. (2009). One size does not fit all: How assessment guides instruction in word study with English learners. *New England Reading Association Journal, 44,* 17–24.

Taylor, B., & Pearson, P. D. (2002). *Teaching reading: Effective schools, accomplished teachers.* Hillsdale, NJ: Lawrence Erlbaum.

Zucker, T., & Invernizzi, M. (2008). My e-sorts and digital extensions of word study. *The Reading Teacher, 61,* 654–658.

## Children's Literature Cited

Martin, B. (2008). *Brown bear, brown bear, what do you see?* (40th anniversary ed.). E. Carle (Illus.). New York: Henry Holt.

# Strategy 7

# Reflective Word Study

Best practices in phonics instruction emphasize active manipulation of word identification skills and metacognition (Taylor & Pearson, 2002). When students think about the letters and sounds in a word, they are processing letter/sound patterns for decoding (Cunningham & Cunningham, 2002). In order to become independent code breakers, students need a toolbox of strategies to use while reading for word identification (Vellutino & Scanlon, 2002).

The purpose of *Reflective Word Study* is to facilitate students' metacognition while decoding. Reflective Word Study allows students to share their knowledge about letters and sounds in order to develop a habit of strategic reading. As students internalize the process, they are encouraged to implement it during independent reading.

---

### IRA/NCTE Standards for English Language Arts

6. Students apply knowledge of language structure, language conventions (e.g., spelling and punctuation), media techniques, figurative language, and genre to create, critique, and discuss print and nonprint texts.

11. Students participate as knowledgeable, reflective, creative, and critical members of a variety of literacy communities.

*Source:* International Reading Association and National Council of Teachers of English (1996).

---

## USING REFLECTIVE WORD STUDY

*When to use the strategy:* Reflective Word Study is designed for guided reading lessons. However, it is easily adaptable for intervention sessions for individual students. Teachers may also choose to model the process for the whole class.

*Strategy modifications for grade levels:* This strategy may be modified for older students by focusing the word study on multisyllabic words. Using assessment data, teachers provide students with word patterns that they are struggling to master.

## IMPLEMENTING THE REFLECTIVE WORD STUDY STRATEGY: STEP BY STEP

1. **Define the term *strategy*.** Teachers ask students to define the word *strategy* and discuss strategies they use to study or tackle a difficult problem.

2. **Discuss word identification process.** Teachers lead students in a discussion of the process they currently use when they encounter unknown vocabulary words.

3. **Display the word study sheet.** Teachers ask students to read each word study prompt and tell what it means to them (see Figure 7.1).

4. **Demonstrate selected word study prompt.** Teachers use the whiteboard to write a sentence with a new vocabulary word. Teachers demonstrate the prompt "Think of the beginning and ending sound in the word" and conduct a think-aloud of their thoughts.

5. **Support practice.** Teachers place students in dyads to practice using the word study prompt with a new example on the whiteboard. Teachers ask students to think aloud as they attempt to decode the new word.

6. **Reflect on process.** Students discuss how they can use the word study prompt while reading. The process is repeated for the following lesson with a new word study prompt from Figure 7.1.

| Figure 7.1 | Word Study Guide | |
|---|---|---|
| **Vocabulary Word** | **Strategy I Used** | **What I Learned** |
| ***PREPAYMENT*** | *I broke the word into the parts that I knew.* | *I learned that if you do not know a word, then you should try to find the parts you do know.* |
| | | |
| | | |
| | | |

## APPLYING THE REFLECTIVE WORD STUDY STRATEGY: SECOND-GRADE LESSON ON MULTISYLLABIC WORDS

The teacher gathers a small guided reading group of four students for intervention. Using the Word Study Guide (see Figure 7.1), the teacher demonstrates how to use the guide to decode the multisyllabic word *prepayment*:

- Think of the beginning and ending letters/sounds (Pp, Tt). What sounds do those letters make?

- Break the word into parts we already know (pre/pay/ment). We know the words *he/day/tent* and can use them to read these chunks.

- Read to see if it makes sense. Substitute the word you think it is, and see if the sentence makes sense. If it doesn't, then you need to begin again.

- Talk with your partner about your word-solving skills and identify new concepts about letters and sounds that you learned.

As dyads complete the activity, the teacher asks them to share their use of strategies to identify *prepayment*. The teacher records their strategies and new concepts on chart paper to use as a reference tool for the next lesson and for independent reading.

---

### IRA/NCTE Standards for English Language Arts

10. Students whose first language is not English make use of their first language to develop competency in the English language arts and to develop understanding of content across the curriculum.

*Source:* International Reading Association and National Council of Teachers of English (1996).

---

## DIFFERENTIATING INSTRUCTION FOR ENGLISH LANGUAGE LEARNERS

English language learners need additional explicit support in learning letter-sound relationships (Rogers & Helman, 2009). One adaptation of Reflective Word Study for second-language learners is to focus on spelling patterns such as silent [e], as in *came,* or vowel digraphs, as in *loud.* English language learners use letter tiles to manipulate the spelling patterns and to generate additional words with the same spelling pattern. As new words are learned, students write them on their personal word walls for future reference.

## DIFFERENTIATING INSTRUCTION FOR STUDENTS WITH SPECIAL NEEDS

Students with special needs require explicit coaching in the application of word identification strategies (Taylor & Pearson, 2002). One modification for striving readers is to ask them to keep a daily log for 1 week of the word identification strategies they used either at home or in school. During individual conferences or intervention sessions, the teacher meets with students with special needs to discuss which strategies they used and any words they were unable to identify. Building on the strategies they are already using well, the teacher facilitates the use of additional strategies such as "chunking" to guide students toward fluency. As students with special needs become more skilled, the weekly log can be gradually phased out.

## References

Cunningham, P. M., & Cunningham, J. W. (2002). What we know about how to teach phonics. In A. Farstrup & S. J. Samuels (Eds.), *What research has to say about reading instruction* (pp. 87–110). Newark, DE: International Reading Association.

International Reading Association and National Council of Teachers of English. (1996). *Standards for the English language arts.* Newark, DE: International Reading Association and Urbana, IL: National Council of Teachers of English.

Rogers, C., & Helman, L. (2009). One size does not fit all: How assessment guides instruction in word study with English learners. *New England Reading Association Journal, 44,* 17–24.

Taylor, B., & Pearson, P. D. (2002). *Teaching reading: Effective schools, accomplished teachers.* Hillsdale, NJ: Lawrence Erlbaum.

Vellutino, F., & Scanlon, D. (2002). The interactive strategies approach to reading intervention. *Contemporary Educational Psychology, 27,* 573–635.

# Phonics Through Shared Reading

# Strategy 8

## SPEAKING BRIEFLY: AN OVERVIEW OF THE LITERACY STRATEGY

*Phonics Through Shared Reading* provides emergent and early readers with an explicit model of how to apply their phonics skills while reading. Shared reading allows developing readers to see how new vocabulary words are identified by fluent readers (Gill, 2006). Its explicit modeling and application of word identification skills in context of use enable teachers to target instruction for specific skill sets.

Phonics Through Shared Reading may be used with picture books, songs, or poetry. Through repeated readings, developing readers learn to listen for rhymes, discriminate among sounds, and identify onset/rimes within a risk-free environment (Invernizzi, 2003). Observational data during shared reading may also aid the teacher in designing intervention lessons for striving readers or students with special needs.

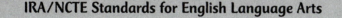

---

### IRA/NCTE Standards for English Language Arts

2. Students read a wide range of literature from many periods in many genres to build an understanding of the many dimensions (e.g., philosophical, ethical, aesthetic) of human experience.

11. Students participate as knowledgeable, reflective, creative, and critical members of a variety of literacy communities.

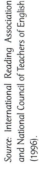

*Source:* International Reading Association and National Council of Teachers of English (1996).

## USING PHONICS THROUGH SHARED READING

*When to use the strategy:* Phonics Through Shared Reading is designed for a whole class session. The teacher may follow the session with guided reading lessons that provide further scaffolding of the targeted skill or strategy.

*Strategy modifications for grade levels:* The teacher may adapt this lesson for intermediate grade learners by selecting text that focuses on multisyllabic word patterns.

## IMPLEMENTING THE PHONICS THROUGH SHARED READING STRATEGY: STEP BY STEP

1. **Select text for targeted instruction.** Using assessment data, teachers select a poem, song, or picture book to teach a rhyme or identification of an onset/rime. Text must be short enough to allow for repeated readings in one lesson.

2. **Read for fluency and meaning.** Teachers first read aloud the text and focus on comprehension and fluency.

3. **Highlight targeted sound or strategy.** Teachers read the text again and ask students to listen for a targeted rhyme, onset, or word pattern. Teachers may ask students to write the letter or rime on whiteboards each time it is repeated.

4. **Apply strategy in context.** Teachers read the text for the third time and mask targeted words with the onset or rime. Teachers stop before the masked word and ask students to problem solve using their word identification skills. As the letters are slowly revealed, students share their strategies for correctly decoding the word. After students have supplied the word, the teacher encourages cross-checking by asking, "Does it sound right? Does it look right? Does it match the picture?"

5. **Review target sounds.** After the third repeated reading, teachers dictate words with the targeted onset or rime for students to encode on whiteboards. For younger students, teachers may review the sounds orally or focus on initial/final sounds.

## APPLYING THE PHONICS THROUGH SHARED READING STRATEGY: FIRST-GRADE LESSON

After analyzing assessment data from the prior week's lessons, the teacher decides to focus on identification of word patterns to move students toward fluency. Today's shared reading will use the poem "Ickle Me, Pickle Me, Tickle Me Too" by Shel Silverstein (1974) to focus on the [ickle] word pattern. The teacher begins with the following:

- "Let's read the poem title and see if we can figure out what it is going to be about." After discussing the title, the teacher calls attention to the poet. "What do we know about Shel Silverstein poetry?" The teacher guides students toward knowledge about Silverstein's nonsensical and humorous poetry. After discussing the poet's style, the teacher reads aloud the poem for enjoyment.

- "Can you figure out the sounds in this word pattern, [ickle]?" Teacher takes several attempts and asks students who decoded the pattern correctly to share how they figured it out.

- The teacher then reads the poem again and asks students to listen for words with the targeted word pattern. After the second reading, students come up to write the targeted words on chart paper.

- The poem is read for the third time, with selected students reading the line "Ickle me, pickle me, tickle me too." After reading the selected lines, students use colored markers to frame the targeted rimes.

- After the shared reading, students work in dyads to generate more words with the targeted rimes on their whiteboards. Teachers orally review their words and ask selected students to write their words on chart paper.

At the conclusion of the session, students are given individual copies of the poem to read independently and to share with their parents for homework.

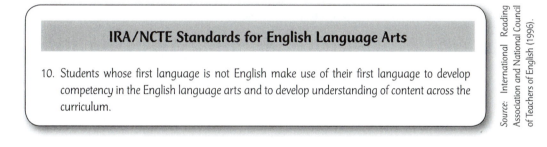

### IRA/NCTE Standards for English Language Arts

10. Students whose first language is not English make use of their first language to develop competency in the English language arts and to develop understanding of content across the curriculum.

*Source:* International Reading Association and National Council of Teachers of English (1996).

## DIFFERENTIATING INSTRUCTION FOR ENGLISH LANGUAGE LEARNERS

Shared reading provides English language learners with an explicit model of how to apply word identification skills while reading (Gill, 2006). It is critically important that second-language learners receive explicit demonstrations of how to decode unfamiliar words and then be given opportunities to practice their skills with support (Allington, 2001). One way to ensure that second-language learners receive this support is to scan the shared reading text onto a SMART Board and then save the entire lesson with high-lighted words to a computer. Second-language learners may revisit the session with a more proficient reading partner to practice their decoding of the masked words. Teachers may collect assessment data by asking English language learners to write down any questions or problems they still have with word identification.

## DIFFERENTIATING INSTRUCTION FOR STUDENTS WITH SPECIAL NEEDS

Students with special needs require motivation to engage in reading and application of word identification skills. One adaptation for students with special needs is to use comic books as text for shared reading (McVicker, 2007). The visual representation provides students with special needs with additional support for cross-checking and also moti-vates them to problem solve while reading. Teachers may scan the comic book and then use a SMART Board to highlight text for demonstration purposes.

## REFERENCES

Allington, R. (2001). *What really matters for struggling readers.* New York: Longman.

Gill, S. (2006). Teaching rimes with shared reading. *The Reading Teacher, 60,* 191–194.

International Reading Association and National Council of Teachers of English. (1996). *Standards for the English language arts.* Newark, DE: International Reading Association and Urbana, IL: National Council of Teachers of English.

Invernizzi, M. (2003). Concepts, sounds, and the ABCs: A diet for the very young reader. In D. M. Barone & L. M. Morrow (Eds.), *Literacy and young children: Research-based practices* (pp. 140–157). New York: Guilford.

McVicker, C. (2007). Comic strips as a text structure for learning to read. *The Reading Teacher, 61,* 85–89.

## Children's Literature Cited

Silverstein, S. (1974). Ickle me, pickle me, tickle me too. *Where the sidewalk ends.* New York: Harper & Row.

# Strategy 9

# Constructing Words

*Constructing Words* is an instructional strategy that engages students in word study across the grades (Cunningham, 1991). The purpose of the activity is to provide opportunities for readers to recognize word patterns and generate new words. As students actively manipulate onsets and rimes to explore different combinations of letters and sounds, they are applying their knowledge of phonics and decoding skills. In fact, this activity was found to be especially effective as an intervention for striving readers (Snow, Burns, & Griffin, 1998).

This activity is best suited for a guided reading lesson or as an intervention activity. In order to increase its effectiveness, teachers may use assessment data to target certain word patterns or sound stems for students to manipulate. It is also easily adaptable during the lesson to provide further support for striving readers or students with special needs.

---

### IRA/NCTE Standards for English Language Arts

6. Students apply knowledge of language structure, language conventions (e.g., spelling and punctuation), media techniques, figurative language, and genre to create, critique, and discuss print and nonprint texts.

11. Students participate as knowledgeable, reflective, creative, and critical members of a variety of literacy communities.

*Source: International Reading Association and National Council of the Teachers of English (1996).*

## Using Constructing Words

*When to use the strategy:* Constructing Words is designed as a guided reading lesson. However, it may also be used for an intervention session. In order to implement this instructional activity, the teacher will need letter tiles and magnetic boards. It is possible to use this activity with paper letters and file folders with pockets if magnetic boards are not available.

*Strategy modifications for grade levels:* Teachers may modify this lesson for intermediate grade students by creating a peer-tutoring activity. Students may work with a more advanced reader on constructing multisyllabic words.

### IMPLEMENTING THE CONSTRUCTING WORDS STRATEGY: STEP BY STEP

1. **Read aloud from selected text.** Teachers read aloud from a text that contains stem words for the Constructing Words activity. After the read-aloud, the highlighted words are defined and studied.

2. **Model constructing words.** Teachers write the rimes to use as stems on chart paper with selected onset letters. Using letter tiles, the teacher demonstrates how to create a new word with different onset letter tiles.

3. **Distribute word study sheet.** Teachers distribute Constructing Words sheet (see Figure 9.1) to students. Working in dyads, students use the letter tiles and magnetic boards to create new words. One partner uses the letter tiles to construct the word while the other records it on the sheet. Students take turns reversing roles for the activity.

4. **Summarize new vocabulary.** Students report words that were created and discuss their definitions. Teachers record their creations on chart paper or a SMART Board.

5. **Review new concepts.** Teachers ask students to share how their knowledge about onsets and rimes has changed as a result of the activity. At the conclusion of the session, teachers ask students how they may apply their new knowledge while reading independently.

### APPLYING THE CONSTRUCTING WORDS STRATEGY: FIRST-GRADE LESSON ON WORD STUDY

Students gather on the rug for a read-aloud of *Casey at the Bat* by Ernest Lawrence Thayer (1997). The teacher conducts a picture walk and asks students to use the title and pictures to make predictions. After the read-aloud, students discuss what happened

| Figure 9.1 | Constructing Words | |
|---|---|
| **Words We Created** | **Definitions** |
| | |
| | |
| | |
| | |

to Casey during the baseball game and check their predictions. Then the teacher highlights the following words in the text: *game, hip,* and *air.* The teacher models how to construct new words with the stem [dirt] and generates the word [shirt] by changing the onset letters. Using the Constructing Words sheet shown in Figure 9.1, the teacher directs students to do the following:

- Use the following letter tiles to create new words: s, t, h, 1, f.
- Write the words you created on the Constructing Words sheet.
- Define your new words with your partner.

After students have completed their sheets, the teacher asks them to report their new creations. Students are asked to share how they used their knowledge of letters and sounds to complete the activity.

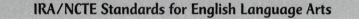

### IRA/NCTE Standards for English Language Arts

10. Students whose first language is not English make use of their first language to develop competency in the English language arts and to develop understanding of content across the curriculum.

*Source:* International Reading Association and National Council of Teachers of English (1996).

## DIFFERENTIATING INSTRUCTION FOR ENGLISH LANGUAGE LEARNERS

English language learners benefit from the integration of technology and word study. The "Alphabet Soup" activity on the Between the Lions website (PBS Kids, 2009) provides second-language learners with a multimodal method for engaging in word study. English language learners use the keyboard to respond to visual stimuli as they create new words. As each word is constructed, the student receives auditory feedback as well. Students may also save their work for the teacher to collect as assessment data.

## DIFFERENTIATING INSTRUCTION FOR STUDENTS WITH SPECIAL NEEDS

Research indicates that Constructing Words is an effective strategy for at-risk students (Snow et al., 1998). One way to increase its effectiveness for striving readers is to provide them with letter tiles that have raised bumps. These special letter tiles enable striving readers to trace over the onsets before attaching them to the stem word. As striving readers trace the raised letter tile and say the sound, they are processing the blending of sounds in order to decode.

## REFERENCES

Cunningham, P. M. (1991). *Phonics they use: Words for reading and writing.* New York: HarperCollins.

International Reading Association and National Council of Teachers of English. (1996). *Standards for the English language arts.* Newark, DE: International Reading Association and Urbana, IL: National Council of Teachers of English.

PBS Kids. (2009). *Between the lions: Alphabet soup.* Retrieved Feb. 12, 2010, from http://pbskids.org/lions/games/soup.html

Snow, C., Burns, M., & Griffin, P. (1998). *Preventing reading difficulties in young children.* Washington, DC: National Academy Press.

## Children's Literature Cited

Thayer, E. L. (1997). P. Polacco (Illus.). *Casey at the bat: A ballad of the republic, sung in the year 1888.* New York: Putnam.

# Strategy 10

## Picture It

### Speaking Briefly: An Overview of the Literacy Strategy

*Picture It* is an instructional strategy that focuses on the acquisition of the alphabetic principle. The alphabetic principle is the concept that words are composed of letters, which represent sounds (Harris & Hodges, 1995). Striving readers and students with special needs often struggle with this concept. One method for instructing all learners is to facilitate the association of a letter with an image or symbol. Research indicates that multimodal, explicit instruction in letter-sound relationships engages learners in the application of their knowledge and skills (Adams, 2003).

The purpose of the Picture It activity is to provide developing and striving readers with multimodal instruction in letters and sounds. As students begin to associate a visual image with a letter, they also are instructed to focus on the mouthing of the sound. Associating imagery and sound with graphemes will enable all readers to process the alphabetic principle.

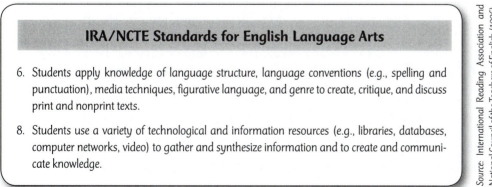

### IRA/NCTE Standards for English Language Arts

6. Students apply knowledge of language structure, language conventions (e.g., spelling and punctuation), media techniques, figurative language, and genre to create, critique, and discuss print and nonprint texts.

8. Students use a variety of technological and information resources (e.g., libraries, databases, computer networks, video) to gather and synthesize information and to create and communicate knowledge.

*Source:* International Reading Association and National Council of the Teachers of English (1996).

### Using Picture It

*When to use the strategy:* Picture It is designed as an intervention activity for a small group of students. However, it may be adapted for a whole class with modifications.

The activity will take several sessions to complete, as students must create photographs for letters. If teachers do not have access to a digital camera or phone camera, they may use images from the Internet as a substitution.

*Strategy modifications for grade levels:* Teachers may modify this lesson for younger students by facilitating the creation of a picture book that illustrates the targeted letter/sound/rime.

## IMPLEMENTING THE PICTURE IT STRATEGY: STEP BY STEP

1. **Select the targeted letter/sound.** Teachers present the targeted letter card on poster board and explicitly provide the sound.

2. **Invite students to provide examples.** Teachers attach a photograph of an item that begins with the targeted letter/sound and invite students to generate other examples from objects in the classroom.

3. **Provide digital cameras.** Teachers provide pairs of students with digital cameras and instruct them to photograph objects that begin with the targeted letter.

4. **Download images.** Teachers download and print images from the digital cameras. Students attach the images to their own letter cards.

5. **Say the sound.** Teachers scaffold students' pronunciation of the sound as they trace the letter on their cards. As they pronounce the sound, teachers call students' attention to how their mouth forms it.

6. **Repeat process with new letter/sounds.** Teachers use their assessment data to create new letter cards for additional sounds. Students retain the letter cards and bring them home to practice with their parents or caregivers.

## APPLYING THE PICTURE IT STRATEGY: KINDERGARTEN INTERVENTION ACTIVITY

The kindergarten teacher directs students to the letter card [Bb] on the easel. The teacher tells the students, "This is the letter [Bb] as in *boy*. The letter [Bb] says [bbb]. Let's say the sound together." After asking students to echo the sound, the teacher displays a picture of a bee and asks them to identify it. The picture is attached to the [Bb] letter card. The teacher asks students to look around the room to find objects that begin with the targeted letter/sound. Students' responses of *box*, *ball*, and *book* are written on chart paper. The teacher directs students to do the following:

- Work with your partner to take photos of objects in the room that begin with [Bb].

- Place the photo on your letter card and say the name of the sound.

- Watch your partner's mouth as he or she says the sound. What did you notice?

- Trace the letter on your card and say the sound again. Recite the name of the picture.

When students have completed the activity, they share their completed letter cards and photos with the other dyads.

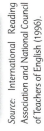

*Source:* International Reading Association and National Council of Teachers of English (1996).

> ### IRA/NCTE Standards for English Language Arts
>
> 10. Students whose first language is not English make use of their first language to develop competency in the English language arts and to develop understanding of content across the curriculum.

## DIFFERENTIATING INSTRUCTION FOR ENGLISH LANGUAGE LEARNERS

Pictures are effective tools for aiding English language learners' development of the alphabetic principle and phonics skills (Rogers & Helman, 2009). One adaptation for second-language learners is to extend the activity to a letter book. Using the digital camera, English language learners take several pictures of objects in the classroom that begin with the targeted letter. Working with the teacher or a more proficient partner, second-language learners create an alphabet book for each targeted letter by writing the names under each photo. The books can be taken home to share with their parents or may be placed in the classroom library for all to enjoy.

## DIFFERENTIATING INSTRUCTION FOR STUDENTS WITH SPECIAL NEEDS

The majority of students with special needs struggle with the alphabetic principle. One modification for this population is to create a tactile extension. Using an aluminum pan filled with cornmeal, students with special needs trace the targeted letter in cornmeal and say its sound. As students acquire words that begin with the initial sound, they may trace words as well. The multisensory nature of the experience helps striving readers associate the letter with the sound it represents.

## REFERENCES

Adams, M. (2003). Alphabetic anxiety and explicit, systematic phonics instruction: A cognitive science approach. In S. Neumann & D. K. Dickinson (Eds.), *Handbook of early literacy research* (pp. 66–81). New York: Guilford.

Harris, T., & Hodges, R. E. (1995). *The literacy dictionary: The vocabulary of reading and writing.* Newark, DE: International Reading Association.

International Reading Association and National Council of Teachers of English. (1996). *Standards for the English language arts.* Newark, DE: International Reading Association and Urbana, IL: National Council of Teachers of English.

Rogers, C., & Helman, L. (2009). One size does not fit all: How assessment guides instruction in word study with English learners. *New England Reading Association Journal, 44,* 17–24.

# SECTION III

# Essential Strategies for Teaching Reading Fluency

## A BRIEF OVERVIEW OF READING FLUENCY

Reading fluency is an essential mark of the proficient reader. Recently, fluency has been heralded by many educators as the key connector between reading words and comprehension. Samuels (2006) explains that when students are fluent readers, they read words quickly and accurately, freeing their attention and memory to work on comprehending the print. Research showing the correlation between reading fluency and reading achievement is well documented (Chard, Vaughn, & Tyler, 2002; Dowhower, 1994; Rasinski & Hoffman, 2003). Unfortunately, not all young students become fluent readers by the end of the third grade. Studies of reading fluency in upper and elementary grades have shown that fluency is a significant factor in students' reading achievement and suggest that fluency remain a part of their reading instructional program (Rasinski, Rikli, & Johnston, 2009). A review of the research by the National Reading Panel (National Institute of Child Health and Human Development, 2000) revealed that 44% of fourth-graders tested were dysfluent in reading. Emphasized as "one of the several critical factors necessary for reading comprehension," yet "often neglected in the classroom," reading fluency has become one of the building blocks within the reading program (Center for the Improvement of Early Reading Achievement, 2003, p. 11). Currently, research strongly supports the need to include fluency instruction in the reading program. Within this section, the following important aspects of fluency are discussed: the definition of fluency, characteristics of fluent and dysfluent readers, and what research has to say about appropriate instruction for developing fluency in young readers.

*What is fluency?* Teachers know when their students are fluent readers. Such students demonstrate "accurate, quick, meaningfully expressive, and appropriate phrased reading" (Rasinski & Padak, 2001, p. 162). Fluency is defined by the behaviors demonstrated by proficient readers while they read aloud. Understanding the definition or the components that contribute to reading fluency is important for teachers who plan instruction and assess children's reading fluency. The first essential component of fluency is *accurate reading*. Reading words correctly is dependent on students' decoding skills, their use of context to figure out words, and a large bank of sight words that allows them to instantly recognize a word (Torgesen & Hudson, 2006). *Reading rate* is the second essential component of reading. Fluency is characterized by quick, smooth, and effortless reading at a rate that is comfortable for both the reader and the listener. As teachers, we know that accurate reading supports a reader's rate of reading. When students do not have well-developed decoding skills or large sight-word vocabularies, they become "word readers" who labor at the sight of each word as they try to recognize or decode it. Much of their attention is spent on decoding words, with little focused on constructing meaning from the text. Samuels (2006) used the term *automaticity* to describe accurate and quick reading. Being able to recognize a body of words instantly, coupled with decoding skills, provides the foundation for fluent reading. Although some readers may be able to read lists of words, this is not fluency; fluent readers are expected to read words that appear in connected text quickly and accurately (Hudson, Lane, & Pullen, 2005). *Prosody* is the last essential component of reading fluency, and it describes the features that contribute to expressive reading. For example, the quality of oral fluent reading is expressive. The readers' pitch and tone change as they interpret the text; fluent readers attend to the phrasing and punctuation within the text, and they use these features to adjust their reading to convey meaning.

*What are the major differences between fluent and dysfluent reading?* Most teachers can identify fluent reading and know when students are struggling to read a passage by listening to their oral reading. All students read differently depending on the level of the text they read. All readers, for example, slow down when given a difficult text that is unfamiliar to them. As teachers begin to discern more fluent and less fluent reading among their students, they need to be aware of the level of text that is being read. At the same time, teachers need to be aware that fluent reading for a second- or third-grader may be different from that of a sixth-grader. Figure III.1 depicts a comparison of the reading behaviors of more fluent and less fluent readers. By observing and assessing students' reading behaviors associated with reading fluency, teachers plan more effective instruction for developing students' reading fluency.

*What does research say about instructional strategies to promote reading fluency?* The research on using the appropriate approach for developing strategies for teaching reading fluency is gaining ground. Samuels (2006, pp. 29–30) has outlined a number of instructional strategies that use repeated oral readings and have shown to be effective for increasing reading fluency. These include repeated readings, the use of commercially prepared and teacher-made audiotapes, stories on CD-ROM, partner reading, guided pairs, Readers Theatre, Choral Reading, and integrated instruction in fluency reading. The Center for the Improvement of Early Reading Achievement (2003) strongly supports guided repeated readings as a method for promoting reading fluency and suggests a second approach: Provide students with good models of reading. Children at all grade levels benefit from hearing excellent articulation of words and expressive reading—including phrasing, tone, and pitch—that delivers the meaning to listeners. This means it is important for students to hear teachers read aloud, as well as to hear other fluent readers.

The third approach for developing fluent readers is engaging students in silent reading. Although the research is sparse regarding independent reading programs, most classroom teachers encourage students to read on their own, at home as well as in the classroom. Reutzel and Cooter (2008) outline some disadvantages of engaging all

**Figure III.1**   Reading Behaviors of More Fluent Reading and Less Fluent Reading

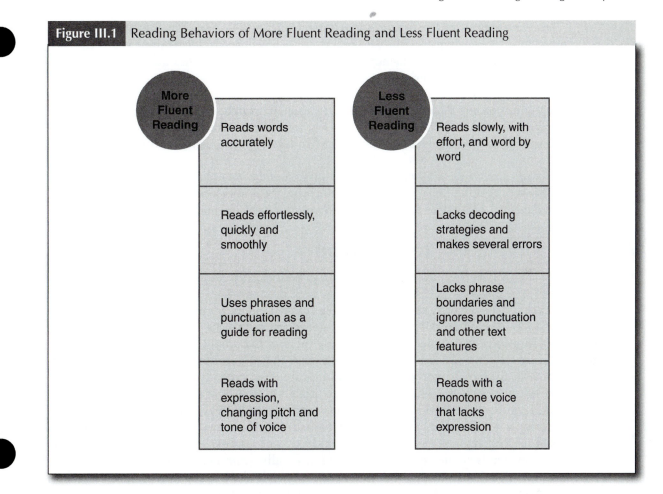

students in free reading, self-selecting their own books with no monitoring or accountability. Only when independent reading is carefully monitored by the teacher will students' fluency improve and develop. Many researchers claim that fluency and comprehension instruction for struggling readers should go hand in hand (Pressley, Gaskins, & Fingeret, 2006). Teachers who utilize in fluency instruction need to provide opportunities for students to engage in meaningful discussions of the text (Griffith & Rasinski, 2004). Finally, Applegate, Applegate, and Modla (2009) warn that reading fluency is important and contributes to comprehension; however, not all students who read the text fluently will necessarily comprehend it. Therefore, teachers need to understand that although developing reading fluency promotes comprehension, it does not secure it!

## GUIDELINES FOR TEACHING READING FLUENCY

*Incorporate read-alouds across the curriculum.* Students at all grade levels, from kindergarten through high school, benefit from hearing books read aloud. In addition to developing students' vocabularies and love for reading, they hear excellent models of reading fluency. Teachers should read aloud every day using outstanding children's literature.

*Provide students with authentic and interesting reading practices.* Reading fluency is developed through instruction and practice. Teachers need to incorporate repeated readings to promote reading fluency by using motivating approaches and genuine reasons for practicing oral reading.

*Integrate reading fluency across the curriculum.* Throughout the day, students read and write in a range of content areas. Teachers may take advantage of the abundant opportunities that varied subject areas present for developing students' oral reading fluency.

*Provide direct instruction in teaching reading fluency.* In addition to providing excellent models of reading fluency, teachers need to engage in direct instruction that encourages students to read words accurately, at an appropriate rate, and with expression.

## A STRATEGY FOR ASSESSING READING FLUENCY

Teachers can identify students who are fluent readers by asking them to read their text aloud. However, when they are engaged in monitoring students' progress of oral reading fluency, teachers need to assess the specific components of reading fluency. Reading fluency includes the following three major components that need to be systematically monitored: accuracy, reading rate, and prosody. *Accuracy* for word recognition refers to whether students read printed words correctly. With large sight-word vocabularies, fluent readers can instantly recognize most words or use appropriate decoding skills and word-learning strategies to determine unknown words. *Reading rate* is an important indicator of reading fluency and refers to how fast one reads connected discourse or text. Finally, *expressive reading* is an important aspect of reading fluency that is frequently overlooked in the assessment of reading fluency. It is characterized by reading that is smooth, natural, and conversational, with the reader using correct phrasing and a quality of tone and pitch that helps convey the meaning of the passage.

## ASSESSING THE PROGRESS OF A STUDENT'S ORAL READING FLUENCY

To facilitate the assessment and monitoring of students' oral reading fluency, use the rubric shown in Figure III.2 to assist in establishing levels of reading fluency. The rubric is based on Rasinski's (2003) Multidimensional Fluency Scale and clearly describes observable behaviors for three different components of oral reading fluency on four different levels of reading fluency. The rubric serves as a guide to the teacher in determining the student's level of proficiency for the following components of reading fluency: (1) word accuracy and reading rate, (2) reading with phrasing and rhythm, and (3) reading with expression. For each of the components, the rubric includes four levels of oral reading fluency—low fluency level, moderate fluency level, proficient fluency level, and advanced fluency level—with a set of reading behaviors for each criterion. To establish a student's level of reading fluency, follow the procedures for word accuracy and reading rate and phrasing, rhythm, and expression. Then match the student's results on each of the measures to the reading behaviors on the rubric to determine a level of oral reading proficiency for the specific component. For reading phrasing, rhythm, and expression, the teacher observes the student reading and determines the level of reading fluency by identifying matching oral reading behaviors.

| Figure III.2 | Rubric for Monitoring Oral Reading Fluency | | | |
|---|---|---|---|---|
| **Components for Oral Reading Fluency** | **Levels of Reading Fluency** | | | |
| | **Low Fluency Level** | **Moderate Fluency Level** | **Proficient Fluency Level** | **Advanced Fluency Level** |
| **Reading words correctly and reading rate** | Has poor word recognition skills, reading WCPM* below the 50th percentile for grade level; reads with effort at a slow and laborious pace; stops at each word | Has moderate word recognition skills, reading WCPM at the 50th to 75th percentile for grade level; reads at a moderate pace; stopping at some words | Has strong word recognition skills, reading WCPM at the 75th to 90th percentile for grade level; reads at a moderately comfortable pace; but slows or stops at challenging words | Has excellent word recognition skills, reading WCPM at or above the 90th percentile for grade level; reads effortlessly, at a conversational pace, adjusting pace to the reading selection |
| **Reading with phrasing and rhythm** | Reads word by word, with a lack of rhythm and no attention to phrase boundaries | Reads with proper phrasing at some times; has many false stops that frequently obstructs the rhythm of the language and interferes with the meaning of the text | Reads with proper phrasing at most times; has some false stops that obstructs the rhythm of the language but does not interfere with the meaning of the text | Reads with proper phrasing and appropriate rhythm of the language; smooth reading clearly helps to communicate the meaning of the text |
| **Reading with expression** | Reads without expression and enjoyment, simply calling out words; reads at a low volume that is inaudible | Reads with little expression and enthusiasm; at times demonstrates expression, appropriate pitch, and volume while reading; reading does not sound like natural langue | Reads with some enthusiasm and expression; reads with appropriate pitch, volume, and expression throughout most of the text; oral reading sounds like natural language through most of the text | Reads with enthusiasm and excellent expression, adjusting pitch, volume, and expression to interpret the meaning of the text; oral reading sounds like natural language throughout the reading of the text |

*words correct per minute

## PROCEDURE FOR ESTABLISHING FLUENCY LEVELS FOR READING RATE AND WORD ACCURACY

To determine the reading rate and accuracy, the teacher uses the *1-minute reading sample* method suggested by Rasinski (2003). By listening to students read grade-level text for 1 minute, their reading rate and word accuracy can be established. The practice for assessing students' words correct per minute (WCPM), taken three times per year, is an effective approach for progress monitoring (Hasbrouck & Tindal, 2006). To determine a student's WCPM, as well as the reader's reading fluency level for this component, use the following procedure:

1. Mark off 300 words from a passage in a book that is at the student's reading level and make two copies, one for the student and a second for the teacher.

2. As the student reads the passage aloud, record the errors on the teacher's copy. Errors include word omissions and substitutions as well as hesitations in reading a word that last longer than 3 seconds. Self-corrections made within a considerable period of time, 3 to 5 seconds, are not considered errors.

3. After one minute of reading, mark the word completed by the student.

4. Count the number of errors and subtract it from the total number of words the student read within 1 minute. For example, if a third-grader who was assessed in the fall read 102 words within 1 minute and had three errors, the student's WCPM would be 99. Using the norms established for WCPM, the student's performance would be at the 75th percentile. The norms for students in grades 1 through 8 for fall, winter, and spring in Figure III.3 have been established by Hasbrouck and Tindal (2006).

5. Use the reading norms and the student's results to determine the percentile for his/her performance. Determine the student's reading fluency level for reading accuracy and rate by consulting the rubric in Figure III.3.

| Figure III.3 | Oral Reading Fluency Norms for Grades 1–8 |

| Words Correct Per Minute (WCPM) | | | | |
| --- | --- | --- | --- | --- |
| | | **Fall** | **Winter** | **Spring** |
| **Grade** | **Percentile** | **WCPM** | **WCPM** | **WCPM** |
| **1** | 90 | | 81 | 111 |
| | 75 | | 47 | 82 |
| | 50 | | 23 | 56 |
| | 25 | | 12 | 28 |
| | 10 | | 6 | 15 |
| **2** | 90 | 106 | 125 | 142 |
| | 75 | 79 | 100 | 117 |
| | 50 | 51 | 72 | 89 |
| | 25 | 25 | 42 | 61 |
| | 10 | 11 | 18 | 31 |
| **3** | 90 | 128 | 146 | 162 |
| | 75 | 99 | 120 | 137 |
| | 50 | 71 | 92 | 107 |
| | 25 | 44 | 62 | 78 |
| | 10 | 21 | 36 | 48 |
| **4** | 90 | 145 | 166 | 180 |
| | 75 | 119 | 139 | 152 |
| | 50 | 94 | 112 | 123 |
| | 25 | 68 | 87 | 98 |
| | 10 | 45 | 61 | 72 |
| **5** | 90 | 166 | 182 | 194 |
| | 75 | 139 | 156 | 168 |
| | 50 | 110 | 127 | 139 |
| | 25 | 85 | 99 | 109 |
| | 10 | 61 | 74 | 83 |

| Grade | Percentile | Fall | Winter | Spring |
|---|---|---|---|---|
| | | WCPM | WCPM | WCPM |
| **6** | 90 | 177 | 195 | 204 |
| | 75 | 153 | 167 | 177 |
| | 50 | 127 | 140 | 150 |
| | 25 | 98 | 111 | 122 |
| | 10 | 68 | 82 | 93 |
| **7** | 90 | 180 | 192 | 202 |
| | 75 | 156 | 165 | 177 |
| | 50 | 128 | 136 | 150 |
| | 25 | 102 | 109 | 123 |
| | 10 | 79 | 88 | 98 |
| **8** | 90 | 185 | 199 | 199 |
| | 75 | 161 | 173 | 177 |
| | 50 | 133 | 146 | 151 |
| | 25 | 106 | 115 | 124 |
| | 10 | 77 | 84 | 97 |

*Source:* Hasbrouck, J., & Tindal, G. (2006). Oral reading fluency norms: A valuable assessment tool for reading teachers. *The Reading Teacher, 59*(7), 636–644.

## PROCEDURE FOR ESTABLISHING FLUENCY LEVELS FOR READING WITH RHYTHM, PHRASING, AND EXPRESSION

An excellent way to determine a student's expressive reading is through analyzing the student's taped oral reading. When taking a 1-minute sample of the student's reading to determine reading accuracy and rate, the teacher tapes the student's reading. At a later time, the teacher listens to the tape to determine the student's phrasing, rhythm, and expressive reading. Using the rubric in Figure III.2, determine the student's fluency level on the two components of reading fluency.

## A GUIDE FOR USING RESPONSE TO INTERVENTION FOR READING FLUENCY

As educators, we recognize that an important milestone in becoming literate is the development of reading fluency. Teachers of young students monitor their progress in oral reading fluency and analyze their performances on oral reading assessments. When a student's accuracy for word recognition, rate of reading, or reading with rhythm, phrasing, and expression does not reach the established level, the teacher offers an intervention strategy. The following serves as an example for using Response to Intervention.

The teacher of second-graders analyzed her observations of children's oral reading and identified those students who did not reach the established fluency level for reading with rhythm and expression. Within a small group, the teacher offered a mini-lesson that included direct instruction of these skills. The small-group instruction was followed by the students' engagement in paired-assisted reading to provide them with practice on these skills.

## Professional Resources

Opitz, M. F., & Rasinski, T. V. (2008). *Good-bye round-robin reading: 25 effective oral reading strategies* (Updated ed.). Portsmouth, NH: Heinemann.

Prescott-Griffin, M. L., & Witherell, N. (2004). *Fluency in focus: Comprehension strategies for all young readers.* Portsmouth, NH: Heinemann.

Rasinski, T. V. (2005). *The fluent reader: Oral reading strategies for building word recognition, fluency, and comprehension.* New York: Scholastic.

Rasinski, T. V., & Blachowicz, C. (2006). *Fluency instruction: Research-based practices.* New York: Guilford.

## References

Applegate, M. D., Applegate, A. J., & Modla, V. B. (2009). "She's my best reader; she just can't comprehend": Studying the relationship between fluency and comprehension. *The Reading Teacher, 62*(6), 512–521.

Center for the Improvement of Early Reading Achievement. (2003). *Put reading first: The research building blocks of reading instruction, kindergarten through grade 3* (2nd ed.). Washington, DC: National Institute for Literacy through the Educational Research and Development Centers Program, PR Award Number R305R70004 by the Office of Educational Research and Improvement, U.S. Department of Education.

Chard, D. J., Vaughn, S., & Tyler, B. (2002). A synthesis of research on effective interventions for building fluency with elementary students with learning disabilities. *Journal of Learning Disabilities, 35,* 386–406.

Dowhower, S. L. (1994). Repeated reading revisited: Research into practice. *Reading & Writing Quarterly, 10,* 343–358.

Griffith, L. W., & Rasinski, T. V. (2004). A focus on fluency: How one teacher incorporated fluency with her reading curriculum. *The Reading Teacher, 58*(2), 126–137.

Hasbrouck, J., & Tindal, G. (2006). Oral reading fluency norms: A valuable assessment tool for reading teachers. *The Reading Teacher, 59*(7), 636–644.

Hudson, R. F., Lane, H. B., & Pullen, P. C. (2005). Reading fluency, assessment, and instruction: What, why, and how? *The Reading Teacher, 58,* 702–714.

National Institute of Child Health and Human Development. (2000). *Report of the National Reading Panel. Teaching children to read: An evidence-based assessment of the scientific literature on reading and its implications for reading instruction* (NIH Publication No. 00–4769). Washington, DC: U.S. Government Printing Office.

Pressley, M., Gaskins, I. W., & Fingeret, L. (2006). Instruction and development of reading fluency in struggling readers. In S. J. Samuels & A. E. Farstrup (Eds.), *What research has to say about fluency instruction* (pp. 47–69). Newark, DE: International Reading Association.

Rasinski, T. V. (2003). Reading first: Fluency is fundamental. *Instructor, 113*(4), 15–20.

Rasinski, T. V., & Hoffman, J. V. (2003). Theory and research into practice: Oral reading in the school literacy curriculum. *Reading Research Quarterly, 38*(4), 510–532.

Rasinski, T. V., & Padak, N. D. (2001). *From phonics to fluency: Effective teaching of decoding and fluency in the elementary school.* New York: Longman.

Rasinski, T. V., Rikli, A., & Johnston, S. (2009). Reading fluency: More than automaticity? More than a concern for primary grades? *Literacy Research and Instruction, 48,* 350–361.

Reutzel, D. R., & Cooter, R. B. (2008). *Teaching children to read: The teacher makes the difference* (5th ed.). Upper Saddle River, NJ: Merrill Prentice Hall.

Samuels, S. J. (2006). Toward a model of reading fluency. In S. J. Samuels & A. E. Farstrup (Eds.), *What research has to say about fluency instruction* (pp. 24–46). Newark, DE: International Reading Association.

Torgesen, J. K., & Hudson, R. F. (2006). Reading fluency: Critical issues for struggling readers. In S. J. Samuels & A. E. Farstrup (Eds.), *What research has to say about fluency instruction* (pp. 130–158). Newark, DE: International Reading Association.

# Paired-Assisted Reading

# Strategy
# 11

The *Paired-Assisted Reading* strategy provides a structured approach for partnering students to practice oral reading. Often called partner reading, two students are paired for the purpose of listening to each other as they practice reading aloud. The strategy is based on peer-mediated learning: The more fluent reader gives assistance to the less fluent reader when needed. Research has demonstrated that Paired-Assisted Reading is a powerful strategy for promoting oral reading while developing fluency (Samuels, 2006). Reading fluency in young children performing at varying levels improved as a result of peer-assisted learning in oral reading (Fuchs et al., 2001). Further, Nes (2003) reported that the Paired-Assisted Reading strategy used with upper elementary students led to a significant improvement in their reading fluency. In his discussion of the research on Paired-Assisted Reading, Topping (2006) describes this strategy as a highly effective approach for developing reading fluency.

Paired or partner reading was first used as a suggestion to parents in helping their children practice reading at home. Soon, the strategy was used in the primary grades to promote practice in reading; eventually, it had been adapted to a variety of classroom settings. In all cases, its purpose remains the same: to establish a context for students to engage in repeated oral readings and develop fluency. Simply put, two students read together, with one more fluent student modeling reading and guiding the less fluent reader. Depending on the resources of the classroom, the procedure for assisting the reader may change. For example, in classrooms where teacher assistants are available to work with the classroom teacher and share instructional responsibilities, greater support and more frequent monitoring of students by adults during paired reading would increase their fluency. However, when resources are scarce, using Paired-Assisted Reading with two students of different reading ability levels would allow time for practicing reading, with assistance given to the less fluent reader. In one study reported by Griffith and Rasinski (2004), the teacher used a 30-minute block for partner reading with results showing an improvement in reading fluency for less fluent students. Part of the success for this strategy, as well as many others, occurs when teachers establish routines for its use and diligently monitor the students to ensure their engagement in reading.

*Source:* International Reading Association and National Council of Teachers of English (1996).

### IRA/NCTE Standards for English Language Arts

3. Students apply a wide range of strategies to comprehend, interpret, evaluate, and appreciate texts. They draw on their prior experience, their interactions with other readers and writers, their knowledge of word meaning and of other texts, their word identification strategies, and their understanding of textual features (e.g., sound-letter correspondence, sentence structure, context, graphics).

## USING PAIRED-ASSISTED READING

*When to use the strategy:* Teachers may use the strategy within a variety of contexts. Most teachers establish routines for having students practice reading after they have received instruction on vocabulary, read the text, and engaged students in a discussion on the story. Teachers may also use the strategy after a shared reading experience.

*Strategy modifications for grade levels:* Children in kindergarten and first grade will need more guidance in using the Paired-Assisted Reading strategy. Some students in the early primary grades may need help in taking turns. For these younger students, the teacher may start with paired reading to help students learn to take turns and listen to their partners read. After students understand turn taking, helping them offer assistance when their partners do not know a word is the next step.

### IMPLEMENTING THE PAIRED-ASSISTED READING STRATEGY: STEP BY STEP

1. **Organize the classroom for paired reading.** Have students seated close to each other in a comfortable and quiet location that has few or no distractions.

2. **Select appropriate reading materials.** The passages to be read should be within the students' reading instructional range. Students receiving assistance from a more fluent reader will benefit from selections that they can read with little difficulty that contain a few words they have just learned. Texts that are too easy or too difficult will not promote fluency and may cause boredom or frustration for the readers and result in diverting the students from the task of reading. The fluent reader should be capable of reading the text assigned to the less fluent reader with ease. If the paired students are being assisted by a tutor or a teacher assistant, the students may be at a similar fluency level and, therefore, be reading the same text that is appropriate to their reading level.

3. **Establish a procedure that will work for the students.** There are a number of factors to consider when using this instructional strategy. Each classroom is different with respect to the students' backgrounds, ages, reading levels, motivation, and interest in learning. Another important factor to consider is the resources available to the teachers. Some classes have very large student enrollments and no teacher assistants, and others have a small class size and one or two teacher assistants to aid in instruction. Therefore, decide on a procedure that is appropriate

for the context of the classroom. Once the procedure is decided, implementing the Paired-Assisted Reading strategy may take several trials with refinements and changes to make it work for the students. Consider the following different ways of implementing the strategy:

- Pair two students, one more fluent and the second less fluent in reading, each having different reading levels. Have the more fluent reader assist the less fluent reader.

- Pair two students from the same class with similar reading levels. Have students receive assistance from a tutor or the teacher assistant.

- Pair two students from the same class with similar reading levels. The teacher monitors several groups, moving from one group to another and offering assistance to those who need it.

- Use cross-grade pairing of students—an older fluent reader with a younger less fluent reader. Have the older student read and then listen to the less fluent student, offering guidance and assistance during repeated readings.

4. **Assign students to reading pairs.** Select students who are compatible and work well together.

5. **Establish a procedure with carefully defined roles for each student to follow.** When students know what they must do, have clear expectations for accomplishing the task, and are held accountable, they will spend more time engaged in reading. All students need to demonstrate the attitudes, dispositions, and skills of listening and helping their peers. Therefore, the teacher uses the model selected for Paired-Assisted Reading—based on the students' age, grade, reading levels, interests, and motivation for reading—and defines a set of rules for paired reading. Train students to follow the established procedures, and monitor their reading behaviors during the implementation of the strategy.

## APPLYING THE PAIRED-ASSISTED READING STRATEGY: SECOND-GRADE LESSON ON FAMOUS AMERICAN WOMEN

Students in the second grade were reading books on famous American women. After silent reading, students were partnered for Paired-Assisted Reading. The teacher paired two students who were reading the same book and had different levels of fluency; one student was more fluent in reading and was paired with a second student who was less fluent and needed some assistance. One pair of reading partners was reading *Amelia and Eleanor Go for a Ride* by Pam Munoz Ryan (2000). This very inviting picture storybook is based on the true story of two accomplished women, Amelia Earhart and Eleanor Roosevelt, and their admiration and friendship for each other. After students engaged in a 15-minute silent reading of their selected books, they were partnered for paired reading. The students first talked about what they read, and they decided on the passage they would read to each other. The more fluent reader read first and provided a demonstration of effortless reading to the student who needed assistance, while the less fluent reader listened and followed each word with a pointer. As the second reader began to read, the fluent reader followed along in a similar fashion and offered assistance when the partner stopped, hesitated on a word, or asked for assistance. The partner said the word, and the reading proceeded.

*Source:* International Reading Association and National Council of Teachers of English (1996).

> ### IRA/NCTE Standards for English Language Arts
>
> 10. Students whose first language is not English make use of their first language to develop competency in the English language arts and to develop understanding of content across the curriculum.

## DIFFERENTIATING INSTRUCTION FOR ENGLISH LANGUAGE LEARNERS

Students who are learning the English language will benefit from tape-assisted readings. English language learners benefit from demonstrations of reading at an advanced fluency level. Have students first listen to the audiotape as they follow the text. Students practice oral reading by reading along with the tape and then reading to another student who is fluent in reading.

## DIFFERENTIATING INSTRUCTION FOR STUDENTS WITH SPECIAL NEEDS

To modify Paired-Assisted Reading for students with special needs, the teacher works with a small group of students who have low levels of reading fluency or with an individual student who is far below the group's fluency level. First, the teacher reads part of the text aloud at a comfortable reading rate for students, and then the students read aloud with the teacher. When the students are ready to read, they select a small part of the text for reading aloud by themselves. Each student rereads the selection alone as the teacher offers assistance to them when needed. When a student makes an error on a word, the teacher corrects it and proceeds without stopping. After students read their selections, the teacher provides individual feedback and may decide to model a specific component of reading fluency such as expressive reading, appropriate phrasing, reading rate, or word accuracy.

## REFERENCES

Fuchs, D., Fuchs, L., Yen, L., McMaster, K., Svenson, E., Yong, N., et al. (2001). Developing first-grade reading fluency through peer mediation. *Teaching Exceptional Children, 34*(2), 90–93.

Griffith, L. W., & Rasinski, T. V. (2004). A focus on fluency: How one teacher incorporated fluency with her reading curriculum. *The Reading Teacher, 58*(2), 126–137.

International Reading Association and National Council of Teachers of English. (1996). *Standards for the English language arts.* Newark, DE: International Reading Association and Urbana, IL: National Council of Teachers of English.

Nes, S. L. (2003). Using paired reading to enhance the fluency skills on less-skilled readers. *Reading Improvement, 40*(4), 179–192.

Samuels, S. J. (2006). Toward a model of reading fluency. In S. J. Samuels & A. E. Farstrup (Eds.), *What research has to say about fluency instruction* (pp. 24–46). Newark, DE: International Reading Association.

Topping, K. J. (2006). Building reading fluency: Cognitive, behavioral, and socioemotional factors and the role of peer-mediated learning. In S. J. Samuels & A. E. Farstrup (Eds.), *What research has to say about fluency instruction* (pp. 106–129). Newark, DE: International Reading Association.

## Children's Literature Cited

Ryan, P. M. (2000). *Amelia and Eleanor go for a ride: Based on a true story*. New York: Scholastic.

# Strategy

# 12

# Choral Reading

## SPEAKING BRIEFLY: AN OVERVIEW OF THE LITERACY STRATEGY

The *Choral Reading* strategy engages students in group-assisted, repeated readings. Students read aloud in unison within a small group or with the whole class. The purpose of the strategy is to provide practice on reading text with fluency. Students gain confidence in reading, because when they read together as a group, they are supported by their peers, who may be more fluent readers, or they may be assisted by the teacher when necessary. In addition to gaining fluency in reading and vocabulary development, they develop an appreciation of literature.

The teacher chooses a text that is appropriate for repeated reading by a group of students, models fluent reading by reading the text aloud, engages students in a discussion of the reading, provides necessary instruction (e.g., vocabulary instruction, phrasing, etc.) and offers the tips to follow for an effective choral reading of the text. Depending on the selected text and familiarity of the students with Choral Reading, the teacher chooses the arrangement for the repeated reading. Figure 12.1 provides a description of variations in arrangements of Choral Reading that are suitable with different texts, as well as with students' varying ages and levels of reading fluency (Rasinski, 2003; Tierney & Readence, 2005; Yopp & Yopp, 2003).

| Figure 12.1 | Types of Choral Reading |
| --- | --- |
| **Unison Choral Reading** | The traditional approach uses the whole group of students, who read the text as one voice. |
| **Antiphonic Choral Reading** | Antiphonic reading is alternating reading with the text divided into parts. Students are divided into two or more groups. Each group is assigned one or more parts, and each group reads on cue. |
| **Cumulative Choral Reading** | This type of repeated reading creates a crescendo effect; that is, the voice and effect swell as more students join in the oral reading. |
| **Dialogue Choral Reading** | Each group of students reads the dialogue of the assigned character. Another group of students may be assigned to read the narrative part of the text. |

| Refrain Choral Reading | Such choral reading occurs when the text contains a refrain such as a poem, lyrics to a song, or a ballad. Each stanza is read by a different group, with the refrain read by the entire class. |
|---|---|
| Echo Reading | Within this type of oral reading, the teacher reads first and the students "echo" the reading, or read it after the teacher. At times, a student may assume the role of the lead reader. |

Choral Reading is supported by scientific evidence (National Institute of Child Health and Human Development, 2000), because it includes repeated readings of the text. It is important that teacher modeling of fluent reading along with direct instruction of the elements of fluent reading are included as part of the strategy. Further, to help students advance in their development of reading fluency, the teacher needs to provide feedback during practice and on their oral reading performances.

## IRA/NCTE Standards for English Language Arts

3. Students apply a wide range of strategies to comprehend, interpret, evaluate, and appreciate texts. They draw on their prior experience, their interactions with other readers and writers, their knowledge of word meaning and of other texts, their word identification strategies, and their understanding of textual features (e.g., sound-letter correspondence, sentence structure, context, graphics).

4. Students adjust their use of spoken, written, and visual language (e.g., conventions, style, vocabulary) to communicate effectively with a variety of audiences and for different purposes.

*Source:* International Reading Association and National Council of Teachers of English (1996).

# USING CHORAL READING

*When to use the strategy:* Choral Reading may be used with smaller guided reading groups or with larger groups who are doing class work. Students who are engaged in these repeated readings should have read the text or have the text read to them by the teacher. The Choral Reading strategy works well after reading, because students are familiar with the text.

*Strategy modifications for grade levels:* Beginner readers in the primary grades should have shorter texts than students in the upper grades and texts that are at their reading level. Prior to having the whole class read together, beginner readers in kindergarten and first grade should practice reading and rereading their texts with the teacher.

## IMPLEMENTING THE CHORAL READING STRATEGY: STEP BY STEP

1. **Select the text that will be used for repeated readings.** Choose a text appropriate for students' reading levels and interests. Poems that have repetition or repeated

refrains and rhythm work well for students who are not familiar with choral reading as well as for younger children with limited sight-word vocabularies. Repeated refrains will provide multiple exposures to words during a single reading.

2. **Prepare the text for Choral Reading and introduce the activity to the students.** Choose an arrangement for the oral reading and mark the text accordingly. For younger students with shorter text, the teacher may write the text on chart paper. For longer text that is more appropriate for older students, the teacher may prepare individual copies that are marked to indicate parts to be read together. Introduce the activity by offering an overview and providing a purpose for engaging in Choral Reading.

3. **Model reading the text fluently and offer direct instruction when necessary.** Begin by reading the entire text aloud. Engage students in a lively discussion on the meaning of the text. Offer direct instruction of reading words accurately, phrasing, or reading with expression. Depending on the text, provide a mini-lesson on words that students may not know and model reading with rhythm and correct phrasing as well as reading with expression to denote the meaning. Students may find it difficult at first to read together or in unison. Therefore, suggestions regarding keeping the same reading rate and tone may be necessary.

4. **Monitor repeated reading of the text.** If the text is short and the group is small, rehearsal of the text may be conducted by the teacher with a small group of students—in pairs through partner reading or in small groups with readers taking turns. As students are reading, the teacher monitors for the important elements of fluent reading. For Choral Reading to be effective with respect to reading words accurately and with automaticity, as well as reading with correct phrasing and expression, students must reread the text a minimum of four times. During the rehearsal, the teacher may have observed and offered feedback of specific reading behaviors that were exceptionally good or that needed correction. Reminders of such reading behaviors prior to reading may offer support to students.

5. **Conduct the Choral Reading of the text.** After students have had sufficient time to rehearse their parts through repeated readings, engage them in Choral Reading of the text. For students who are not familiar with Choral Reading, offer a reminder with regard to when and what they are to read.

## APPLYING THE CHORAL READING STRATEGY: FOURTH-GRADE LESSON ON ANTARCTICA

In the fourth grade, students were studying about Antarctica. During their independent reading time, the teacher put out a number of books on life in Antarctica, including numerous books on penguins. As part of the unit, the teacher engaged students in a read-aloud of *Antarctic Antics: A Book of Penguin Poems* by Judy Sierra (1998). After students responded to the poems, the teacher selected poems from the book and distributed copies to the students, who were divided into groups of four. Each group selected a poem that they wanted to read together to the class. The groups practiced reading the poem together as the teacher monitored their accuracy for reading words, reading rate, phrasing, and expressive reading. After rehearsing their poems through several repeated readings, students were given an opportunity to read their poems to the class. Each group stood in front of the class and read their poems in unison.

*Source:* International Reading Association and National Council of Teachers of English (1996).

> ### IRA/NCTE Standards for English Language Arts
>
> 10. Students whose first language is not English make use of their first language to develop competency in the English language arts and to develop understanding of content across the curriculum.

## DIFFERENTIATING INSTRUCTION FOR ENGLISH LANGUAGE LEARNERS

Choral Reading provides English language learners (ELLs) a safe environment as they practice oral reading within a small group of readers. As they are supported by more fluent readers, group reading provides a sheltered, nonthreatening, and low-anxiety environment in which ELLs are not singled out for errors in their oral performances. To help ELLs make gains in fluent reading, carefully select text that students can understand and to which they can relate. Begin with poetry that is short and has a lively rhythm and is easy to understand and interpret. Students enjoy and are encouraged by humorous poetry that is highly predictable. Such poems allow students to predict words, thereby aiding them in developing their sight-word vocabularies as well as word recognition skills. Because students are beginning to learn a new language, it is important to assist their understanding of English through encouraging nonverbal cues to accompany their oral performance in reading (McCauley & McCauley, 1992).

## DIFFERENTIATING INSTRUCTION FOR STUDENTS WITH SPECIAL NEEDS

Students with special needs benefit from repeated readings and receive a boost in self-confidence when they can join their peers in a Choral Reading activity. The teacher first provides additional support to students prior to Choral Reading through a read-aloud to model how a fluent reading of the text sounds and a discussion of the meaning of the text. Each student then receives individual assistance before the Choral Reading activity. Such assistance given to the student with special needs may be in the form of Echo Reading. The teacher reads one sentence, and the student reads that sentence after hearing the teacher read it. Further, research is quite specific with respect to how the activity is to be conducted with striving readers if rapid progress is to be made. Pressley, Gaskins, and Fingeret (2006) describe successful interventions where "students practiced daily echo and choral reading of text saturated with decodable and high-frequency words, both at school and at home" (p. 55).

## REFERENCES

International Reading Association and National Council of Teachers of English. (1996). *Standards for the English language arts.* Newark, DE: International Reading Association and Urbana, IL: National Council of Teachers of English.

McCauley, J. K., & McCauley, D. S. (1992). Using choral reading to promote language learning in ESL students. *The Reading Teacher, 45*(7), 526–533.

National Institute of Child Health and Human Development. (2000). *Report of the National Reading*

*Panel. Teaching children to read: An evidence-based assessment of the scientific literature on reading and its implications for reading instruction* (NIH Publication No. 00–4769). Washington, DC: U.S. Government Printing Office.

Pressley, M., Gaskins, I. W., & Fingeret, L. (2006). Instruction and development of reading fluency in struggling readers. In S. J. Samuels & A. E. Farstrup (Eds.), *What research has to say about fluency instruction* (pp. 47–69). Newark, DE: International Reading Association.

Rasinski, T. V. (2003). *The fluent reader: Oral reading strategies for building word recognition, fluency, and comprehension.* New York: Scholastic.

Tierney, R. J., & Readence, J. E. (2005). *Reading strategies and practices: A compendium* (6th ed.) Boston: Allyn & Bacon.

Yopp, R. H., & Yopp, H. K. (2003). Time with text. *The Reading Teacher, 57*(3), 284–287.

## Children's Literature Cited

Sierra, J. (1998). *Antarctic antics: A book of penguin poems.* San Diego, CA: Gulliver Books.

# Strategy
# 13

# Read-Arounds

## SPEAKING BRIEFLY: AN OVERVIEW OF THE LITERACY STRATEGY

The *Read-Arounds* strategy provides students with an opportunity to share with their peers a selection from a book they especially enjoyed. Students read a featured book and identify a passage that they wish to share with others. They prepare to read their selection to their peers through rereadings and assistance from their teacher and peers.

Consider how learning to read fluently occurs within the context of Read-Arounds. According to the constructivist theory, learning is a social activity (Vygotsky, 1962, 1978). Through the joint participation of the student and an expert (the teacher or another skilled student), the reader is assisted in learning an important cultural activity, reading. Rogoff (1990) explains that learning takes place by entering an apprenticeship where the acquisition of knowledge or a skill, such as reading, occurs through social activity. Therefore, supported by the teacher and their peers, students become fluent readers through assistance from members of the classroom community and their shared book experiences.

Tompkins (2007) suggests that Read-Arounds may be considered as celebrations of featured books, to be used at the end of a unit. Students enjoy the activity of sharing the parts of the book with others and listening to their friends as they read their selections. However, the strategy may be used for a number of different purposes and within a variety of contexts. For example, Read-Arounds may be used as part of guided reading. Within this context, the students select a few sentences or a short passage from the book they have read, engage in repeated readings of the selection, with the teacher offering assistance and feedback, and finish through engaging in the Read-Around. Students then explain why they have selected that text. Another variation of Read-Arounds may be used as part of a writing activity with students who have completed a research paper on a topic from a particular content area. Students may share their research with their peers by reading the summary paragraph of their papers. As with other applications, practice reading orally precedes the Read–Around and a discussion of the meaning of the text follows.

*Source:* International Reading Association and National Council of Teachers of English (1996).

---

### IRA/NCTE Standards for English Language Arts

3. Students apply a wide range of strategies to comprehend, interpret, evaluate, and appreciate texts. They draw on their prior experience, their interactions with other readers and writers, their knowledge of word meaning and of other texts, their word identification strategies, and their understanding of textual features (e.g., sound-letter correspondence, sentence structure, context, graphics).

4. Students adjust their use of spoken, written, and visual language (e.g., conventions, style, vocabulary) to communicate effectively with a variety of audiences and for different purposes.

12. Students use spoken, written, and visual language to accomplish their own purposes (e.g., for learning, enjoyment, persuasion, and the exchange of information).

---

# USING READ-AROUNDS

*When to use the strategy:* After students finish reading a book that they enjoyed, they will select a short passage that they especially liked. To develop fluency, they will practice reading the passage prior to sharing it with the class.

*Strategy modifications for grade levels:* Fluent readers and students in the intermediate and middle grades selecting and rehearsing the passage for the Read-Arounds will not need assistance in following the procedure. Beginner readers, less fluent readers, and English language learners will need assistance in selecting an appropriate passage for reading aloud to their peers. Passages should be shorter and within the students' reading level range. Assistance such as teacher feedback, instruction, and staying on task may be needed during the repeated reading of the passage.

## IMPLEMENTING THE READ-AROUNDS STRATEGY: STEP BY STEP

The procedure for implementing the Read-Arounds strategy is simple and straightforward and may be changed to fit the purpose and context of the activity. It is important, however, that the following elements are included to promote fluency development: modeling of fluent reading by the teacher, silent reading, oral repeated reading with assistance and feedback from the teacher, and a shared Read-Around by students.

1. **Establish a purpose for performing the Read-Arounds.** The teacher uses the Read-Arounds as part of the literacy program. This activity may be integrated in one of many routines, such as guided reading, literature circles, independent reading, content area reading, writing, etc.

2. **Explore the reading passage with the students.** After students have read and discussed the text, the teacher guides them in their selection of a passage to be read. The length of the passage will depend on the purpose and context for reading. For example, older students sharing their research may read a summary that is longer than that of a first-grader who is reading one or two sentences from a shared-reading book.

3. **Explain the process of practicing reading, and model fluent reading.** Organize students for practice reading their selected passages. They may engage in repeated readings independently, paired with another student, or with a small group of three or four students. The teacher sets the purpose for rehearsing the Read-Around and models reading one of the passages. The teacher will instruct the students to focus on an aspect of fluent reading such as accurate reading, expressive reading, the tone or volume, or the rate of reading.

4. **Assist students as they engage in repeated readings of their selected passages.** As students work individually or in small groups practicing their reading, the teacher observes the reading and offers feedback to each student. Students should be given time for at least four rereadings to benefit from practice.

5. **Engage students in reading their passages to the class or small group.** During the Read-Arounds, students read orally to their peers. The teacher encourages the audience to use listening skills during the performance of the Read-Around. Feedback from the teacher or peers is not given during the Read-Around as it is during practice. At the end of the Read-Arounds, the teacher and students congratulate all participants.

## APPLYING THE READ-AROUNDS STRATEGY: FIRST-GRADE LESSON

The first-grade teacher reads *Stone Soup: An Old Tale* by Marcia Brown (1947) to the class. After hearing the story, the teacher engages them in a lively discussion of the story. The students then read the story silently and select the page that they enjoyed and wish to share with others in their Read-Around. The teacher assigns students to learning partners for practice reading. Taking turns reading to their partners, students engage in reading aloud at least three times. After their practice session, students read their passages to the class, telling them why they selected that part to read.

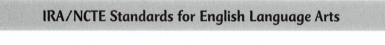

**IRA/NCTE Standards for English Language Arts**

10. Students whose first language is not English make use of their first language to develop competency in the English language arts and to develop understanding of content across the curriculum.

*Source:* International Reading Association and National Council of Teachers of English (1996).

## DIFFERENTIATING INSTRUCTION FOR ENGLISH LANGUAGE LEARNERS

English language learners will derive much assistance in developing reading fluency as well as oral language proficiency through engaging in a modified Read-Around strategy. After students have selected their passages for the Read-Around, have them first listen to the teacher or the audiotape as it is read aloud. This demonstration of fluent reading will help students learn the pronunciation of words and correct phrasing of the text. They practice their passage by engaging in repeated readings of their selected passage as the teacher or another reader offers feedback and assistance.

## DIFFERENTIATING INSTRUCTION FOR STUDENTS WITH SPECIAL NEEDS

Read-Arounds may be differentiated for students with special needs through the use of taped repeated readings. The teacher reads the text or part of the text aloud while the student listens. A brief discussion of the text follows the read-aloud. The teacher then decides on the fluency skill that the students need and models it with the selected text. The student selects a sample of the text to read and practices by reading it aloud two or three times using the tape recorder. The student listens to the tape with the teacher, who provides feedback on the target fluency skill. Finally, the student uses the input and rereads the text once again.

## REFERENCES

International Reading Association and National Council of Teachers of English. (1996). *Standards for the English language arts.* Newark, DE: International Reading Association and Urbana, IL: National Council of Teachers of English.

Rogoff, B. (1990). *Apprenticeship in thinking.* New York: Oxford University Press.

Tompkins, G. (2007). *Literacy for the 21st century: Teaching reading and writing in prekindergarten through grade 4.* Upper Saddle River, NJ: Merrill Prentice Hall.

Vygotsky, L. S. (1962). *Thought and language.* Cambridge: MIT Press.

Vygotsky, L. S. (1978). *Mind in society.* Cambridge, MA: Harvard University Press.

## CHILDREN'S LITERATURE CITED

Brown, M. (1947). *Stone soup: An old tale.* New York: Simon & Schuster.

# Strategy
# 14

# Radio Reading

## SPEAKING BRIEFLY: AN OVERVIEW OF THE LITERACY STRATEGY

The *Radio Reading* strategy is a simple instructional tool used by teachers for developing reading fluency, and its effectiveness has been supported by research (Samuels, 2006). Simply stated, students become radio announcers by reading to their peers, who serve as their audience. Like real radio announcers, students must hold their audience's interest by their fluent reading; therefore, Radio Reading promotes authentic purposes for reading to a real audience. This goal compels students to practice reading their parts through repeated reading of texts. During their oral reading, students focus on meaning and components of fluency that will help communicate their message—word accuracy, reading rate, as well as using an appropriate tone, phrasing, and expression during reading.

The primary purpose of Radio Reading is to provide an activity for students to develop their communication skills (Searfoss, 1975), rather than developing reading fluency. The procedure of the original strategy does not include repeated readings and feedback from the teacher to produce fluent reading. We have adapted the original strategy by incorporating repeated readings as well as feedback and assistance from the teacher for developing reading fluency.

Radio Reading is most effective with short passages (Reutzel & Cooter, 2008) that are more appropriate for developing reading fluency skill. When students practice reading their text three to five times and receive feedback from the teacher, they will benefit from improved automaticity for word recognition as well as improved expressive reading (Rasinski, 2003). An added benefit of Radio Reading is the development of listening comprehension skills in the audience. After the oral readings, the listeners may be asked to respond or to pose a question. The listening audience may ask the radio reader to clarify an aspect of the text by rereading a certain part or by answering a question. When all students are involved in this way, there is an expectation for deeper levels of listening by the audience and an understanding of the text by radio readers, along with their improved reading fluency.

*Source:* International Reading Association and National Council of Teachers of English (1996).

> ### IRA/NCTE Standards for English Language Arts
>
> 3. Students apply a wide range of strategies to comprehend, interpret, evaluate, and appreciate texts. They draw on their prior experience, their interactions with other readers and writers, their knowledge of word meaning and of other texts, their word identification strategies, and their understanding of textual features (e.g., sound-letter correspondence, sentence structure, context, graphics).
>
> 4. Students adjust their use of spoken, written, and visual language (e.g., conventions, style, vocabulary) to communicate effectively with a variety of audiences and for different purposes.
>
> 12. Students use spoken, written, and visual language to accomplish their own purposes (e.g., for learning, enjoyment, persuasion, and the exchange of information).

## USING RADIO READING

*When to use the strategy:* The strategy is appropriate for developing reading fluency through repeated readings of a text. Prior to practicing the passage for reading to an audience, clarification of the text is needed. Students should have read the text silently and aloud to a partner or to the teacher several times, and when confident, the student will be ready to read it aloud to an audience.

*Strategy modifications for grade levels:* Students at all grade levels may participate in Radio Reading. In the primary grades, using narrative and informational literature at students' reading levels would be more appropriate. For intermediate and middle grades, the strategy may be used with literature as well as content-area texts, newspaper and magazine articles, and texts written by students. It is important that texts are selected within students' reading levels and that students practice reading their parts before presenting the broadcast.

### IMPLEMENTING THE RADIO READING STRATEGY: STEP BY STEP

1. **Select materials for the readers.** Prior to conducting Radio Reading, the teacher prepares or selects a script for each reader that is appropriate in difficulty and length. For the benefit of the reader and the listener, the script should be interesting and challenging but not frustrating (Tierney & Readence, 2005). The materials may be any kind: news articles from papers, text from informational books, or narrative from children's literature. Depending on the grade level and reading ability, the script may be a single reading or it may include two or three different selections read by the student throughout the performance.

2. **Prepare the students for participating in the activity by explaining their roles.** Discuss the purpose of the activity and procedure that will be followed. Familiarize students with the role of the news anchor, who organizes and introduces the various reporters when it is their turn to read the news. Emphasize the importance of communicating the message to the audience using an appropriate tone and

reading expression that will hold their audience's attention; stress the importance of good listening skills to the audience, who will not be reading the script but will learn from listening to the announcer.

3. **Guide students in reading their texts.** After students have selected or have been given assigned passages to read, engage them in a discussion. Encourage students to talk about the meaning. One approach that teachers may use to ensure understanding of assigned texts is to ask students to retell their passage in their own words. The teacher provides clarification and feedback when necessary.

4. **Provide time to practice reading.** Provide students with time to practice reading and rereading their texts. They may work with a partner; each partner listens to the reader and offers assistance and feedback. As students work together, the teacher observes and offers assistance and feedback when necessary, ensuring that each student is ready and confident to perform for the audience.

5. **Organize the radio readers and audience for the radio broadcast.** The teacher may organize a production for radio that is formal or less formal. In any case, the radio readers sit around a table in the order in which they are performing. The audience is seated in front of the performers ready to listen to the readings. A student or teacher may serve as the moderator who introduces each student and the title of the text. Each radio reader is expected to read through the text with no interruptions.

6. **Allow time for response from the audience.** The audience is encouraged to respond to the readings. They ask questions to clarify the meanings of the text, or they may ask a reader to reread a part of the passage they especially liked or did not understand.

## Applying the Radio Reading Strategy: Eighth-Grade Lesson

Eighth-graders are in literature circles reading selected works of Jan Cheripko. Among the books are *Rat* (2002), *Imitate the Tiger* (1998), and *Sun Moon Stars Rain* (2006). As part of the daily routine, each group of students in a literature circle selects the same book to read. During reading time, students read silently, raise questions related to the story, engage in 15-minute discussion on the questions, and use their journals to enter their written responses. The teacher has incorporated the Radio Reading strategy within the students' regular routines for literature circles. Since students' discussions of their readings focused on different dilemmas that challenged the main characters, the teacher directed group members to select a paragraph from their daily reading that clearly described the problem that their character must solve. After discussion, they practiced reading their parts to their group. On the following day, prior to the regular routine established for the literature circle, each group presented the main character's dilemma through Radio Reading of their group's selected passages.

---

### IRA/NCTE Standards for English Language Arts

10. Students whose first language is not English make use of their first language to develop competency in the English language arts and to develop understanding of content across the curriculum.

*Source:* International Reading Association and National Council of Teachers of English (1996).

## Differentiating Instruction for English Language Learners

English language learners (ELLs) need models of fluent reading. The teacher may assist ELLs during rehearsal by partnering fluent readers with ELLs. The fluent reader models how to read the passage by reading it first, followed by the ELL. The fluent reader listens to his/her partner and offers feedback and assistance. Students need to read the passage at least three to four times before participating in Radio Reading.

## Differentiating Instruction for Students With Special Needs

Students with special needs frequently lack reading fluency and will therefore benefit from Radio Reading. To promote students' fluency development, select a short passage that the student is able to read. Model to students how their passage should be read by reading it aloud to them while they follow along. Emphasize to them the importance of word accuracy, expressive reading, phrasing, and intonation during the oral reading. Have each student read the passage and record their reading. Analyze each student's oral reading of the passage, and decide on specific skills that need to be taught. Listen to the passage once more with the student and offer appropriate feedback and instruction to improve the student's oral reading. When the students are prepared to read the selected passage, have them engage in radio reading to a small group.

## References

International Reading Association and National Council of Teachers of English. (1996). *Standards for the English language arts*. Newark, DE: International Reading Association and Urbana, IL: National Council of Teachers of English.

Rasinski, T. V. (2003). Reading first: Fluency is fundamental. *Instructor, 113*(4), 15–20.

Reutzel, D. R., & Cooter, R. B. (2008). *Teaching children to read: The teacher makes the difference* (5th ed.). Upper Saddle River, NJ: Merrill Prentice Hall.

Samuels, S. J. (2006). Toward a model of reading fluency. In S. J. Samuels & A. E. Farstrup (Eds.), *What research has to say about fluency instruction* (pp. 24–46). Newark, DE: International Reading Association.

Searfoss, L. W. (1975). Radio reading. *The Reading Teacher, 29*, 295–296.

Tierney, R. J., & Readence, J. E. (2005). *Reading strategies and practices: A compendium* (6th ed.). Boston: Allyn & Bacon.

## Children's Literature Cited

Cheripko, J. (1998). *Imitate the tiger*. Honesdale, PA: Boyds Mills.

Cheripko, J. (2002). *Rat*. Honesdale, PA: Boyds Mills.

Cheripko, J. (2006). *Sun moon stars rain*. Asheville, NC: Front Street.

# Strategy
# 15

# Readers Theatre

## SPEAKING BRIEFLY: AN OVERVIEW OF THE LITERACY STRATEGY

The *Readers Theatre* strategy provides a motivational and authentic context for students to develop all aspects of fluency—accuracy in reading words, an appropriate reading rate, and expressive, smooth, and conversational reading. Unlike many typical oral reading routines where students read to their teacher, they perform for an audience, reading scripts adapted from the best models of children's literature as well as other materials. The mood created by this strategy is described by Martinez, Roser, and Strecker (1998–1999): "Readers Theatre is an interpretive reading activity in which readers use their voices to bring characters to life" (p. 326).

The Readers Theatre strategy incorporates script writing, modeling and teaching the elements of reading fluency, rehearsing the reading of the script, and performing for a "real" audience. The basis for the strategy that ensures fluency development is assisted repeated readings, and it has been heralded as one of the most successful approaches for developing reading fluency in children (Griffith & Rasinski, 2004). In addition to their practice of reading texts, students are given instruction in fluent reading as well as feedback during rehearsal of texts. For these reasons, Readers Theatre has received support from scientific-based research as a reading strategy that promotes reading fluency development (National Reading Panel, 2000; Samuels, 2006). Additional research indicates that the Readers Theatre strategy is a powerful tool for developing reading fluency for average and low-achieving readers (Keehn, 2003) and for students with special needs (Corcoran & Davis, 2005).

The selection of texts for reading is very important. To ensure success, texts should be interesting and relevant to the students. A variety of commercially prepared scripts are available, with a large selection accessible from the Internet or books containing scripts that are written on grade level. Although many teachers and students collaborate in writing a script for a class performance, frequently scripts are simply adapted from children's literature, both fictional and informational trade books, and textbooks. When adapting a piece of fiction, select a story with a strong plot and much dialogue. Stories that contain an abundance of dialogue with very little narration require little adaptation.

*Source:* International Reading Association and National Council of Teachers of English (1996).

## IRA/NCTE Standards for English Language Arts

3. Students apply a wide range of strategies to comprehend, interpret, evaluate, and appreciate texts. They draw on their prior experience, their interactions with other readers and writers, their knowledge of word meaning and of other texts, their word identification strategies, and their understanding of textual features (e.g., sound-letter correspondence, sentence structure, context, graphics).

4. Students adjust their use of spoken, written, and visual language (e.g., conventions, style, vocabulary) to communicate effectively with a variety of audiences and for different purposes.

11. Students participate as knowledgeable, reflective, creative, and critical members of a variety of literacy communities.

12. Students use spoken, written, and visual language to accomplish their own purposes (e.g., for learning, enjoyment, persuasion, and the exchange of information).

## USING READERS THEATRE

*When to use the strategy:* Readers Theatre may be used within most phases of reading and language arts instruction, such as reading and writing workshop, guided reading, or independent reading. Prior to writing their scripts, students read and discuss the book; when scripts are written by students, they use writing workshops. For successful performances, students read and reread their parts before performing for the class.

*Strategy modifications for grade levels:* The Readers Theatre strategy works effectively for students at all grade levels. Because students in the early primary grades may not be fluent readers and writers, the teacher and students may collaborate in writing a script that should be carefully adapted to the students' reading levels. Students in the upper grades may work in cooperative groups to write their own scripts. In all cases, the teacher uses the students' reading levels, as well as ages, to determine the length of the text for Readers Theatre.

### IMPLEMENTING THE READERS THEATRE STRATEGY: STEP BY STEP

1. **Select the script for reading.** Commercially available scripts, scripts written by students, or scripts written by the teacher adapted from children's literature are appropriate. Material for scripts may come from adaptations of children's literature, both fictional and informational texts, commercially prepared scripts, or student- or teacher-authored scripts. Teachers should follow the guidelines when selecting or preparing a script for Readers Theatre:

   • Scripts should be appealing and engaging, with content and language relating to students' experiences and interests.

   • Scripts should be written at students' instructional reading level. Students will benefit from reading and rereading text that contains mostly words they already know and some new words they learn through instruction.

- The length of the scripts should be appropriate to the reading level and age of the students. For example, kindergarten students may be able to read one line of text, whereas fifth-graders may do well with several sentences.

2. **Prepare students by reading and discussing the script.** Assist students in reading the script orally by providing time for them to read it silently. After silent reading of the script, engage students in a discussion of the script to ensure understanding of the plot and characters, their actions, feelings, emotions, etc. If the script is informational text based on content, ensure that students understand the concepts and academic vocabulary within the script. Offer direct instruction of any new vocabulary within the reading for which students may need help such as word meanings or decoding.

3. **Facilitate students' rehearsal of their parts.** Have students select their parts and rehearse them through repeated reading. When appropriate, students may engage in partner reading for rehearsing their parts. As students read their parts aloud, offer assistance and feedback to improve the students' reading fluency. For example, students may be reading without expression, they may be word reading and need help with phrasing, or they may need to improve their reading rate. Finally, help students in using their voice, gestures, and body language to interpret their parts.

4. **Explain the staging to the students.** The type of staging for Readers Theatre does not involve costumes and scenery or an actual stage for the presentation. Have students arrange chairs in an appropriate place in the classroom for their production. Emphasize that the importance lies in accurate reading with a tone and expression that will convey meaning to the audience.

5. **Performing for others.** Students rehearse until they read their parts fluently. When they are ready, their dramatic performances may be shared among themselves or with other classes throughout the school.

## APPLYING THE READERS THEATRE STRATEGY: THIRD-GRADE LESSON

Students in the third grade studied the solar system as part of their science unit on space. The teacher integrated science and literacy by having students read a book from the following text set: (1) *Eleven Planets: A New View of the Solar System* by David A. Aguilar (2008), (2) *Going Around the Sun: Some Planetary Fun* by Marianne Berkes (2008), (3) *The Planets* by Gail Gibbons (2008), (4) *Solar System* by Dr. Mike Goldsmith (2004), (5) *Boy, Were We Wrong About the Solar System* by Kathleen V. Kudlinski (2008), and (6) *Our Solar System* by Seymour Simon (2007). The books are written at varying levels of difficulty; therefore, the teacher guided the students in their selection of books. Students discussed their books within their small groups and wrote ideas in their learning journals. Following their discussion, the teacher and students wrote a documentary play for Readers Theatre, shown in Figure 15.1. Each student received a copy, selected a part, and rehearsed it within their groups by rereading it orally to one another as the teacher provided feedback with respect to their accuracy of reading, reading rate, and expression. When the students were rehearsed, they arranged their chairs to resemble the solar system and took their places and read their parts.

**Figure 15.1** Script for Readers Theatre

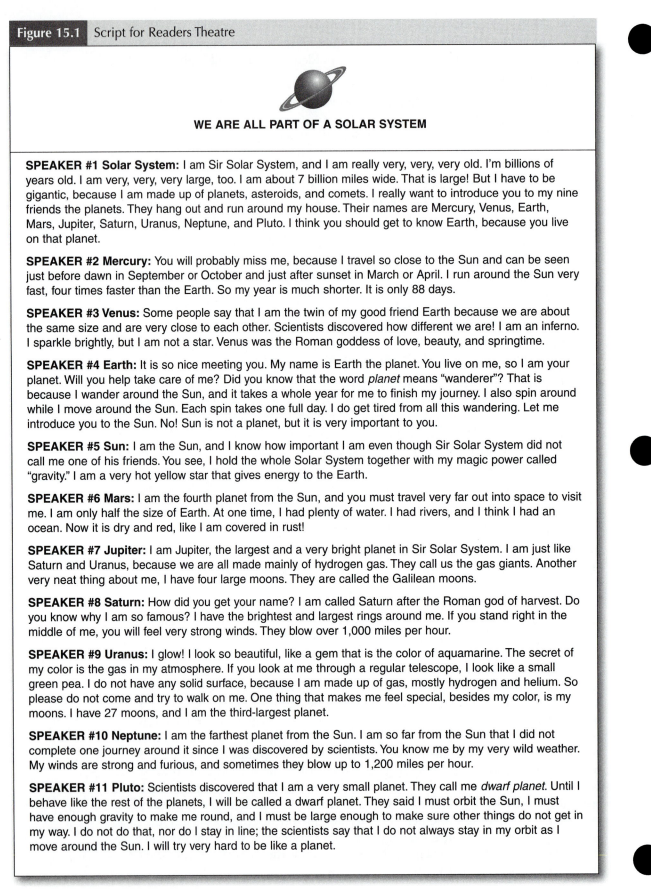

**WE ARE ALL PART OF A SOLAR SYSTEM**

**SPEAKER #1 Solar System:** I am Sir Solar System, and I am really very, very, very old. I'm billions of years old. I am very, very, very large, too. I am about 7 billion miles wide. That is large! But I have to be gigantic, because I am made up of planets, asteroids, and comets. I really want to introduce you to my nine friends the planets. They hang out and run around my house. Their names are Mercury, Venus, Earth, Mars, Jupiter, Saturn, Uranus, Neptune, and Pluto. I think you should get to know Earth, because you live on that planet.

**SPEAKER #2 Mercury:** You will probably miss me, because I travel so close to the Sun and can be seen just before dawn in September or October and just after sunset in March or April. I run around the Sun very fast, four times faster than the Earth. So my year is much shorter. It is only 88 days.

**SPEAKER #3 Venus:** Some people say that I am the twin of my good friend Earth because we are about the same size and are very close to each other. Scientists discovered how different we are! I am an inferno. I sparkle brightly, but I am not a star. Venus was the Roman goddess of love, beauty, and springtime.

**SPEAKER #4 Earth:** It is so nice meeting you. My name is Earth the planet. You live on me, so I am your planet. Will you help take care of me? Did you know that the word *planet* means "wanderer"? That is because I wander around the Sun, and it takes a whole year for me to finish my journey. I also spin around while I move around the Sun. Each spin takes one full day. I do get tired from all this wandering. Let me introduce you to the Sun. No! Sun is not a planet, but it is very important to you.

**SPEAKER #5 Sun:** I am the Sun, and I know how important I am even though Sir Solar System did not call me one of his friends. You see, I hold the whole Solar System together with my magic power called "gravity." I am a very hot yellow star that gives energy to the Earth.

**SPEAKER #6 Mars:** I am the fourth planet from the Sun, and you must travel very far out into space to visit me. I am only half the size of Earth. At one time, I had plenty of water. I had rivers, and I think I had an ocean. Now it is dry and red, like I am covered in rust!

**SPEAKER #7 Jupiter:** I am Jupiter, the largest and a very bright planet in Sir Solar System. I am just like Saturn and Uranus, because we are all made mainly of hydrogen gas. They call us the gas giants. Another very neat thing about me, I have four large moons. They are called the Galilean moons.

**SPEAKER #8 Saturn:** How did you get your name? I am called Saturn after the Roman god of harvest. Do you know why I am so famous? I have the brightest and largest rings around me. If you stand right in the middle of me, you will feel very strong winds. They blow over 1,000 miles per hour.

**SPEAKER #9 Uranus:** I glow! I look so beautiful, like a gem that is the color of aquamarine. The secret of my color is the gas in my atmosphere. If you look at me through a regular telescope, I look like a small green pea. I do not have any solid surface, because I am made up of gas, mostly hydrogen and helium. So please do not come and try to walk on me. One thing that makes me feel special, besides my color, is my moons. I have 27 moons, and I am the third-largest planet.

**SPEAKER #10 Neptune:** I am the farthest planet from the Sun. I am so far from the Sun that I did not complete one journey around it since I was discovered by scientists. You know me by my very wild weather. My winds are strong and furious, and sometimes they blow up to 1,200 miles per hour.

**SPEAKER #11 Pluto:** Scientists discovered that I am a very small planet. They call me *dwarf planet*. Until I behave like the rest of the planets, I will be called a dwarf planet. They said I must orbit the Sun, I must have enough gravity to make me round, and I must be large enough to make sure other things do not get in my way. I do not do that, nor do I stay in line; the scientists say that I do not always stay in my orbit as I move around the Sun. I will try very hard to be like a planet.

*Source:* International Reading Association and National Council of Teachers of English (1996).

| IRA/NCTE Standards for the English Language Arts |
|---|

10. Students whose first language is not English make use of their first language to develop competency in the English language arts and to develop understanding of content across the curriculum.

## DIFFERENTIATING INSTRUCTION FOR ENGLISH LANGUAGE LEARNERS

English language learners (ELLs) benefit from Readers Theatre in numerous ways. In addition to developing accuracy in reading words and strengthening their sight-word vocabularies, ELLs learn the rhythm of the English language, which is frequently different from their home language. Teachers may assist ELLs by listening to their pronunciation of words, highlighting words that are not pronounced correctly or words that they do not know. Target these words for individual instruction and practice. Teachers may also provide students with assistance in their reading of the text with respect to students' pitch, phrasing, and stress. They may model their parts and provide positive feedback.

## DIFFERENTIATING INSTRUCTION FOR STUDENTS WITH SPECIAL NEEDS

Provide support to students with special needs through individual assistance during repeated readings. Select a text that relates to students' experiences and one they will be able to read. In focusing on appropriate phrasing, use direct instruction in teaching students to read meaningful chunks of text by doing the following: (1) Use a highlighter to mark the phrases within the text; (2) read the text aloud to students, model appropriate phrasing, and use a pointer to sweep across the text by phrases; and (3) assist the students in reading the text for phrasing by using the pointer and offering feedback to encourage and correct the students' performance.

## REFERENCES

Corcoran, C. A., & Davis, A. D. (2005). A study of the effects of Readers Theatre on second- and third-grade special education students' fluency growth. *Reading Improvement, 42*(2), 105–111.

Griffith, L. W., & Rasinski, T. V. (2004). A focus on fluency: How one teacher incorporated fluency with her reading curriculum. *The Reading Teacher, 58*(2), 126–137.

International Reading Association and National Council of Teachers of English. (1996). *Standards for the English language arts.* Newark, DE: International Reading Association and Urbana, IL: National Council of Teachers of English.

Keehn, S. (2003). The effect of instruction and practice through Readers Theatre on young readers. *Reading Research and Instruction, 42*(4), 41–61.

Martinez, M., Roser, N. L., & Strecker, S. (1998–1999). "I never thought I could be a star": A Readers Theatre ticket to fluency. *The Reading Teacher, 52*(4), 326–334.

National Reading Panel. (2000). *Teaching children to read: An evidence-based assessment of the scientific literature on reading and its implications for reading instruction.* Washington, DC: National Institute of Child Health and Human Development.

Samuels, S. J. (2006). Toward a model of reading fluency. In S. J. Samuels & A. E. Farstrup (Eds.), *What research has to say about fluency instruction* (pp. 24–46). Newark, DE: International Reading Association.

## Children's Literature Cited

Aguilar, D. A. (2008). *Eleven planets: A new view of the solar system.* Washington, DC: National Geographic.

Berkes, M. (2008). *Going around the sun: Some planetary fun.* Nevada City, GA: Dawn Publications.

Gibbons, G. (2008). *The planets* (3rd ed.). New York: Holiday House.

Goldsmith, M. (2004). *Solar system.* Boston: Kingfisher.

Kudlinski, K. V. (2008). *Boy, were we wrong about the solar system.* New York: Dutton Children's Books.

Simon, S. (2007). *Our solar system* (Updated ed.). New York: Collins.

# SECTION IV

# Essential Strategies for Teaching Vocabulary

## A BRIEF OVERVIEW OF VOCABULARY DEVELOPMENT

The term *vocabulary* has a range of meanings. For example, some teachers use the term to mean *sight-word vocabularies,* referring to students' immediate recognition of words in print; other teachers refer to words students understand as their *meaning vocabularies*. Still other teachers use the term to mean *listening vocabularies,* or students' understanding of words that they hear in the spoken language. Content teachers use the term *academic vocabulary* to refer to content-specific words. Within this section, we use the term *vocabulary* to refer to students' understanding of oral and print words. Vocabularies include conceptual knowledge of words that goes well beyond a simple dictionary definition. Students' vocabulary knowledge is a building process that occurs over time as they make connections to other words, learn examples and nonexamples of the word and related words, and use the word accurately within the context of the sentence (Snow, Griffin, & Burns, 2005).

Why is vocabulary development such an important aspect of a student's academic life? Think about the relationship of vocabulary to overall literacy development. A number of studies have shown that vocabulary size in young children is a strong predictor for success in later grades: The larger the children's vocabularies in the primary grades, the greater their academic achievement in the upper grades. The National Reading Panel (NRP; National Institute of Child Health and Human Development, 2000) analyzed scientific studies that led them to conclude that readers' vocabulary is strongly related to their understanding of text. The NRP explained that when students are taught key words before reading text, they have greater comprehension than students who do not receive such instruction. Clearly, the preponderance of such evidence led the NRP to emphasize vocabulary instruction as an essential element of the literacy program.

Reflecting on the nature of children's learning of words confirms the strong relationship between vocabulary and comprehension and calls attention to the prominent place that vocabulary instruction should hold in the literacy program. Research related to vocabulary instruction and word knowledge shows that there is a robust correlation between knowing words and comprehending text (Beck, McKeown, & Kucan, 2008). Many educators feel that a strong vocabulary program just makes sense. Consider that words are labels for their meanings and when we know a word, we know what it represents. Some words are more complex than others, having multiple meanings, while others are conceptually rich and networked to countless other words. There are those words that may have different syntactic uses depending on their context within a sentence. For example, the word *run* can be used as a noun or a verb. Thus, learning a new word takes place over time. As students hear and read the word in many different contexts, their understanding and use of the word will develop and increase. Thus, the students within our classroom may have an understanding of a word, but the degree to which they know a word may differ. The Partnership for Reading (2003) has used the following three levels to describe students' knowledge for word meanings:

- *Unknown:* The word is completely unfamiliar and its meaning is unknown.

- *Acquainted:* The word is somewhat familiar; the student has some idea of its basic meaning.

- *Established:* The word is very familiar; the student can immediately recognize its meaning and use the word correctly. (p. 43)

## GUIDELINES FOR TEACHING VOCABULARY

Learning words does not occur in a vacuum; that is, children do not acquire meanings of words in isolation. All learning—both personal and academic—occurs within the sociocultural environment of the home, community, and classroom. "Literacy is a social practice, so students learn academic vocabulary through social interactions as members of the learning community" (Scott, Nagy, & Flinspach, 2008, p. 197). Therefore, effective teachers of language and literacy provide practices that stimulate rich uses of language, designing their instructional programs within a social context that promotes literacy learning.

Teachers know that students who are learning to read and write and those who are reading to learn—that is, learning in content areas—will benefit from a sound instructional vocabulary program. This is especially true for classrooms where children have small vocabularies and are English language learners. Knowledge of words is acquired incidentally, where vocabulary is developed through immersion in language activities. Words are also learned through direct instruction, where students learn words through a structured approach. Thus, vocabulary programs should be designed to support children's word learning through a combination of approaches to teaching, direct instruction, and incidental word learning. Michael Graves (2006) offers a framework for successful vocabulary programs that supports effective teaching and students' development of word knowledge. The foundation of his instructional program includes a four-part approach to developing robust vocabularies: (1) Provide rich and varied language experiences, (2) teach individual words, (3) teach word-learning strategies, and (4) foster word consciousness (pp. 4–8).

*Providing rich and varied language experiences:* Incidental word learning takes place when teachers offer and encourage students to participate in a variety of rich language experiences that occur throughout the day and across the curriculum. Examples of such experiences that promote rich and powerful vocabularies at all grade levels include

(1) interactive read-alouds of outstanding children's literature, (2) dialogic-based instructional activities, (3) independent reading, (4) interactive writing, and (5) creating a print-rich environment where the "walls are dripping with words."

*Teaching individual words:* Although many words may be learned incidentally and vocabularies do become stronger when they are supported with a language-rich environment, children benefit from systematic and direct instruction of words. The research is clear with respect to effective teaching of words (Graves, 2006). Vocabulary instruction should (1) provide students with information that contains the context as well as the meaning of the word, (2) design instruction that engages students and allows sufficient time for word learning, (3) make sure students have multiple exposures to the words with review and practice, and (4) create a dialogue around the words.

*Teaching word-learning strategies:* An important aspect of developing students' robust vocabularies is teaching them tools to unlock the meaning of unknown words. The most effective tools use the context of the surrounding words or sentences to infer the meaning of a word, using meaningful word parts to make sense out of the unknown word and using the dictionary effectively to help define an unknown word.

*Building word consciousness in readers and writers:* An important aspect of a strong vocabulary program is to engage students in learning new words. As teachers, we need to develop word consciousness within our students and maintain their interest in words. Graves and Watts-Taffe (2008) suggest that teachers "(1) create a word-rich environment, (2) recognize and promote adept diction, (3) promote word play, (4) foster word consciousness through writing, (5) involve students in original investigations, and (6) teach students about words" (p. 186).

## A STRATEGY FOR ASSESSING VOCABULARY DEVELOPMENT

Assessing student learning is a critical component of effective teaching and achievement. Therefore, part of the teacher's literacy instructional plan needs to include the assessment of students' vocabulary development. We aligned our progress monitoring of vocabulary with the following instructional goals: (1) to enhance vocabulary development and use, (2) to develop word-learning strategies, and (3) to build word consciousness. One approach in assessing students' vocabulary development is through the use of the rubric in Figure IV.1. The rubric contains six criteria related to the goals of the vocabulary instructional program. By monitoring students' progress, teachers may use the results to modify their instruction to meet the needs of individual students, those of the class, and the instructional program.

| Figure IV.1 Rubric for Assessing Vocabulary Development | | | |
| --- | --- | --- | --- |
| **Criterion** | **Level #3 Advanced (3 Points)** | **Level #2 Developing (2 Points)** | **Level #1 Striving (1 Point)** |
| **Word identification** | The student is proficient in saying, reading, or writing the word. | The student has some difficulty saying, reading, or writing the word. | The student has a lot of difficulty saying, reading, or writing the word. |

*(Continued)*

(Continued)

| Word meaning | The student knows the comprehensive meaning of the word and can discuss multiple meanings of the word. | The student knows a partial meaning of the word but has difficulty discussing a full meaning of the word. | The student does not know the meaning of the word and cannot discuss it. |
|---|---|---|---|
| **Reading the word** | The student offers a rich explanation of the contextual meaning of the word. | The student offers a partial explanation of the contextual meaning of the word. | The student is not able to explain the contextual meaning of the word. |
| **Writing the word** | The student uses the word with a high degree of accuracy within the context of writing. | The student uses the word with some degree of accuracy within the context of writing. | The student does not attempt to use the word within the context of writing. |
| **Word-learning strategies** | The student uses a range of word-learning strategies, along with varied resources, to learn new words. | The student uses few word-learning strategies and resources to learn new words. | The student does not use word-learning strategies and resources to learn new words. |
| **Word consciousness** | The student demonstrates an awareness and interest in learning and using new words. | The student demonstrates a minimal awareness and interest in learning and using new words. | The student does not demonstrate an awareness and interest in learning and using new words. |
| **Overall level of vocabulary development** | **Advanced level 18–13 points** | **Developing level 12–7 points** | **Striving level 6–0 points** |

## A Guide for Using Response to Intervention for Vocabulary

Word knowledge is more than just reading a word! As we have discussed in this section, knowing words is multidimensional and the process occurs over time. Therefore, effective instruction and assessment in vocabulary will take into account the students' development in reading words correctly, knowing the meaning of a word within several different contexts, using words in reading as well as writing, using word-learning strategies, and being word conscious. The rubric in Figure IV.1 provides a multidimensional approach to assess word learning that teachers may use to monitor students' vocabulary development in reading and writing. As teachers apply the rubric for evaluating students' performances, they will see patterns emerge in each of these areas that need improvement and may use the results for selecting a Response to Intervention strategy. For example, one teacher of students with special needs analyzed the assessment results and found that four students were not "word conscious." The students had little or no awareness of new and exciting words, and their lack of a positive disposition for words hindered their vocabulary development. The teacher used these results for selecting a Response to Intervention strategy. She chose and implemented the Vocabulary Self-Collection strategy and found there was an overall difference in her students' stance toward learning new words.

## PROFESSIONAL RESOURCES

Allen, J. (2004). *Inside words: Tools for teaching academic vocabulary, grades 4–12.* Portland, ME: Stenhouse.

Baumann, J. F., & Kame'enui, E. J. (Eds.). (2004). *Vocabulary instruction: Research to practice.* New York: Guilford.

Brand, M. (2004). *Word savvy: Integrated vocabulary, spelling, and word study, grades 3–6.* Portland, ME: Stenhouse.

Frey, N., & Fisher, D. (2009). *Learning words inside and out, grades 1–6: Vocabulary instruction that boosts achievement in all subject areas.* Portsmouth, NH: Heinemann.

## REFERENCES

Beck, I. L., McKeown, M. G., & Kucan, L. (2008). *Creating robust vocabulary: Frequently asked questions and extended examples.* New York: Guilford.

Graves, M. F. (2006). *The vocabulary book: Learning and instruction.* New York: Teachers College Press.

Graves, M. F., & Watts-Taffe, S. (2008). For the love of words: Fostering word consciousness in young readers. *The Reading Teacher, 62*(3), 185–193.

National Institute of Child Health and Human Development. (2000). *Report of the National Reading Panel. Teaching children to read: An evidence-based assessment of the scientific research literature on reading and its implications for reading instruction* (NIH Publication No. 00-4769). Washington, DC: U.S. Government Printing Office.

Partnership for Reading. (2003). *Put reading first: The research building blocks of reading instruction, kindergarten through grade 3.* (2nd ed.). Washington, DC: Author.

Scott, J. A., Nagy, W. E., & Flinspach, S. L. (2008). More than merely words: Redefining vocabulary learning in a culturally and linguistically diverse society. In A. E. Farstrup & S. J. Samuels (Eds.), *What research has to say about vocabulary instruction* (pp. 182–210). Newark, DE: International Reading Association.

Snow, C. E., Griffin, P., & Burns, M. S. (Eds.). (2005). *Knowledge to support the teaching of reading: Preparing teachers for a changing world.* San Francisco: Jossey-Bass.

# Strategy 16

# Vocabulary Self-Collection Strategy

## SPEAKING BRIEFLY: AN OVERVIEW OF THE LITERACY STRATEGY

The *Vocabulary Self-Collection* strategy (VSS) is an interactive-learning instructional strategy that promotes word consciousness, as students are actively engaged in identifying important words from their reading to share with members of their class. The strategy was first introduced by Haggard (1982, 1986) and since then has been adapted for various grade levels and instructional contexts. Students select words from their readings that are new and interesting, use the context and other resources to determine the meaning of the words, and nominate the words to be learned by others in the group or class. Teachers using the VSS (1) model the process of collecting words, (2) provide guided practice within reading groups and other instructional contexts, and (3) offer consistent encouragement to students to use VSS during independent reading. The major benefits of using VSS are that students engage in their own learning, discover how to recognize unfamiliar or interesting words from their readings, develop their vocabularies, and become word conscious.

A review of the research on vocabulary instruction conducted by Harmon and Hedrick (2005) led them to claim that struggling readers learn vocabulary when teachers "encourage independent learning by allowing students to self-select terms to be studied" (p. 275). They pointed to VSS as an approach to encourage students to select and study words that they feel are important to learn. Research conducted by Calderon et al. (2005) with English language learners demonstrated that, in addition to teaching vocabulary before reading, their discourse around the text after reading leads to students' vocabulary development.

*Source:* International Reading Association and National Council of Teachers of English (1996).

> ### IRA/NCTE Standards for English Language Arts
>
> 3. Students apply a wide range of strategies to comprehend, interpret, evaluate, and appreciate texts. They draw on their prior experience, their interactions with other readers and writers, their knowledge of word meaning and of other texts, their word identification strategies, and their understanding of textual features (e.g., sound-letter correspondence, sentence structure, context, graphics).

## USING VOCABULARY SELF-COLLECTION

*When to use the strategy:* VSS should be introduced before reading and used by students during and after reading. VSS has been used with intermediate, middle, and secondary students within cooperative group settings, but the strategy may be modified for students in the primary grades as the teacher directs and guides them through the process. Primary-grade students would benefit from the use of VSS after group read-alouds, when they return to the book to select new and interesting words.

*Strategy modifications for grade levels:* VSS works well with intermediate and middle school students. However, the strategy may be modified for use with primary-grade students. Teachers in the primary grades would simply add more modeling techniques and think-alouds and incorporate scaffolding to help students select new and unfamiliar words. In other words, VSS can be effective for young children if the teacher (1) uses it as a whole-group activity, (2) directs the group in selecting the new and interesting words from a group reading such as a read-aloud, and (3) guides the students in a discussion around the meanings of the words. After the new and interesting words have been selected and discussed, they may be posted on a wall chart for students' use.

### IMPLEMENTING THE VOCABULARY SELF-COLLECTION STRATEGY: STEP BY STEP

1. **Teachers introduce the purpose of VSS to students.** They tell students that they will be expected to find new and interesting words from their readings that they will learn through a group nomination process.

2. **Teachers model how to select and nominate important words from the readings.** Teachers show why the word they selected is important by providing a strong rationale. For example, they may show students that without knowing the word, they may not understand the sentence or surrounding sentences. They may also nominate the selected word because it is interesting and would be useful in their own writing.

3. **Teachers demonstrate how to use context and other resources to learn the meaning of the word.** For example, they may use the context or they may refer to the glossary, dictionary, diagrams, or illustrations to unlock the meaning of the word.

4. **Teachers write the word, the context in which it was used, its meaning, and the reason for selecting the word on chart paper.** Using a chart similar to the one shown in Figure 16.1, teachers write the word, the sentence or phrase in which the word was used, the meaning, and the reason for selecting the word.

5. **Teachers engage students in the process of vocabulary self-selection.** Students work in small groups of three to five, and they read a short passage from the book with the teacher. They are guided by the teacher to identify a word they wish to select. The teacher demonstrates how to use context and other resources to figure out the meaning of the word. Together, the students and the teacher engage in a discussion on developing a reason for nominating their word, and each small group moves to nominate one word for learning. Students use their own charts to write the word, the sentence from the text in which the word was found, the meaning, and the reason for selecting the word.

6. **After students are familiar with the strategy, teachers provide guided practice to support the use of VSS during reading.** Teachers organize students in small groups for reading. They introduce the book and provide a brief overview of the strategy. To help them recall the steps in the process for nominating one or two words to learn, students are given the following questions, which may appear as a reminder on a classroom wall chart:

   • What is the word that I believe is important to learn?

   • Why would I select it as an interesting or important word to learn?

   • How was the word used? Write the sentence in which the word was used.

   • What is the meaning of the word? Can I get the meaning of the word from the context, dictionary, glossary, or some diagram in the book?

7. **Students in small groups discuss the words they wish to nominate.** Within their small groups, they talk about each word and why they think the class should learn the word. Through consensus, they nominate two words.

8. **Students write the two words on a chart similar to the one shown in Figure 16.1.** Each group presents its two words to the class. On a class chart, one member of the group writes the word, the sentence in which the word was used, its meaning, and the reason for selecting the word.

## Applying the Vocabulary Self-Collection Strategy: Eighth-Grade Lesson on Ann Martin

Within the eighth-grade literature classroom, students are beginning an author study of Ann Martin. Students in each of the four literature circles have chosen the book they will read after the teacher conducts a book talk on four of Martin's works. Prior to their reading, the teacher reminds students to select two words from the first chapter for nomination and then reviews the procedure for using VSS. The students in each literature group read the same book and, during reading, note interesting words that they wish to nominate; they record them on their graphic organizer and continue reading. After reading the first chapter, students discuss the story in their small groups and offer responses and reflections. They end their book discussions with their vocabulary study. Students share the words they have selected and their meanings with their group and conduct the nomination process by presenting a reason why they selected them. The group reaches consensus and presents them to the class. The teacher writes each of the nominated words on the class chart along with their meanings, the sentences in which they appeared, and the reason for selecting the words. Figure 16.1 provides the nomination chart from one literature group that was reading *A Corner of the Universe* by Ann M. Martin (2002).

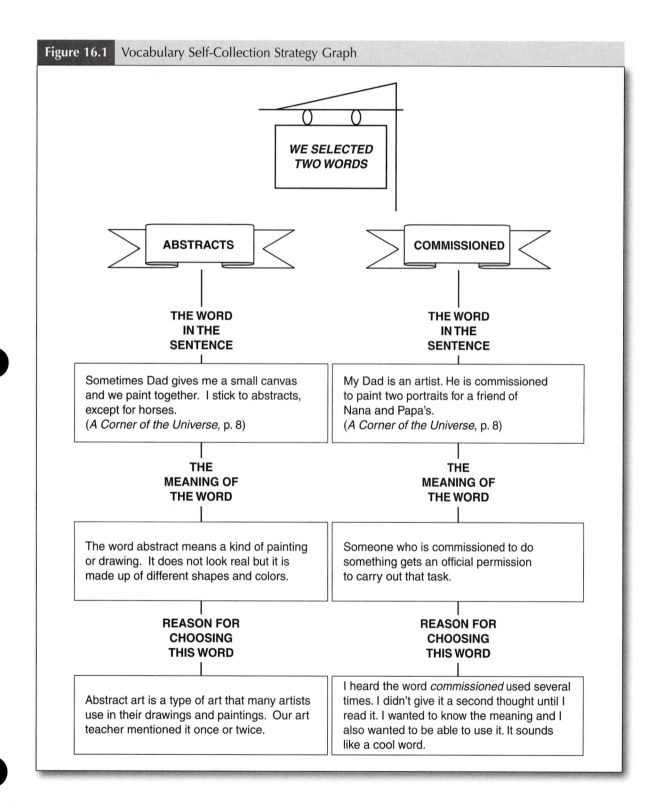

**Figure 16.1**   Vocabulary Self-Collection Strategy Graph

**WE SELECTED TWO WORDS**

**ABSTRACTS**

**COMMISSIONED**

**THE WORD IN THE SENTENCE**

**THE WORD IN THE SENTENCE**

Sometimes Dad gives me a small canvas and we paint together. I stick to abstracts, except for horses.
(*A Corner of the Universe*, p. 8)

My Dad is an artist. He is commissioned to paint two portraits for a friend of Nana and Papa's.
(*A Corner of the Universe*, p. 8)

**THE MEANING OF THE WORD**

**THE MEANING OF THE WORD**

The word abstract means a kind of painting or drawing. It does not look real but it is made up of different shapes and colors.

Someone who is commissioned to do something gets an official permission to carry out that task.

**REASON FOR CHOOSING THIS WORD**

**REASON FOR CHOOSING THIS WORD**

Abstract art is a type of art that many artists use in their drawings and paintings. Our art teacher mentioned it once or twice.

I heard the word *commissioned* used several times. I didn't give it a second thought until I read it. I wanted to know the meaning and I also wanted to be able to use it. It sounds like a cool word.

*Source:* International Reading Association and National Council of Teachers of English (1996).

---

### IRA/NCTE Standards for English Language Arts

10. Students whose first language is not English make use of their first language to develop competency in the English language arts and to develop understanding of content across the curriculum.

---

## DIFFERENTIATING INSTRUCTION FOR ENGLISH LANGUAGE LEARNERS

Teachers may highlight and use the resources that all students bring to the classroom. A significant contribution that English language learners may make to the class is sharing their language with other students. When a word is nominated as an interesting and new word to learn and use, the word may be translated in the home language of students who are learning English. English-only students will benefit from learning words from world languages, and English language learners will benefit from making connections to their home language for a greater understanding of the new words.

## DIFFERENTIATING INSTRUCTION FOR STUDENTS WITH SPECIAL NEEDS

Students with special needs experiencing problems in reading will also have difficulty identifying words they wish to learn. Once they are able to identify new and interesting words, students with special needs will most likely be unable to use context to determine the meaning of the word. Research has shown that the interaction with others regarding word learning will offer them the support they need (Ruddell & Shearer, 2002). Therefore, teachers should carefully select students to work together using a mixed-grouping format and emphasize that it is important to discuss how and why words are selected. This will benefit students who do not know how to identify words for learning. Offer time and guidance to students with special needs by providing mini-lessons on word identification skills, how to use context to guess at the meaning of the word, and how to use other resources within the text such as pictures, graphics, glossaries, and diagrams.

## REFERENCES

Calderon, M. A., August, D., Slavin, R., Duran, D., Madden, N., & Cheung, A. (2005). Bringing words to life in classrooms with English language learners. In E. H. Hiebert & M. L. Kamil (Eds.), *Teaching and learning vocabulary: Bringing research to practice* (pp. 115–137). Mahwah, NJ: Erlbaum.

Haggard, M. R. (1982). The Vocabulary Self-Collection strategy: An active approach to word learning. *Journal of Reading, 27*(3), 203–207.

Haggard, M. R. (1986). The Vocabulary Self-Collection strategy: Using student interest and word knowledge to enhance vocabulary growth. *Journal of Reading, 29*(7), 634–642.

Harmon, J. M., & Hedrick, W. B. (2005). Research on vocabulary instruction in content areas: Implications for struggling readers. *Reading & Writing Quarterly, 21*, 261–280.

International Reading Association and National Council of Teachers of English. (1996). *Standards for the English language arts.* Newark, DE: International Reading Association and Urbana, IL: National Council of Teachers of English.

Ruddell, M. R., & Shearer, B. A. (2002). "Extraordinary," "tremendous," "exhilarating," "magnificent": Middle school at-risk students become avid word learners with Vocabulary Self-Collection strategy (VSS). *Journal of Adolescent and Adult Literacy, 45*(5), 352–363.

## CHILDREN'S LITERATURE CITED

Martin, A. M. (2002). *A corner of the universe.* New York: Scholastic.

# Strategy
# 17

# Word Mapping

The purpose of the *Word Mapping* strategy is to promote the students' deeper understanding of words through depicting varying relationships between and among words. Word maps are visual displays of word meanings organized to depict relationships with other words. Research reveals that to develop students' vocabularies, teachers need to promote in-depth word knowledge (Beck, McKeown, & Kucan, 2002). The Word Mapping strategy, or semantic mapping, is one of the most powerful approaches to teaching vocabulary because it engages students in thinking about word relationships (Graves, 2008). The strategy promotes students' active exploration of word relationships, thereby leading to a deeper understanding of word meanings by developing their conceptual knowledge related to words. The effectiveness of Word Mapping is supported by research. For example, a study comparing mapping word relationships and a contextual approach to learning words indicated that semantic mapping produced greater gains in word learning (Margosein, Pascarella, & Pflaum, 1982). Students learn about words through mapping because it helps them examine the characteristics of the word concepts, categorize words, and see relationships among words that are similar as well as those that may be different. Such activities that are part of the Word Mapping strategy are cognitive strategies that lead to a deeper understanding of words and the concepts that they represent.

The Word Mapping strategy is referred to by different names, such as semantic mapping, concept mapping, and word clusters. The strategy may be adapted to the nature of vocabulary instruction, the learning outcomes, and students' grade levels. For example, for learning some words, it may be more appropriate to have students explore the synonyms, antonyms, and origin of the words; whereas for other words, it may be more helpful to find examples and nonexamples of the words. Sinatra, Stahl-Gemake, and Berg (1984) used word maps successfully for vocabulary instruction with students in the elementary grades who were disabled readers. Further, Reutzel and Cooter (2008) suggest the use of word maps with English language learners for vocabulary instruction because it offers a way for them to demonstrate and connect their prior knowledge to new concepts and, at the same time, serves as a useful tool to categorize information.

*Source:* International Reading Association and National Council of Teachers of English (1996).

## IRA/NCTE Standards for English Language Arts

3. Students apply a wide range of strategies to comprehend, interpret, evaluate, and appreciate texts. They draw on their prior experience, their interactions with other readers and writers, their knowledge of word meaning and of other texts, their word identification strategies, and their understanding of textual features (e.g., sound-letter correspondence, sentence structure, context, graphics).

6. Students apply knowledge of language structure, language conventions (e.g., spelling and punctuation), media techniques, figurative language, and genre to create, critique, and discuss print and nonprint texts.

12. Students use spoken, written, and visual language to accomplish their own purposes (e.g., for learning, enjoyment, persuasion, and the exchange of information).

# USING WORD MAPPING

*When to use the strategy:* The strategy is most effective when used before, during, and after reading. Most teachers use the Word Mapping strategy to introduce new vocabulary before reading. As a follow-up to reading and discussion of the text, they encourage students to develop their word maps by using the new information they acquired through reading. Students may also use word maps during reading, as they add new ideas and words to further build word knowledge and extend understanding of word relationships.

*Strategy modifications for grade levels:* Word maps may be used at any grade level from kindergarten through the eighth grade and beyond. Teachers of the primary grades adjust the word maps to students' literacy development by exploring fewer word relationships at a time. For the intermediate and middle grades, word maps become more complex as students search for varied word relationships and rich word meanings. As older and more proficient readers learn the process of mapping words, they will use them independently and more creatively.

## IMPLEMENTING THE WORD MAPPING STRATEGY: STEP BY STEP

1. **Select words for vocabulary instruction.** Prepare for vocabulary instruction by carefully selecting the words to be taught. Choose words by considering the readings and the words that are key to understanding the text.

2. **Project a blank word map on the screen.** Model how to construct a word map and demonstrate to students how to use the word map for building and exploring word relationships.

3. **Write the key words on the word map.** In each blank, write and say the key word that will be taught.

4. **Use a think-aloud to model how to explore relationships between words.** Use the think-aloud strategy to (a) demonstrate how to explore word relationships; (b) think about the meaning of the key word or related words; (c) model how to further the meaning of the word by examples and nonexamples, or synonyms and antonyms, of the word; (d) find the definition of the word in a glossary or dictionary and find its use in context or a discussion with another student about the word's meaning; and (e) draw a picture of the word to illustrate its meaning in context.

5. **Record ideas that have been used to explore the word meanings and relationships.** During the think-aloud, record information about the word in the appropriate space on the word map.

6. **Students are directed to use the word maps during and after reading to add information about the key words.** Students use the word maps for recording new information while they are reading. After reading, they may further develop their word meanings by looking for dictionary definitions, drawing pictures of words, and adding new words from their readings.

7. **Students share their maps with others.** Have students share their maps with the class. During this sharing period, students use the information on their word maps to develop and expand the class map. Students write new information on the group map and are encouraged to revise their own word maps to incorporate these new ideas.

## Applying the Word Mapping Strategy: Fifth-Grade Lesson on the Founding Fathers

Within the fifth grade, the teacher has used an integrated language arts and social studies unit to help students learn about the American colonies and their conflict with Great Britain. One of the aspects of the unit was to study the contributions of our Founding Fathers. The teacher created a text set that included the following literature: *Thomas Jefferson: A Picture Book Biography* by J. C. Giblin (1994), *Thomas Jefferson* by C. Harness (2004), *The Revolutionary John Adams* by C. Harness (2003), *A Picture Book of Dolley and James Madison* by D. A. Adler and M. S. Adler (2009), and *Farmer George Plants a Nation* by Peggy Thomas (2008). Students were divided into four literature circles, and members in each group were reading the same book. To introduce the key vocabulary for understanding each book, the teacher created four word maps, one for each book. Using the Word Mapping strategy, the teacher taught the key words to each literature circle through the use of direct instruction and guided discussion. Students were then directed to (1) use their word maps during and after reading by elaborating or building on word meanings from their readings and discussions within the literature circles and (2) find new words and meanings to add to their word maps, along with pictures and diagrams that illustrate the words' meanings. Figure 17.1 depicts the word map that was used by the teacher before reading and the word map that students created during and after reading. Students then shared their word maps with members of their literature groups and later with the class during discussions of their readings.

**Figure 17.1**   Word Maps for Vocabulary in *Thomas Jefferson* by Cheryl Harness

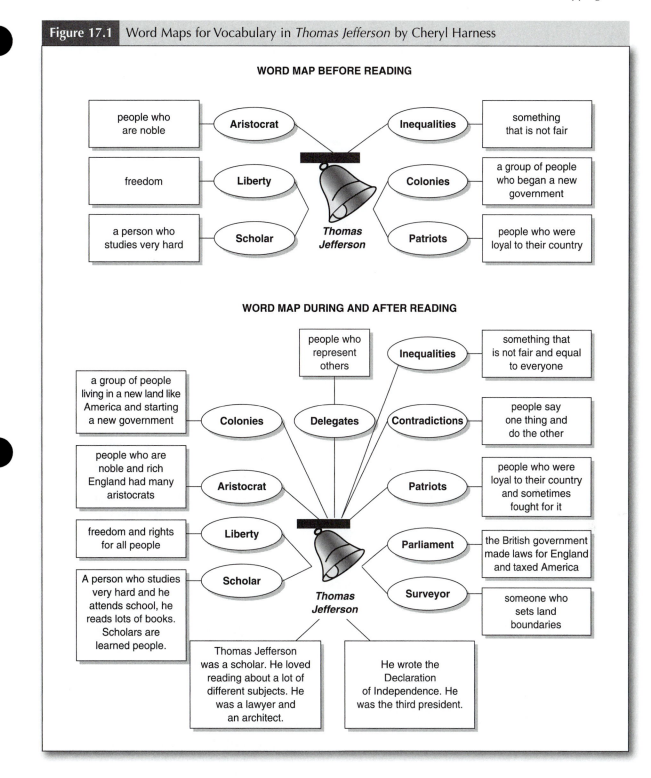

*Source:* International Reading Association and National Council of Teachers of English (1996).

### IRA/NCTE Standards for English Language Arts

10. Students whose first language is not English make use of their first language to develop competency in the English language arts and to develop understanding of content across the curriculum.

## DIFFERENTIATING INSTRUCTION FOR ENGLISH LANGUAGE LEARNERS

Using the Word Mapping strategy is an excellent approach for teaching vocabulary to English language learners. The word map offers a visual that depicts relationships among words. To optimize the English language learner's potential for word learning, write each key word in English as well as his/her home language and add pictures and diagrams to illustrate the meanings of the words.

## DIFFERENTIATING INSTRUCTION FOR STUDENTS WITH SPECIAL NEEDS

Mapping words and showing relationships are excellent approaches that teachers may use to develop meaning vocabularies for students with special needs. Teachers need to offer greater support to students who are striving to become proficient readers. During reading, teachers should provide individualized help to disabled readers by helping them see word relationships, expanding on the meanings of words, and helping them use references such as glossaries and dictionaries to develop the meanings of the words. Encourage students to use their own maps as a resource and to consult them for reviewing vocabulary and using the words in their writing.

## REFERENCES

Beck, I., McKeown, M. G., & Kucan, I. (2002). *Bringing words to life: Robust vocabulary instruction.* New York: Guilford.

Graves, M. (2008). Instruction on individual words: One size does not fit all. In A. E. Farstrup & S. J. Samuels (Eds.), *What research has to say about vocabulary instruction* (pp. 56–79). Newark, DE: International Reading Association.

International Reading Association and National Council of Teachers of English. (1996). *Standards for the English language arts.* Newark, DE: International Reading Association and Urbana, IL: National Council of Teachers of English.

Margosein, C. M., Pascarella, E. T., & Pflaum, S. W. (1982). The effects of instruction using semantic mapping on vocabulary and comprehension. *Journal of Early Adolescence, 2*(2), 185–194.

Reutzel, D. R., & Cooter, R. B. (2008). *Teaching children to read: The teacher makes the difference* (5th ed.). Upper Saddle River, NJ: Merrill Prentice Hall.

Sinatra, R. C., Stahl-Gemake, J., & Berg, W. (1984). Improving reading comprehension of disabled readers through semantic mapping. *The Reading Teacher, 38*(1), 22–29.

## Children's Literature Cited

Adler, D. A., & Adler, M. S. (2009). *A picture book of Dolley and James Madison.* New York: Holiday House.

Giblin, J. C. (1994). *Thomas Jefferson: A picture book biography.* New York: Scholastic.

Harness, C. (2003). *The revolutionary John Adams.* Washington, DC: National Geographic Society.

Harness, C. (2004). *Thomas Jefferson.* Washington, DC: National Geographic Society.

Thomas, P. (2008). *Farmer George plants a nation.* Honesdale, PA: Calkins Creek.

# Strategy
# 18
# Graphic Morphemic Analysis

The *Graphic Morphemic Analysis* strategy is an approach to word learning that will help readers unlock the meaning of new and challenging words by analyzing the meaningful parts within a word. A morpheme is the smallest unit of meaning within a word. Most of us know morphemes as root words and affixes or prefixes and suffixes. When teachers employ morphemic analysis, they help students see more than just the parts of words. Rather, they lead students to examine the word for its meaningful parts, which will lead them to discover the word's meaning. The Graphic Morphemic Analysis strategy employs a systematic approach to deconstructing a word into its meaningful parts (morphemes) to figure out what the word means through the use of a graphic. Similar to morpheme triangles (Winters, 2009) and morpheme circles (Harmon, Wood, & Hedrick, 2006), the Graphic Morphemic Analysis strategy helps students use a visual analysis of the word to deconstruct it and construct meaning from word relationships and contextual meanings. Utilizing graphics as part of the strategy provides readers with a visual adjunct that helps them see the meaningful parts within the word in isolation for a systematic analysis.

Why is morphemic analysis important to vocabulary development? There are a number of studies that show the relationship between vocabulary and comprehension. Additional research by Kieffer and Lesaux (2007) demonstrates the relationship of comprehension and morphemic analysis by elementary students as well as English language learners in a large urban school district. As students move through the grades, they are expected to read more complex texts that have an increasing number of derivational words (Nagy & Anderson, 1984). Thus, it makes instructional sense to provide students with a cognitive strategy to learn new words from complex texts.

What are some guidelines for using effective morphology instruction with students? Kieffer and Lesaux (2007) draw from research to present the following four principles for effective instruction in morphemic analysis: (1) Teach morphology in the context of rich, explicit vocabulary instruction; (2) teach students to use morphology as a cognitive strategy with explicit steps; (3) teach underlying morphological knowledge in two ways—both explicitly and in context; and (4) for students with developed knowledge of Spanish, teach morphology in relation to cognates (pp. 139–142). Many words from the content areas have cognates, or words derived from languages other than English. "Since a substantial percentage of these cognates are more common in Spanish conversation than in English, attention to this group of words in instruction could build on a potential fund of knowledge held by Spanish-speaking students" (Hiebert & Lubliner, 2008, p. 108). Therefore, English language learners will benefit when morphology instruction is linked to their language.

---

### IRA/NCTE Standards for English Language Arts

3. Students apply a wide range of strategies to comprehend, interpret, evaluate, and appreciate texts. They draw on their prior experience, their interactions with other readers and writers, their knowledge of word meaning and of other texts, their word identification strategies, and their understanding of textual features (e.g., sound-letter correspondence, sentence structure, context, graphics).

6. Students apply knowledge of language structure, language conventions (e.g., spelling and punctuation), media techniques, figurative language, and genre to create, critique, and discuss print and nonprint texts.

*Source: International Reading Association and National Council of Teachers of English (1996).*

---

## USING GRAPHIC MORPHEMIC ANALYSIS

*When to use the strategy:* Teachers need to provide students with direct instruction of morphemic analysis that is part of a total vocabulary program. The Graphic Morphemic Analysis strategy may be employed before and after reading as part of the vocabulary instructional program. To prepare students for reading the selected text, the teacher may focus on one or two vocabulary words to demonstrate how their meanings are related to the morphemes within the word. After reading, the students have a better understanding of the context in which the words are used; therefore, the teacher directs them to use the Graphic Morphemic Analysis strategy to determine word meanings utilizing each word's context and morphemes.

*Strategy modifications for grade levels:* What is the appropriate grade to introduce morphemic analysis? Researchers found that fourth- and fifth-grade students learn and use morphemic analysis for increasing word learning (Baumann et al., 2002; Kieffer & Lesaux, 2007). This does not mean that it should not be introduced and taught at the primary grade levels. Because the analysis of words is a developmental process, Moats (2000) suggests that teaching first-graders about roots and affixes increases their proficiency in word recognition. It also helps heighten their awareness of word parts and facilitates their ability to examine words for their meaningful parts. Morphemic analysis presented to primary-grade students should focus on the root words and their meanings (Biemiller, 2004). As students learn to see the meaningful parts of the word, the teacher may introduce prefixes and suffixes.

### IMPLEMENTING THE GRAPHIC MORPHEMIC ANALYSIS STRATEGY: STEP BY STEP

1. **Select a word from the assigned readings for teaching the strategy.** Words that are selected should be within students' experiential backgrounds and have rich contextual meanings.

2. **Engage students in a discussion on the purpose of the strategy.** Lead the discussion on the importance of examining parts of words to determine their meanings. Tell students they will learn the procedure for learning to figure out the meanings of unknown words.

3. **Use a think-aloud to demonstrate how to divide a word into its parts.** Using the selected word, model how to detach the prefix from the root word. Then show students how to take the suffix off the root word.

4. **Demonstrate how to examine each word part for its meaning.** Using a think-aloud, begin with the root word and say the meaning aloud; continue with the prefix, thinking aloud how it will change the meaning when added to the root word, and do the same with the suffix.

5. **Guide students through the process of using the graphic organizer to analyze a word and determine its meaning.** Project the graphic organizer shown in Figure 18.1 on the SMART Board or a transparency. On the graphic organizer, say and write the word in the appropriate box. Ask students to detach the prefix from the root word, as well as the suffix from the root word, writing them in the labeled boxes. Ask students for the meanings of each word part and lead a discussion on how the prefix and suffix change the meaning of the root word.

6. **In the appropriate box, write the sentence that contains the target word.** Use a guided discussion with students on what the context of the sentence tells them about the meaning of the word, along with what the meaning of the root word and the affixes tells them.

7. **Show students how to figure out the meaning of the word.** Lead a discussion on how the meaning of the word is dependent on the context of the sentence and conduct an analysis of the word parts. Decide on the meaning of the word and write it in the appropriate box on the graphic organizer.

8. **Check the meaning of the word with the dictionary definition.** Write the dictionary definition in the appropriate box on the graphic organizer and demonstrate how to use it to check on the meaning from the context of the sentence.

### Applying the Graphic Morphemic Analysis Strategy: Fourth-Grade Lesson on the Transcontinental Railroad

Students in the fourth grade were learning about how the Transcontinental Railroad helped build America. The teacher engaged the class through a read-aloud of *Railroad Fever: Building the Transcontinental Railroad, 1830–1870* by Monica Halpern (2003). This book provides a historically accurate depiction of the building of the railroad by immigrants and slaves as well as its effects on a growing country. After a discussion of each major part of the book, the teacher engaged students in the study of the important words that were needed to understand the major concepts and ideas within the selected passage. After discussing Chapter 3, "The Workers," the teacher focused on where the workers came from and used the Graphic Morphemic Analysis strategy to teach the word *immigrants*. Using the graphic shown in Figure 18.1, the teacher taught students how to analyze the word to look for its meaningful parts.

**Figure 18.1** Graphic Morphemic Analysis of the Word *immigrants*

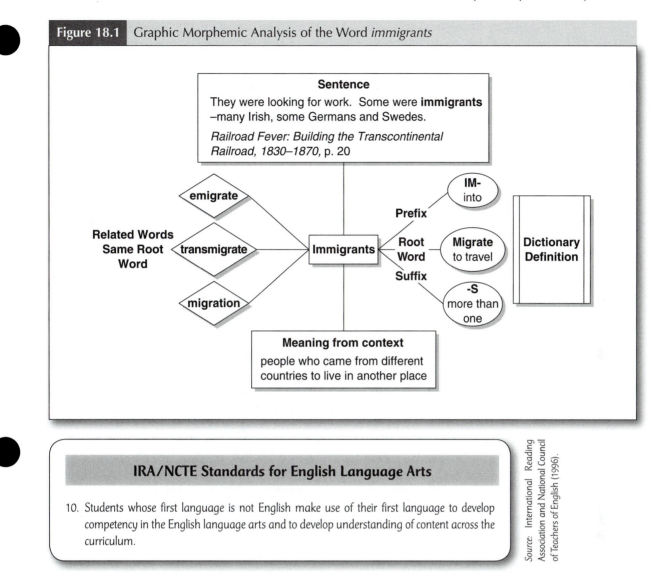

## DIFFERENTIATING INSTRUCTION FOR ENGLISH LANGUAGE LEARNERS

English language learners (ELLs) benefit from the study of morphemic analysis. ELLs oftentimes do not hear the suffix that appears at the end of the word. Further, many of the suffixes change the word's tense or change it from a singular to a plural noun. Although this subtle change is not obvious for most English-only students, it is important that ELLs receive additional attention in learning words that contain suffixes such as *-s, -ing, -ed,* and *-ly.*

Another way to modify instruction for ELLs is to use words with cognates (a word part originating from a language other than English) that relate to their first language. Hiebert and Lubliner (2008) argue that a high number of words in content-area curriculum have Spanish cognates, many of which are part of everyday discourse in their native language. However, because ELLs cannot make the connection between the new vocabulary word and the cognate, teachers need to assist them in creating this relationship.

## Differentiating Instruction for Students With Special Needs

Prior to showing students how to look for root words and affixes within words, modify the lesson on morphemic analysis by teaching them first to build new words by adding prefixes and suffixes to root words. Have students record each new word within their Vocabulary Journals, writing the word, each of its parts, and its meaning. After students have learned a number of words, have them look for and highlight the root word and affixes.

## References

Baumann, J. F., Edwards, E. C., Font, G., Tereshinski, C. A., Kame'enui, E. J., & Olejinik, S. (2002). Teaching morphemic and contextual analysis to fifth-grade students. *Reading Research Quarterly, 37,* 150–176.

Biemiller, A. (2004). Teaching vocabulary in the primary grades. In J. F. Baumann & E. J. Kame'enui (Eds.), *Vocabulary instruction: Research to practice* (pp. 28–40). New York: Guilford.

Harmon, J. M., Wood, K. D., & Hedrick, W. B. (2006). Vocabulary instruction in middle and secondary content classrooms: Understandings and directions from research. In A. E. Farstrup & S. J. Samuels (Eds.), *What research has to say about vocabulary instruction* (pp.150–181).

Hiebert, E. H., & Lubliner, S. (2008). The nature, learning, and instruction of general academic vocabulary. In A. E. Farstrup & S. J. Samuels (Eds.), *What research has to say about vocabulary instruction* (pp. 106–129). Newark, DE: International Reading Association.

International Reading Association and National Council of Teachers of English. (1996). *Standards for the English language arts.* Newark, DE: International Reading Association and Urbana, IL: National Council of Teachers of English.

Kieffer, M. J., & Lesaux, N. K. (2007). Breaking down words to build meaning: Morphology, vocabulary, and reading comprehension in the urban classroom. *The Reading Teacher, 61*(2), 134–144.

Moats, L. C. (2000). *Speech to print: Language essentials for teachers.* Baltimore: Paul H. Brookes.

Nagy, W. E., & Anderson, R. C. (1984). How many words are there in printed school English? *Reading Research Quarterly, 19,* 304–330.

Winters, R. (2009). Interactive frames for vocabulary growth and word consciousness. *The Reading Teacher, 62*(8), 685–690.

## Children's Literature Cited

Halpern, M. (2003). *Railroad fever: Building the Transcontinental Railroad, 1830–1870.* Washington, DC: National Geographic Society.

# Interactive Word Wall

# Strategy 19

## SPEAKING BRIEFLY: AN OVERVIEW OF THE LITERACY STRATEGY

The *Interactive Word Wall* strategy promotes a vocabulary-rich classroom environment where walls are alive with words. The key to implementing the word wall strategy is *interactivity*. The classroom walls are adorned with new and interesting words that the students learn through interacting with their texts, the teacher, and one another. They are encouraged to use the words posted on the word wall for their own reading and writing. To promote interaction and dialogue around the words, it is important to keep the words relevant; that is, "the posted words should be the focal point for thinking about and noticing how they are used" (Beck, McKeown, & Kucan, 2008, p. 52). Researchers stressed the importance of students' active engagement in using word walls (Harmon, Wood, Hedrick, Vintinner, & Willeford, 2009). Their study with seventh-grade students demonstrates that older as well as younger children need a print-rich environment that engages them in their own word learning and vocabulary development.

Word walls have been used by teachers for different types of word-study activities (Wagstaff, 1999). These include helping young children learn high-frequency words (Cunningham, 2005) as well as developing academic vocabulary or specialized words in content-area classrooms with older students. Many teachers use the word wall during reading time to help students expand their vocabulary. The following are tips for supporting an interactive word wall:

- Incorporate the Interactive Word Wall strategy as part of the word study instructional routine.

- Select the display wall carefully, making sure that it is at eye level and large enough to post the words.

- Decide on how you wish to display the words, such as alphabetically or organized by themes or content areas.

- Write the words legibly on oak tag or paper, demonstrating appropriate handwriting.

*Source:* International Reading Association and National Council of Teachers of English (1996).

> ### IRA/NCTE Standards for English Language Arts
>
> 3. Students apply a wide range of strategies to comprehend, interpret, evaluate, and appreciate texts. They draw on their prior experience, their interactions with other readers and writers, their knowledge of word meaning and of other texts, their word identification strategies, and their understanding of textual features (e.g., sound-letter correspondence, sentence structure, context, graphics).
>
> 4. Students adjust their use of spoken, written, and visual language (e.g., conventions, style, vocabulary) to communicate effectively with a variety of audiences and for different purposes.

## USING THE INTERACTIVE WORD WALL

*When to use the strategy:* The Interactive Word Wall strategy may be used before, during, or after reading. The teacher may use the word wall to introduce new vocabulary prior to reading. During reading, students are encouraged to find words that are unfamiliar and that should be placed on the word wall to learn. After reading, the class may return to the word wall to expand on the meaning of the words that are posted or to add new words to the wall. The word wall may also be used outside reading as a review or practice, such as when the teacher asks the students to "read the wall." Word walls are resources for students and should be used when they are looking for new and interesting words to use in their writing.

*Strategy modifications for grade levels:* Word walls may be used at any grade level with very little modification. The purpose of the word wall dictates its use. For example, word walls for children in kindergarten and first grade reflect their learning needs, including sight words and high-frequency words. As primary-grade students learn strategies for decoding words, they may have a word wall designed around word families. Within intermediate and middle school classrooms, one might see word walls filled with vocabulary across the curriculum or words selected from a unit of study.

### IMPLEMENTING THE INTERACTIVE WORD WALL STRATEGY: STEP BY STEP

1. **Establish a purpose for using the word wall.** Word walls may be used to help students learn high-frequency words, or they may be used to develop vocabulary around a theme. For example, themes for word walls may include the tropical rain forest, going green, or staying healthy. Some teachers may use word walls for literature units or author studies. Once the purpose has been established, share it with the students.

2. **Select the words that are targeted for instruction.** Select a few words for teaching and post them on the wall in advance or write them as they are presented for discussion. Words on the wall need to be spelled correctly and written legibly, as students will be encouraged to use the word wall as a resource for their reading and writing.

3. **Before reading, teach the words.** Engage students in a lively discussion of the words. Teachers may decide to write a brief meaning of the word.

4. **After reading, students may post words to the word wall.** Because word walls are effective when they are interactive, teachers guide discussion of the readings to include new and interesting words that students discovered in their readings. These words, along with their meanings, may be posted on the word wall.

5. **Initiate activity around the word wall.** For the word wall to be effective, members of the learning community must use them. The teacher plays an important role in initiating activity that leads to interactive word walls. For example, using word walls as references in finding interesting words for writing and playing word games will encourage students to make the word walls their own.

## APPLYING THE INTERACTIVE WORD WALL STRATEGY: SECOND-GRADE LESSON

The second-grade teacher conducted a dialogic read-aloud of the picture storybook titled *Martin's Big Words: The Life of Dr. Martin Luther King, Jr.* (Rappaport, 2001). After the teacher introduced the book, she read the biography aloud without stopping. When she completed the read-aloud, the teacher conducted a text talk by showing the pictures, talking about the text, and encouraging children to respond. Later that day and several days after, the teacher returned to the book and revisited it with a discussion around selected key words, asking the children to "talk about what you think the word(s) are saying" while showing them the pictures. As the children responded, the teacher posted the word on the word wall and further developed its meaning, as shown on the word wall in Figure 19.1. After rereading the book, the teacher placed it on the open-faced book rack and invited the children to read it independently. They frequently referred to the word wall while reading and to use the newly learned words in their writing.

| **Figure 19.1** | Word Wall for *Martin's Big Words: The Life of Dr. Martin Luther King, Jr.* | | | | |
|---|---|---|---|---|---|
| **Aa** | **Bb** | **Cc** | **Dd** | **Ee** | **Ff** |
| Alabama | Bible<br>blistering<br>bombed | courage<br>convinced<br>continued<br>citizens | decided<br>dream | | |
| **Gg** | **Hh** | **Ii** | **Jj** | **Kk** | **Ll** |
| governors<br>garbage<br>collectors | hymns | Indian nation | judges<br>jailed | | |

*(Continued)*

(Continued)

| Mm | Nn | Oo | Pp | Qq | Rr |
|---|---|---|---|---|---|
| mayors<br>movement<br>murdered<br>Martin<br>minister<br>Montgomery | Nobel Peace<br>Prize | | preach<br>police chief<br>protest | | remembered<br>Rosa Parks |
| **Ss** | **Tt** | **Uu** | **Vv** | **Ww** | **Xx** |
| Segregation<br>South<br>Southerners<br>Southern cities<br>separate | towns<br>threatened | United States | voted | Washington | |
| **Yy** | **Zz** | | | | |
| | | | | | |

*Source:* International Reading Association and National Council of Teachers of English (1996).

---

### IRA/NCTE Standards for English Language Arts

10. Students whose first language is not English make use of their first language to develop competency in the English language arts and to develop understanding of content across the curriculum.

## DIFFERENTIATING INSTRUCTION FOR ENGLISH LANGUAGE LEARNERS

Supporting English language learners during vocabulary instruction may be accomplished in a number of ways. Key words that are targeted for learning should be related to the experiences of all students, especially those who are linguistically diverse. When posting the key word on the word wall, write the word in the student's first language, asking him/her to pronounce the word and explain it to the class.

## DIFFERENTIATING INSTRUCTION FOR STUDENTS WITH SPECIAL NEEDS

Students with special needs benefit from practice and repeated exposure to new vocabulary words. Have students create personal word walls that are portable. Students design their own interactive word walls from a blank file folder. Using the four sides of the folder, they draw 26 boxes, one for each letter of the alphabet. They post words from their classroom word wall on their portable word wall as well as new words they learn from their own readings. Students may be encouraged to post additional words from their readings. Words will be available to them on demand, at home and in school.

## REFERENCES

Beck, I. L., McKeown, M. G., & Kucan, L. (2008). *Creating robust vocabulary: Frequently asked questions and extended examples.* New York: Guilford.

Cunningham, P. M. (2005). *Phonics they use: Words for reading and writing* (4th ed.). New York: HarperCollins.

Harmon, J. M., Wood, K. D., Hedrick, W. B., Vintinner, J., & Willeford, T. (2009). Interactive word walls: More than just reading and writing on the walls. *Journal of Adolescent and Adult Literacy, 52*(5), 398–409.

International Reading Association and National Council of Teachers of English. (1996). *Standards for the English language arts.* Newark, DE: International Reading Association and Urbana, IL: National Council of Teachers of English.

Wagstaff, J. (1999). *Teaching reading and writing with word walls.* New York: Scholastic.

## CHILDREN'S LITERATURE CITED

Rappaport, D. (2001). *Martin's big words: The life of Dr. Martin Luther King, Jr.* New York: Hyperion Books for Children.

# Strategy
# 20
## Vocabulary Journals

## SPEAKING BRIEFLY: AN OVERVIEW OF THE LITERACY STRATEGY

*Vocabulary Journals* are valuable in helping students explore the meanings of words that they encounter while reading. These journals are a specific type of learning log where students record "their ideas and information from content areas in a notebook and responses" (Popp, 1997, p. 1) about new words that they have learned from reading literature or textbooks. Journals are not notebooks used to record notes. Rather, Vocabulary Journals are used by students to respond and transact with words, concepts, and ideas through the use of their own language. Students select words from their readings that are difficult, novel, or used in different contexts. They use their journals to explore the words' meanings, make connections between the new words and their own experiences and ideas they already know, and produce rich definitions.

The primary purpose for using Vocabulary Journals is to encourage students to become word conscious by collecting new and interesting words and learning their meanings through engaged explorations. Vocabulary Journals may be used as part of guided reading lessons, during independent reading, and during their readings across the content areas. Teachers may use Vocabulary Journals effectively with students at all grade levels by adjusting their instructional procedures. For example, Bone (2000) used Vocabulary Journals with eighth-grade students in her literature class. She encouraged students to explore the meanings of words by using different graphic organizers in their journals. Students used graphics for making connections between word meanings, for building knowledge with concept ladders, and for working through the meanings of words with a K-W-L chart.

*Source:* International Reading Association and National Council of Teachers of English (1996).

---

### IRA/NCTE Standards for English Language Arts

3. Students apply a wide range of strategies to comprehend, interpret, evaluate, and appreciate texts. They draw on their prior experience, their interactions with other readers and writers, their knowledge of word meaning and of other texts, their word identification strategies, and their understanding of textual features (e.g., sound-letter correspondence, sentence structure, context, graphics).

12. Students use spoken, written, and visual language to accomplish their own purposes (e.g., for learning, enjoyment, persuasion, and the exchange of information).

# USING VOCABULARY JOURNALS

*When to use the strategy:* Vocabulary Journals may be used before, during, or after reading depending on how the teacher will use the journals. For example, oftentimes the teacher will use direct instruction for teaching the key words before reading the text. Students will then record the words and their initial ideas in their journals, but they will return to the words during and after reading to personalize the meanings of the words. During independent reading, students will use their journals during and after reading.

*Strategy modifications for grade levels:* The Vocabulary Journal strategy may be used at all grade levels. For the primary grades, teachers will need to monitor students' use of the journals to a greater extent. Additionally, it may take time for first- and second-graders to identify words for their journals; therefore, teachers should suggest words for their journals and then encourage them to add a word or two.

## IMPLEMENTING THE VOCABULARY JOURNAL STRATEGY: STEP BY STEP

1. **Introduce Vocabulary Journals to students.** Talk about the purpose of the journal and how to identify words from their readings to explore a word's meaning and use.

2. **Demonstrate how to select words from a reading.** Conduct a read-aloud to show the students which words might be selected for their Vocabulary Journals.

3. **Use a think-aloud to model how to construct meanings from words.** Engage in a think-aloud on how to interact with text to construct and build word meaning. Demonstrate to students how to

   a. consult other resources such as glossaries and dictionaries to show meanings of words or search illustrations, diagrams, and subtitles;

   b. use the context of the sentence or sentences around the word to explore the meaning of the word;

   c. show word relationships such as synonyms, antonyms, homonyms, etc.; and

   d. explore meaning through making connections to the word, such as what they know that is similar to the meaning of the word or other readings in which the word might have been used.

4. **Record ideas that have been used to explore the meaning of the word.** Display different techniques that were used to represent word meanings and relationships. For example, discuss the use of word or concept maps and other graphic organizers to show word and concept relationships and the use of pictures to depict meanings.

5. **Encourage students' systematic use and sharing of Vocabulary Journals.** Develop students' interest in words by encouraging their use of Vocabulary Journals and providing a range of contexts where students use their journals. They may be used most effectively in literature circles, guided reading, independent reading, shared reading, read-alouds, and reading across the curriculum. Teachers encourage the students' use of journals during discussions where they may share their words, ideas, and questions.

6. **Encourage students to use their Vocabulary Journals as a resource.** Provide authentic ways to help students use their Vocabulary Journals as a tool for learning. Since journals are a storehouse for new and interesting words and their meanings, spellings of words, concepts, and ideas, students should be encouraged to use their Vocabulary Journals during writing.

## Applying the Vocabulary Journal Strategy: Third-Grade Lesson on Extreme Weather Conditions

Students in the third grade were studying a science unit on extreme weather conditions, including hurricanes, tornadoes, rainstorms, and severe drought. The teacher introduced the topic of tornadoes and provided instruction on the following key words: *tornadoes, cumulonimbus clouds, thunderhead, condensation, downdraft,* and *updraft.* After a brief discussion and a short video of a tornado, students engaged in reading from books on the topic. The teacher directed students to use their Vocabulary Journals to expand the meanings of the key words and to note any important words that relate to the word *tornado* by providing them with the following explicit instructions:

- Show the difference between an updraft and a downdraft using pictures.

- Using a map of the United States, show where most tornadoes hit.

- Compare a hurricane and a tornado.

- Use a word cluster diagram to show words that are related to a tornado.

After their readings, the students shared their Vocabulary Journals with their learning partners to discuss the interesting words and their meanings that they gleaned from their readings. Figure 20.1 shows a sample page from a student's Vocabulary Journal, written after reading *Tornadoes!* by Gail Gibbons (2009).

*Source:* International Reading Association and National Council of Teachers of English (1996).

---

### IRA/NCTE Standards for English Language Arts

10. Students whose first language is not English make use of their first language to develop competency in the English language arts and to develop understanding of content across the curriculum.

---

## Differentiating Instruction for English Language Learners

English language learners (ELLs) face a range of challenges related to vocabulary development. Michael Graves (2006) has identified "building a basic vocabulary of the most frequent English words" (p. 86) as one of the most critical skills for ELLs. Thus, Vocabulary Journals should be used for collecting, learning, and using high-frequency and everyday English words. Teachers should serve as guides in directing the students to identify and study these words, as well as encouraging students to use their Vocabulary Journals as resources. ELLs will also benefit from collecting words that have cognates in their home language. For both types of words—high-frequency words and new or interesting words—that students are learning, provide individual assistance by doing the following: (1) Pronounce the new word clearly and then have the student say the word, (2) ask the student to say the word in his/her home language and in English, and (3) encourage students to use the words in their speaking and writing.

**Figure 20.1** Student's Entry in Vocabulary Journal for *Tornadoes!* by Gail Gibbons

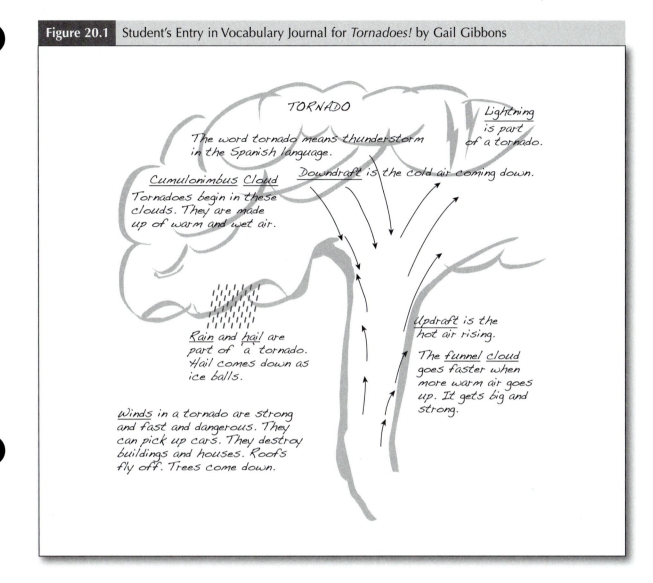

TORNADO

The word tornado means thunderstorm in the Spanish language.

Lightning is part of a tornado.

Downdraft is the cold air coming down.

<u>Cumulonimbus</u> <u>Cloud</u>
Tornadoes begin in these clouds. They are made up of warm and wet air.

<u>Rain</u> and <u>hail</u> are part of a tornado. Hail comes down as ice balls.

<u>Updraft</u> is the hot air rising.

The <u>funnel</u> <u>cloud</u> goes faster when more warm air goes up. It gets big and strong.

<u>Winds</u> in a tornado are strong and fast and dangerous. They can pick up cars. They destroy buildings and houses. Roofs fly off. Trees come down.

## DIFFERENTIATING INSTRUCTION FOR STUDENTS WITH SPECIAL NEEDS

There are differences among students with special needs, especially related to their literacy development. Many students who are disabled readers need assistance in organizational skills as well as in completing tasks. These students will benefit from using the journal to collect words. Demonstrations of how to organize a journal will be helpful. Other students' Vocabulary Journals may be a source for students with special needs and those who are reluctant to use journals. Teachers need to remind students to follow through in using their journals. These reminders may be in the form of journal checks and offering assistance to students in identifying words and finding their meanings from various sources.

## REFERENCES

Bone, B. (2000). Lessons from a Vocabulary Journal. *Voices From the Middle, 7*(4), 17–23.

Graves, M. F. (2006). *The vocabulary book: Learning and instruction.* New York: Teachers College Press.

International Reading Association and National Council of Teachers of English. (1996). *Standards for the English language arts.* Newark, DE: International Reading Association and Urbana, IL: National Council of Teachers of English.

Popp, M. S. (1997). *Learning journals in the K–8 classroom: Exploring ideas and information in the content areas.* Mahwah, NJ: Erlbaum.

## CHILDREN'S LITERATURE CITED

Gibbons, G. (2009). *Tornadoes!* New York: Holiday House.

# SECTION V

# Essential Strategies for Teaching Story Comprehension

## A Brief Overview of Story Comprehension

Comprehension is fundamental to the act of reading and stands out as the singular purpose for reading any text. Although the comprehension process has been defined and explained in a variety of ways, for the purpose of presenting strategies for teaching story comprehension within Section V, we view reading comprehension through a constructivist lens and provide a brief overview of the critical elements that are fundamental to understanding and responding to stories.

Applying the constructivist view of learning to the process of reading comprehension includes critical elements of understanding as a reader interacts with the text (Kucer, 2001; Rosenblatt, 1978). Three components—the reader, the text, and transaction—are essential to consider in teaching reading to children. Research supports the constructivist model for developing comprehension in young readers. The National Reading Panel (National Institute of Child Health and Human Development, 2000) has summarized research related to the process of comprehension, defining it as "intentional thinking during which meaning is constructed through interactions between text and reader" and further describing comprehension as a problem-solving thinking process (p. 14). Reading comprehension is a highly strategic process, and for readers to understand any text demands their active engagement to construct meaning before, during, and after the reading (Sweet & Snow, 2003). Thus, our description of developing readers constructing meaning from reading stories focuses on the reader, the text, and transaction.

*The reader:* The reader is the most important aspect of comprehending stories. Each reader brings specific traits to the reading act that characterize the event as being quite unique. Research by Fletcher (1994) reveals that the students' world knowledge is the most important factor in their comprehension of text; whereas Schallert and Martin

(2003) posit that readers' background knowledge of the text plays a critical role in their understanding. As we think of students within our classrooms, or even ourselves as readers, we can list additional traits that affect their comprehension of text, such as motivation to read, skill development in reading, purpose for reading the text, etc. Thus, for instruction in story comprehension to be effective, it must consider and support the unique traits that the reader brings to the text.

*The text:* The second factor in constructing meaning is the text. Understanding the range of different text types is critical to effective teaching, and the teacher's knowledge of their differences plays an important role in teaching story comprehension. In the previous sections, we read how skill in decoding and vocabulary within text matter when reading; another factor is the reader's familiarity with the content of the story. Knowledge of text structures, in both narrative (stories) and expository (informational) texts, affects how students read. For example, strategic readers use their understanding of the organization of stories for comprehension and recall (Mandler, 1984). According to Pardo (2004), effective teaching of comprehension occurs when text structures are taught and demonstrated to young children. Further research reveals that there are positive effects on students' comprehension when they have in-depth knowledge of a text's organization or structure (Dickson, Simmons, & Kame'enui, 1995; Duke & Pearson, 2002).

Because Section V addresses story comprehension, the structure of the narrative is further explained. Stories are written in the narrative, and such texts comprise a wide range of fictional books, including fantasies, folklore, and realistic fiction (Buss & Karnowski, 2000). Although the genres within this broad category are quite different, they do share a common feature that is related to their structure—that is, how the stories are organized. Authors write their narratives around the common elements of a story, frequently referred to as story schema or story grammars (Mandler, 1984). These story elements or structures include the characters, setting, plot, and story resolution. The following is a brief description of each of the elements of a story:

- *Characters:* Within each story, there are characters; some play a major role and others minor roles. They are very important to the story development, because in many stories it is their actions, personality, and character traits that drive the plot. Characters in realistic fiction are people; however, in some fantasy stories, characters may be animals or even objects that assume human traits. For example, in *Little Blue and Little Yellow* by Leo Lionni (1995), the two characters are colors that take on human characteristics.

- *Story setting:* The time and the place in which the story occurs is its setting. For some stories, the setting is critical to the development of the plot; for other stories, the setting is not as essential to mobilize the story. For example, the historical fiction *Nory Ryan's Song* by Patricia Reilly Giff (2000) takes place in 1845 in Western Ireland on Maidin Bay, where Nory Ryan and her family lived. The time and place—the potato blight and the repression of the Irish by the English landowners—accounts for the development of the story, including the story problem and solution. Whereas in *Little Blue and Little Yellow,* the setting is not apparent to readers, who focus on the characters' actions and traits.

- *Plot:* The essence of the story is the plot, consisting of the problem that challenges the protagonist into action. The problem helps define the goal for the main character, who works to gain a resolution to the problem. Some stories are designed with simple plots, whereas other complex stories are composed of a major goal and subgoals that must be achieved to solve the problem. In any case, throughout the story, the main character is confronted through conflict within the story, which produces tension, excitement, and interest. It is the character's response to the conflict that leads to the solution of the problem.

- *Story resolution:* Stories end with a resolution, a solution to the story problem or a nonsolution. Most readers feel satisfied when the protagonist solves the problem or at least when the author proposes a hopeful resolution.

Stories are complex and most do not contain a simple straightforward sequence of story events or elements. Younger students learn to read with simple stories; as they develop as readers, they choose books with more complex plots. Notwithstanding the complexity of a story, they are all organized around the same story elements. When readers are familiar with the text structure of a narrative, they will be able to use it to understand stories by identifying and analyzing the elements within a story, making predictions based on the story elements, and retelling the story they read. Therefore, effective instruction of story comprehension includes teaching text structure.

*The transaction:* We have considered two factors affecting comprehension, the readers and the text. The reader transacts with the text, which leads to the construction of meaning. Such transactions occur within a context, and that context plays an important role in the process of constructing meaning. The context teachers create for readers frequently contributes to the meaning that they construct from reading. Consider the following two contexts for reading: one student who is reading a short story and given questions to answer when finished and a second reader who is given the same story but is encouraged to make a personal response to the reading. Both readers have different purposes based on the direction of the teacher and will construct different meanings from the text. Transaction leads to the meaning that is constructed when the reader and the text interact within a real context.

## GUIDELINES FOR TEACHING STORY COMPREHENSION

More than 25 years of research targeting the teaching of comprehension reveals that teachers feel more comfortable testing comprehension than teaching it (Gill, 2008). What does the reader need to know about comprehension, and what do teachers need to teach? Using the constructivist model of comprehension, we can focus on the reader by asking what proficient readers do during reading and then compare their reading strategies with those of our students. Duke and Pearson (2002) summarized the research on what good readers do while reading. Effective teachers use their knowledge of good readers' strategies to assist them in planning instruction for reading comprehension. Figure V.1 provides a visual outline of strategies used by good readers during reading (Duke & Pearson, 2002, pp. 205–206).

Although most teachers believe that the primary goal of all reading is comprehension, researchers continually remind us that instruction in reading comprehension does not take front and center stage in most classrooms (Durkin, 1978/1979; Pressley, 2006). For most teachers, reading comprehension instruction is difficult. Therefore, teaching models that promise effective instruction must be clear with respect to what and how reading comprehension should be taught. Guidelines to help teachers implement effective instruction call for (a) daily comprehension instruction for all students, (b) strategy instruction that is explicit, (c) teacher modeling and demonstrations of strategy use, (d) large blocks of time for guided practice and scaffolding students' attempts at strategy use, and (e) time for independent reading (Scharlach, 2008). The National Reading Panel (National Institute of Child Health and Human Development, 2000) provides the

| Figure V.1 | What Proficient Readers Do While Reading |

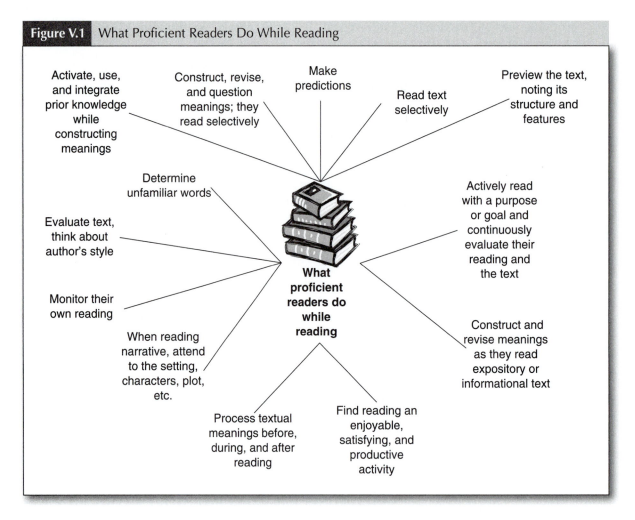

framework for the critical comprehension strategies that need to be part of a school-wide instructional program. They have made recommendations for teaching the following research-based comprehension strategies:

- *Comprehension monitoring:* Teachers help readers become aware of their own understanding of the text.

- *Cooperative learning:* Teachers create literacy environments where students learn reading strategies together.

- *Graphic and semantic organizers:* Teachers guide students in using graphic representations of the material to assist in their comprehension of text.

- *Question answering:* Teachers help students answer questions about the text that are posed by the teacher, who offers immediate feedback.

- *Question generation:* Teachers train readers to ask themselves questions about various aspects of the story before, during, and after reading.

- *Story structure:* Teachers provide instruction on the structure of the story as a means of helping them understand and recall story content.

- *Summarization:* Teachers offer readers direct instruction on summarizing and generalizing ideas they have read.

# A Strategy for Assessing Story Comprehension

Effective teachers monitor students' reading comprehension and use the assessment results to design and develop instruction for students' literacy needs. Although there are a number of standardized tests administered to students during the year, many assessments do not always help teachers understand the students' strengths and their areas for improvement that specifically relate to classroom learning and instruction. Therefore, "it becomes the responsibility of the classroom teacher to make up for the shortcomings" within current assessment systems (Duke, 2005, p. 103). Many teachers who are identified as exemplary use a range of assessments, including rubrics to monitor students' comprehension. Figure V.2 is an example that teachers may use for aligning instruction and assessment to monitor students' reading comprehension. Informal classroom assessments such as rubrics are developed based on performance outcomes defined for students and may be modified for their varying learning needs.

| **Figure V.2** | Rubric for Assessing Story Comprehension | | | | |
|---|---|---|---|---|---|
| **Criterion** | **Proficient (3 Points)** | **Advanced (2 Points)** | **Developing (1–0 Points)** | **Score** | **Comments** |
| **Story characters** | Identifies and describes the characters, offers insights into their intentions and motivations, and makes personal and text connections | Identifies and describes the characters, states their intentions, and makes some personal and text connections | Identifies the characters but is unable to provide complete descriptions, does not refer to the characters' intentions, and cannot make personal or text connections | | |
| **Story goal or problem** | Identifies and fully analyzes the goal of the story and makes a range of predictions that may lead to the story resolution | Identifies the goal of the story briefly | Is unable to identify the goal of the story | | |
| **Story events** | Identifies the story events in their sequence and describes them, showing how each event will lead to the resolution of the story; offers alternatives to story events that may lead to more efficient resolutions | Identifies major story events and places most in correct sequence; makes some attempts to show how story events lead to the story resolution; does not offer alternate ways to achieve a more efficient story resolution | Identifies a few story events and does not place them in correct sequence; does not show the connection between the story events and the ending of the story | | |

*(Continued)*

(Continued)

| Criterion | Proficient (3 Points) | Advanced (2 Points) | Developing (1–0 Points) | Score | Comments |
|---|---|---|---|---|---|
| **Details** | Provides many details with rich descriptions | Provides some details with adequate descriptions | Provides few details with no descriptions | | |
| **Story resolution, conclusion, and theme** | Provides an in-depth discussion of the story resolution, conclusions, and theme | Briefly discusses the story resolution and makes a simple conclusion | Makes a brief allusion to the story ending | | |
| **Connections** | Makes numerous connections to the story, including self-connections, text connections, and world connections | Makes some connections to the story that typically include more self-connections | Makes few if any connections to the story | | |
| **Responses** | Offers personal responses to the story that show critical thinking and reflection | Offers some responses to the story that do not demonstrate reflection | Does not offer personal responses to the story | | |
| **Scoring Guide** <br> **Directions:** Assign a score of [1] for each [+] assessment. If you recorded a [–] mark, assign a score of [0]. <br> Proficient: 12–9 points <br> Advanced: 8–5 points <br> Developing: 4–0 points | | | | | |

# A Guide for Using Response to Intervention for Story Comprehension

Readers' knowledge of story structure endows them with a mechanism for analyzing a story that will lead to deeper levels of story comprehension. When students are engaged in literacy activities, they are frequently required to discuss or write about story parts or make connections and respond to the story. Teachers may use the rubric shown in Figure V.2 as a guide for assessing students' performances in areas related to story comprehension. The teacher engages in student observations during discussions of stories or analyzes students' writing to determine areas related to story comprehension that need improvement. The teacher uses the assessment results to identify those groups of students who need additional instruction and selects the instructional strategy that will assist them. For example, one teacher observed students during their literature circle discussion of a story character and targeted a small group of students who were not able to identify the character's traits or use evidence from the story narrative to confirm their statements. Using small-group instruction with the target group, the teacher used Character Mapping to help students identify the traits of a story character and confirm them with evidence from the text.

## PROFESSIONAL RESOURCES

Caldwell, J. S. (2008). *Comprehension assessment: A classroom guide.* New York: Guilford

Hansen, J. (2004). *Tell me a story: Developmentally appropriate retelling strategies.* Newark, DE: International Reading Association.

Wilhelm, J. D. (2002). *Action strategies for deepening comprehension: Role plays, text-structure tableaux,* talking strategies, and other enactment techniques that engage students with text. New York: Scholastic.

Wilhelm, J. D. (2004). *Reading is seeing.* New York: Scholastic

## REFERENCES

Buss, K., & Karnowski, L. (2000). *Reading and writing literary genres.* Newark, DE: International Reading Association.

Dickson, S. V., Simmons, D. C., & Kame'enui, E. J. (1995). *Text organization and its relationship to reading comprehension: A synthesis of the research.* Washington, DC: National Center to Improve the Tools of Educators.

Duke, N. K. (2005). Comprehension of what for what: Comprehension as a nonunitary construct. In S. G. Paris & S. A. Stahl (Eds.), *Children's reading comprehension and assessment* (pp. 93–106). Mahwah, NJ: Erlbaum.

Duke, N., & Pearson, P. D. (2002). Effective practices for developing reading comprehension. In A. E. Farstrup & S. J. Samuels (Eds.), *What research has to say about reading instruction* (pp. 205–242). Newark, DE: International Reading Association.

Durkin, D. (1978/1979). What classroom observations reveal about reading comprehension instruction. *Reading Research Quarterly, 14*(4), 481–538.

Fletcher, C. R. (1994). Levels of representation in memory for discourse. In M. A. Gernsbacher (Ed.), *Handbook of psycholinguistics* (pp. 589–607). San Diego, CA: Academic Press.

Gill, S. R. (2008). A comprehension matrix: A tool for designing comprehension instruction. *The Reading Teacher, 62*(2), 106–113.

Kucer, S. B. (2001). *Dimensions of literacy: A conceptual base of teaching reading and writing in a school setting.* Mahwah, NJ: Erlbaum.

Mandler, J. M. (1984). *Stories, scripts, and scenes: Aspects of schema theory.* Hillsdale, NJ: Erlbaum.

National Institute of Child Health and Human Development. (2000). *Report of the National Reading Panel. Teaching children to read: An evidence-based assessment of the scientific literature on reading and its implications for reading instruction* (NIH Publication No. 00-4769). Washington, DC: U.S. Government Printing Office.

Pardo, L. S. (2004). What every teacher needs to know about comprehension. *The Reading Teacher, 58*(3), 272–280.

Pressley, M. (2006, April 29). *What the future of reading research could be.* Paper presented at the International Reading Association Reading Research Conference, Chicago, IL.

Rosenblatt, L. R. (1978). *The reader, the text, and the poem: The transaction theory of the literary work.* Carbondale, IL: Southern Illinois University Press.

Schallert, D. L., & Martin, D. B. (2003). A psychological analysis of what teachers and students do in the language arts classroom. In J. Flood, D. Lapp, & J. M. Jensen (Eds.), *Handbook of research of teaching the English language arts* (pp. 21–45). Mahwah, NJ: Erlbaum.

Scharlach, T. D. (2008). START comprehending: Students and teachers actively reading text. *The Reading Teacher, 61*(1), 20–31.

Sweet, A. P., & Snow, C. E. (2003). *Rethinking reading comprehension.* New York: Guilford.

## CHILDREN'S LITERATURE CITED

Giff, P. R. (2000). *Nory Ryan's song.* New York: Random House.

Lionni, L. (1995). *Little blue and little yellow.* New York: HarperCollins.

# Strategy
# 21

# Story Mapping

## SPEAKING BRIEFLY: AN OVERVIEW OF THE LITERACY STRATEGY

The *Story Mapping* strategy provides a visual display of story elements that will assist readers in remembering, comprehending, and retelling the stories they listen to and read. We live in a visual world where language is supported by a range of pictures, icons, and graphics that serve as an adjunct for understanding oral and print language. For example, when we need to drive to an unfamiliar place, the directions that we use may be a set of print or spoken directions accompanied by a map that plots the trip by marking the streets, highways, and bridges with icons and labels. Similar to geographic maps, story maps offer visual representations of the parts of a story that help students navigate their way through the story, from the beginning to the end of the text. This diagram facilitates students in acquiring a story sense that assists them in comprehending the story through the map's organized representation of the structure of narrative text. Clearly, reading with story maps supports students in organizing their ideas around the elements of the text, thereby helping them comprehend stories at deeper levels. Educators agree that students' use of story maps during reading will develop their comprehension and visualization strategies for narrative text (Fiene & McMahon, 2007). Further, the National Reading Panel (National Institute of Child Health and Human Development, 2000) supports the scientific evidence for teaching comprehension strategies that employ graphic organizers, such as story maps with text talk.

*Source:* International Reading Association and National Council of Teachers of English (1996).

### IRA/NCTE Standards for English Language Arts

1. Students read a wide range of print and nonprint texts to build an understanding of texts, of themselves, and of the cultures of the United States and the world; to acquire new information; to respond to the needs and demands of society and the workplace; and for personal fulfillment. Among these texts are fiction and nonfiction, classic and contemporary works.

3. Students apply a wide range of strategies to comprehend, interpret, evaluate, and appreciate texts. They draw on their prior experience, their interactions with other readers and writers, their knowledge of word meaning and of other texts, their word identification strategies, and their understanding of textual features (e.g., sound-letter correspondence, sentence structure, context, graphics).

12. Students use spoken, written, and visual language to accomplish their own purposes (e.g., for learning, enjoyment, persuasion, and the exchange of information).

# USING STORY MAPPING

*When to use the strategy:* When students are unfamiliar with Story Mapping, it is important to use direct instruction and modeling before, during, and after reading. They need to learn how to use the map to organize the story around its elements. This is especially true for young children, who will benefit from listening to a story and seeing its important parts recorded on a story map. The teacher uses the story map before reading to help students make predictions, during reading to identify story parts, and after reading to reconstruct the whole story.

*Strategy modifications for grade levels:* Story Mapping may be used with students at different grade levels. For primary-grade students, teachers provide direct instruction through modeling and demonstrations by using stories that have simple plots and demonstrating how to use the story maps. For kindergarten children, teachers may use felt boards and props to demonstrate story mapping and retelling. After students in the intermediate and middle grades are taught story structure and how to use story maps, they may use the mapping strategy with a variety of literacy activities, such as plotting stories in their journals during independent reading or during literature circles. Further, students may develop story maps using software such as Inspiration 9 for upper grades or Kidspiration 3 for primary grades and then share them through class presentations using SMART Boards.

## IMPLEMENTING THE STORY MAPPING STRATEGY: STEP BY STEP

This strategy consists of two parts. Students learn how to identify and elaborate on the elements of a story, and they use their story maps to guide their oral retellings of the story.

### Direct Instruction of Story Mapping

1. **Select a quality piece of children's literature to use for teaching the elements of a story.** Choose an appropriate story for the students' interests and comprehension levels that also has an explicit story structure. To teach the elements of a story, consider using picture storybooks. They are short and can be completed within a single instructional block of time. Further, there is a wide range of picture storybooks suitable for students at all grade levels.

2. **Read the story aloud to the students.** Introduce the story and read it aloud. Tell the students that they will learn about the story parts of the book that they completed.

3. **Present the story map graphic to the students.** On the SMART Board, project a blank graphic of a story map similar to the one in Figure 21.1. Use the story map to teach each element of a story and provide examples from familiar stories that students have read.

4. **Engage students in a guided discussion of the story using the parts of the story depicted on the map.** Use the story map with the students to identify the elements of the story they read. During the post-reading discussion of the story, use question prompts such as the one shown on the story map in Figure 21.1 to help students recall, reflect, and respond to each of the story elements. Have students use their own story maps to record their ideas and responses.

5. **Summarize students' responses and ideas related to the story elements and record them on the story map.** Write a summary of ideas on the class story map and review it with the students, drawing their attention to each of the story elements.

| Figure 21.1 | Sample Story Map |

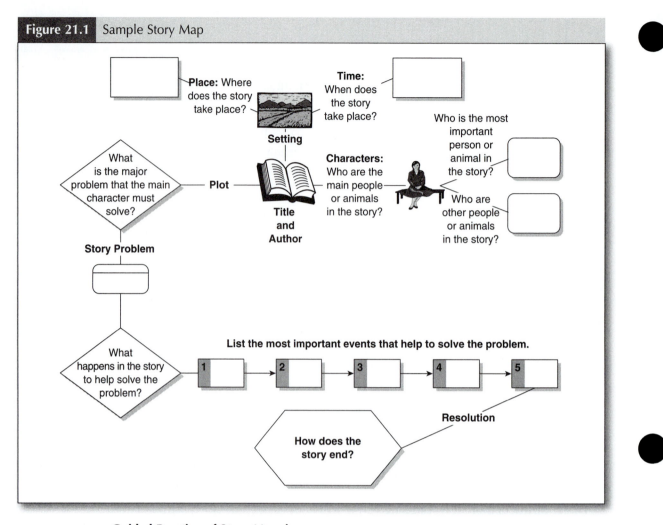

### Guided Practice of Story Mapping

Story Mapping is an effective comprehension strategy that students may use during guided reading, literature circles, or independent reading. After the teacher provides direct instruction in Story Mapping, students need practice in using the strategy to internalize it and "make it their own." Teachers may provide opportunities within the literacy program that require students to reconstruct the story through the use of a visual representation of the story structure. At first, students depend on teacher-constructed story maps to recreate their stories. When students become familiar with Story Mapping, they will no longer be dependent on generic story maps; rather, they will design their own to fit the story. As students use Story Mapping on their own, the teacher assists them by offering constructive feedback. Students will benefit from opportunities to share and compare their story maps with their peers.

### APPLYING THE STORY MAPPING STRATEGY: FOURTH-GRADE LESSON

The teacher in the fourth grade engages students in a read-aloud of *Maggie's Amerikay,* written by Barbara Timberlake Russell (2006) with pictures by Jim Burke. This historical fiction picture storybook is about a young girl's family who leaves Ireland to come to America, where they settle in the bustling port of New Orleans. Life is different! Here Maggie learns about the people and their different ways of living. As she learns to read and write, she befriends Nathan, an African-American boy who plays the cornet.

After reading and discussing the story, the teacher projects the story map on the SMART Board and guides the students through the story. As students discuss each element, the teacher summarizes their responses and records them on the story map, as depicted in Figure 21.2.

**Figure 21.2** Story Map of *Maggie's Amerikay*

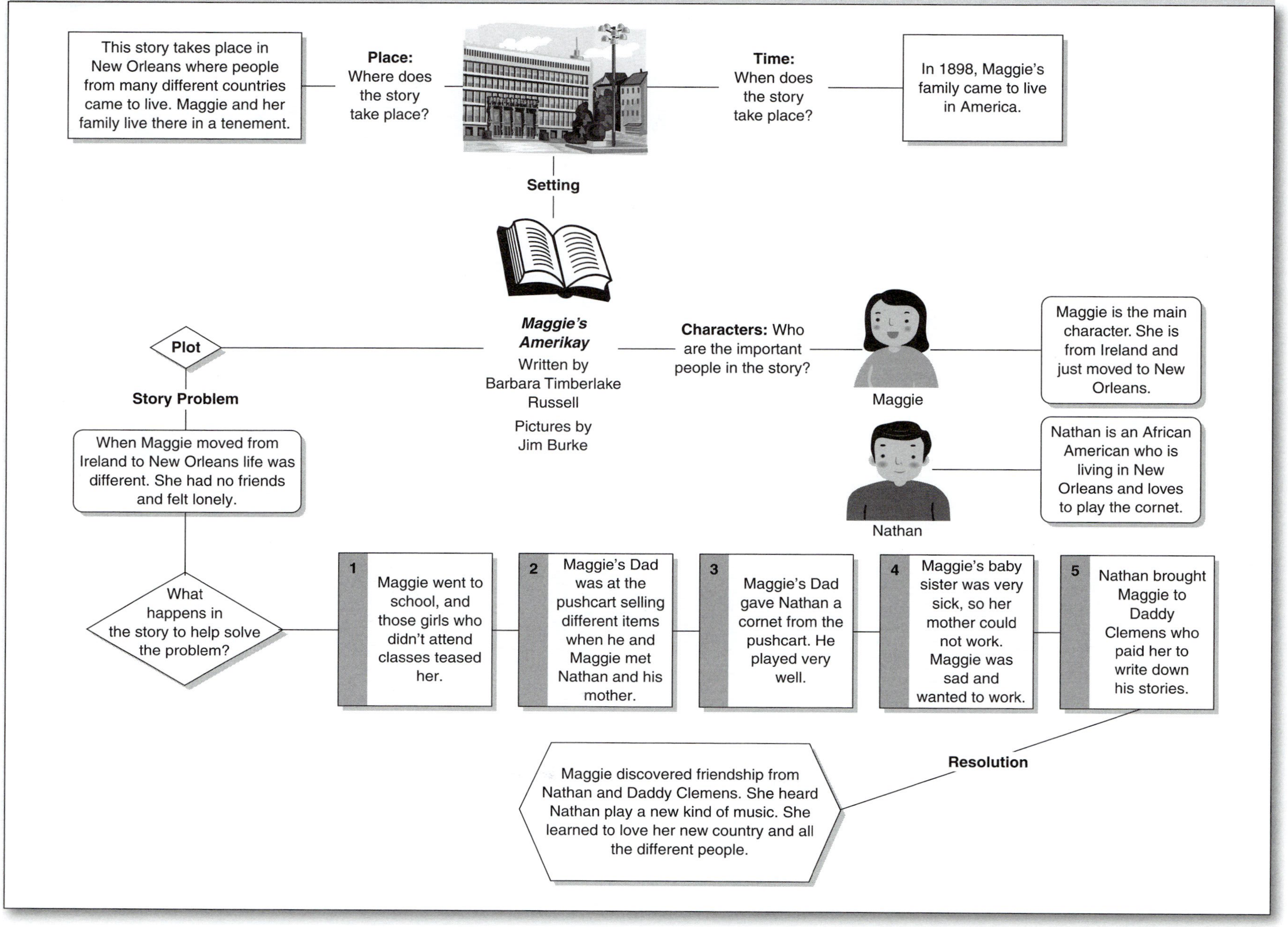

**Setting**

**Place:** Where does the story take place?

This story takes place in New Orleans where people from many different countries came to live. Maggie and her family live there in a tenement.

**Time:** When does the story take place?

In 1898, Maggie's family came to live in America.

*Maggie's Amerikay*
Written by Barbara Timberlake Russell
Pictures by Jim Burke

**Characters:** Who are the important people in the story?

Maggie is the main character. She is from Ireland and just moved to New Orleans.

Maggie

Nathan is an African American who is living in New Orleans and loves to play the cornet.

Nathan

**Plot**

**Story Problem**

When Maggie moved from Ireland to New Orleans life was different. She had no friends and felt lonely.

What happens in the story to help solve the problem?

**1** Maggie went to school, and those girls who didn't attend classes teased her.

**2** Maggie's Dad was at the pushcart selling different items when he and Maggie met Nathan and his mother.

**3** Maggie's Dad gave Nathan a cornet from the pushcart. He played very well.

**4** Maggie's baby sister was very sick, so her mother could not work. Maggie was sad and wanted to work.

**5** Nathan brought Maggie to Daddy Clemens who paid her to write down his stories.

**Resolution**

Maggie discovered friendship from Nathan and Daddy Clemens. She heard Nathan play a new kind of music. She learned to love her new country and all the different people.

125

*Source:* International Reading Association and National Council of Teachers of English (1996).

### IRA/NCTE Standards for English Language Arts

10. Students whose first language is not English make use of their first language to develop competency in the English language arts and to develop understanding of content across the curriculum.

## DIFFERENTIATING INSTRUCTION FOR ENGLISH LANGUAGE LEARNERS

English language learners will benefit from increased visualization strategies and dialogue to assist them in understanding text structure as well as recalling and elaborating on story elements. Farris and Downey (2004) used *concept muraling* with students to teach important concepts across the curriculum and suggest that this approach would assist English language learners in comprehending text. Briefly, the teacher selects the significant ideas to be taught, creates a visual or a picture of the concept, displays it, and engages students in a dialogue to expand and elaborate the information around significant concepts. Students use the pictures and other visuals of important concepts to create an elaborate mural by adding more of their own information to the significant ideas using pictures and other visuals. Although concept muraling was used with content subjects, the approach may be modified to teach the structure of stories by placing pictures, visuals, and icons to represent the story parts. Students work together on the story mural to expand ideas and concepts related to the story elements. Their group interpretations of the story become part of the *story mural*. Story muraling will assist English language learners' comprehension of the text because of its increased emphasis on dialogue, interpretation of the story, and the visualization of big ideas within the story.

## DIFFERENTIATING INSTRUCTION FOR STUDENTS WITH SPECIAL NEEDS

Story Mapping for students with special needs has had positive effects on comprehension of narrative text. Studies show that students with learning disabilities and behavioral problems who are disabled readers improve in story comprehension when they receive instruction in Story Mapping (Babyak, Koorland, & Mathes, 2000; Boulineau, Fore, Hagan-Burke, & Burke, 2004). Researchers show that students with serious emotional and reading problems will benefit when Story Mapping instruction is accompanied by (1) modeling the strategy, (2) rehearsal of specific strategy steps, (3) scaffolded assistance, and (4) corrective feedback (Epstein et al., 1993).

## REFERENCES

Babyak, A. E., Koorland, M., & Mathes, P. G. (2000). The effect of story mapping instruction on students with behavioral disorders. *Behavioral Disorders, 25*(3), 239–258.

Boulineau, T., Fore, C., III, Hagan-Burke, S., & Burke, M. D. (2004). Use of story mapping to increase the story-grammar text comprehension of elementary students with learning disabilities. *Learning Disability Quarterly, 27*(2), 105–121.

Epstein, M., Kauffman, J., Lloyd, J., Cook, L., Cullinan, D., Forness, S., et al. (1993). Improving services for students with serious emotional disturbances. *National Association for Secondary School Principals (NASSP) Bulletin, 76,* 46–51.

Farris, P. J., & Downey, P. M. (2004). Concept muraling: Dropping visual crumbs along the instructional trail. *The Reading Teacher, 58*(4), 376–380.

Fiene, J., & McMahon, S. (2007). Assessing comprehension: A classroom-based process. *The Reading Teacher, 60*(5), 406–417.

International Reading Association and National Council of Teachers of English. (1996). *Standards for the*

*English language arts.* Newark, DE: International Reading Association and Urbana, IL: National Council of Teachers of English.

National Institute of Child Health and Human Development. (2000). *Report of the National Reading Panel. Teaching children to read: An evidence-based assessment of the scientific literature on reading and its implications for reading instruction* (NIH Publication No. 00-4769). Washington, DC: U.S. Government Printing Office.

## CHILDREN'S LITERATURE CITED

Russell, B. T. (2006). *Maggie's Amerikay.* New York: Farrar, Straus, & Giroux.

# Strategy
# 22

# Story Retelling

## SPEAKING BRIEFLY: AN OVERVIEW OF THE LITERACY STRATEGY

Most teachers view retelling a text as a reading- or listening-comprehension assessment tool. Indeed, it is that, but it is far more. The *Story Retelling* strategy encourages reading for meaning and language development. When students are required to retell a story, they reconstruct the story, digging deep into various story events, actions of the characters, and their intentions. Story retellings hand over the responsibility to the student for constructing meaning. In their classic work *Read and Retell*, Brown and Cambourne (1987) observed the language-rich benefits students derived from engaging in retelling stories: Students acquired an understanding of text structures, vocabulary, and text conventions; they developed an awareness of the process that was involved in the reconstruction of text; they gained reading flexibility—that is, they employed different strategies for different reading tasks; and students used a range of text conventions in their own writing (pp. 10–12).

When students retell stories, they engage in oral language as they share their interpretations and responses to the text. Such engagement in language demands active participation in the comprehension process (Hoyt, 1999). For all retellings, students are required to summarize and synthesize the text, which are both complex cognitive processes (Harvey & Goudvis, 2007). Shaw (2005) reminds us that retelling places the demand on students to transform or recreate the story and put it into their own words. As we reflect on what this strategy requires from readers, we recognize the power of the strategy: Story retelling "involves reconstructing the entire text structure, including the major elements, details, and sequence" (Reutzel & Cooter, 2008, p. 241).

Benson and Cummins (2000) take into account that children's learning is developmental. Within their model of developmental retelling, they demonstrate a constructivist approach to comprehending stories. Therefore, the approach they utilize is to prepare students for written retellings by guiding their retellings and offering visual supports such as story maps and graphics.

*Source:* International Reading Association and National Council of Teachers of English (1996).

---

### IRA/NCTE Standards for English Language Arts

3. Students apply a wide range of strategies to comprehend, interpret, evaluate, and appreciate texts. They draw on their prior experience, their interactions with other readers and writers, their knowledge of word meaning and of other texts, their word identification strategies, and their understanding of textual features (e.g., sound-letter correspondence, sentence structure, context, graphics).

4. Students adjust their use of spoken, written, and visual language (e.g., conventions, style, vocabulary) to communicate effectively with a variety of audiences and for different purposes.

6. Students apply knowledge of language structure, language conventions (e.g., spelling and punctuation), media techniques, figurative language, and genre to create, critique, and discuss print and nonprint texts.

12. Students use spoken, written, and visual language to accomplish their own purposes (e.g., for learning, enjoyment, persuasion, and the exchange of information).

---

# USING STORY RETELLING

*When to use the strategy:* When students are learning to retell a story, it is important that teachers begin before the story is introduced. At this phase of the reading process, students learn how to use the text to make predictions about the story as teachers lay the groundwork for retelling. After students learn the strategy, story retellings may be a part of the after-reading activity.

*Strategy modifications for grade levels:* For younger children and students who are developing a story sense and have no experience with story retellings, it is important that the teacher use modeling and demonstrations. These are followed by direct instruction and guided story retellings. Young children will benefit from the use of story props, such as a puppet that becomes the main character who retells the story. For older students and for those with a well-developed sense of story, the teacher may decide to use written retellings. Students who engage in written story retellings will benefit from a guide, such as a series of questions or a checklist of story parts, that serves as a plan for developing a complete story retelling.

## IMPLEMENTING THE STORY RETELLING STRATEGY: STEP BY STEP

Steps for retelling a story may be varied, depending on the students' literacy development as well as the instructional context. Teachers frequently modify steps in the strategy to fit the age and reading level as well as the literacy context. The story retelling session employs the following framework: (1) predict; (2) read, confirm, and review; (3) retell; and (4) share and compare.

### Predict

Prior to reading the story, students make predictions about the story plot, characters, and theme.

1. Read the title of the book to the students. Ask students to tell what they think the story will be about and what clues they get from the title to help make such predictions.

2. Show the book to the students and ask them to focus on the illustration on the cover. Ask them to make further predictions from the clues provided in the illustration. Encourage students to use clues to make predictions about the story events, characters, or even the overall story theme.

3. Predictions may also include vocabulary. Using a brainstorming approach, have students think of their predictions and suggest words the author may use to tell the story.

### Read, Confirm, and Review

1. The teacher may read the story aloud, or the students may read the story silently.

2. After reading the story, the teacher and students confirm their predictions for the story.

3. The teacher and students review the story elements as they relate to the story. The teacher may use questions that are based on the story parts to help students recall the characters, story problem, events and their sequence, and story resolution or ending.

### Retell

Select an appropriate approach to retell the story.

1. *Oral retellings:* The teacher may ask the students to retell the story to their partners. Students may participate in a group retelling that is conducted by the teacher, who uses questions that help students recall specific story parts.

2. *Written retellings:* The teacher may request that students engage in a written retelling of the story. When students are familiar with writing their retellings, they may use their journals to summarize the story. A helpful start to written retellings is to provide students with a graphic organizer that helps them organize the story as they recall the parts.

### Share and Compare

1. *Share:* Provide time for students to share their retellings. Sharing retellings may occur within the context of the whole class, small groups of four to five students, or learning pairs. Students discuss the various parts that they thought were important to the development of the story or that made the story interesting and exciting. They may focus on character development or the actions of the character.

2. *Compare:* Lead the group in a discussion to include comparisons. The teacher may move the discussion to focus on comparisons within the story or across other stories that are familiar to the students.

## APPLYING THE STORY RETELLING STRATEGY: KINDERGARTEN LESSON

The teacher introduces kindergarten students to one of Leo Tolstoy's classics written for children. *Philipok,* retold by Ann Keay Beneduce (2000) and illustrated by Gennady Spirin, has a simple plot and an easy-to-remember set of story events. The story focuses on a young Russian boy, Philipok, who wants to go to school like his older brother Peter. Philipok finds the opportunity to steal out and go to school and faces a few challenges on the way.

The teacher introduces the book and reads the story to the children. Knowing that the students have little experience in retelling stories, the teacher gives a puppet named Philipok to the child who retells the story. To guide the student's oral retelling, the teacher uses the following questions as prompts:

- Who were Peter and Philipok?

- Tell what Philipok wanted to do?

- Why did he want to go to school?

- What did Philipok do when his grandma fell asleep?

- Tell all the things that happened to Philipok on the way to school. (To help sequence the story events, the teacher may wish to use the illustrations to prompt the student's retelling.)

- Tell what happened when little Philipok went into the schoolhouse.

- How does the story end?

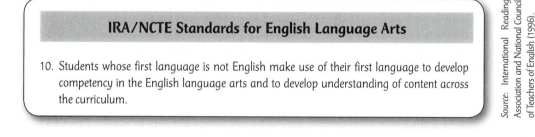

### IRA/NCTE Standards for English Language Arts

10. Students whose first language is not English make use of their first language to develop competency in the English language arts and to develop understanding of content across the curriculum.

*Source:* International Reading Association and National Council of Teachers of English (1996).

## DIFFERENTIATING INSTRUCTION FOR ENGLISH LANGUAGE LEARNERS

Oral story retellings are most appropriate for English language learners who are beginning to learn how to retell stories. To help English language learners retell a story, select a picture storybook that has a well-developed and straightforward plot and a context to which students relate. For example, a story with flashbacks will be confusing, whereas one that contains a set of events that are clearly stated and sequenced will be less confusing. Provide a set of prompts—such as questions developed around the story elements—that will help students remember and talk about the story. When students retell the story and have difficulty retelling a story part, offer assistance by sharing the retelling. When English language learners are familiar with oral story retellings, they may begin written retellings guided by a graphic with familiar prompts.

## DIFFERENTIATING INSTRUCTION FOR STUDENTS WITH SPECIAL NEEDS

Story retellings are appropriate for students with a range of reading abilities when the strategy is used flexibly (Brown & Cambourne, 1987). Differentiate instruction for students with special needs by providing them with prompts during oral story retellings and employing them until the students learn and apply the prompts in their own retellings. One set of prompts is the five-finger story retelling, based on five questions related to story parts:

1. Who are the characters in the story?

2. What happened in the story?

3. Where did the story take place?

4. When did the story take place?

5. What happened at the beginning of the story, what happened next, and how did it end?

## REFERENCES

Benson, V., & Cummins, C. (2000). *The power of retelling: Developmental steps for building comprehension.* Bothell, WA: Wright Group.

Brown, H., & Cambourne, B. (1987). *Read and retell.* Portsmouth, NH: Heinemann.

Harvey, S., & Goudvis, A. (2007). *Strategies that work: Teaching comprehension.* Portland, ME: Stenhouse.

Hoyt, L. (1999). *Revisit, reflect, retell: Strategies for improving reading comprehension.* Portsmouth, NH: Heinemann.

International Reading Association and National Council of Teachers of English. (1996). *Standards for the English language arts.* Newark, DE: International Reading Association and Urbana, IL: National Council of Teachers of English.

Reutzel, D. R., & Cooter, R. B., Jr. (2008). *Teaching children to read: The teacher makes the difference* (5th ed.). Upper Saddle River, NJ: Merrill Prentice Hall.

Shaw, D. (2005). *Retelling strategies to improve comprehension: Effective hands-on strategies for fiction and nonfiction to help students remember and understand what they read.* New York: Scholastic.

## CHILDREN'S LITERATURE CITED

Beneduce, A. K. (2000). *Philipok.* New York: Philomel.

# Strategy

# 23

# Book Talks

The *Book Talk* strategy is a motivational tool used by the teacher to rouse students' interest in books. The teacher uses it to provide a coming attraction to a piece of literature that they will read during literature circles or guided reading or to whet their appetites for particular library books available to them for independent reading (Tompkins, 2006). Although the strategy is used primarily by teachers, literacy specialists, and librarians to encourage reading, Book Talks have been used successfully by students when reporting on books or promoting books to their peers. Within this strategy, we provide guidelines for teachers to use Book Talks as a motivational tool to encourage students to read, as well as for students to use when sharing books with their peers.

*Book Talks conducted by teachers:* The primary goal of the teacher's Book Talk is to motivate the students to pick up the book and read it. To achieve this goal, the teacher must think about the selection of the book. A convincing Book Talk begins with an interesting piece of children's literature—a story that offers students opportunities to make personal, text, and world connections; expands their knowledge of the world; and develops their vocabulary. The teacher's presentation of the book must be persuasive and believable, showing his/her own interest in the book by making personal connections to characters and story events. Finally, since the Book Talk promotes excitement among the students to read the story, the teacher is careful not to tell the entire story.

*Book Talks conducted by students:* The purpose for students to conduct Book Talks is to share their readings with their peers and to entice them to read the book. Students have an opportunity to discuss their personal interpretations and responses to the books they read. Unlike a traditional book report, students offer reflections on different aspects of the story and critique and evaluate the text. Frequently, the teacher offers guidelines for students to follow based on their reading and grade levels. Included in Book Talks are brief read-alouds of the most interesting story part, which will further benefit the student's development in reading fluency (Rasinski, 2003).

Students' engagement in Book Talks involves text talk that should lead to higher-level thinking for the discussant as well as the listener. The teacher offers guidelines that students follow to develop their talks. Fischbaugh (2004) helped students develop questions that they used for planning their presentations by providing them with an opportunity to establish the criteria for writing their questions and to use a rating scale to evaluate their questions. Their questions became the planning tool for their Book Talk.

*Source:* International Reading Association and National Council of Teachers of English (1996).

---

### IRA/NCTE Standards for English Language Arts

3.  Students apply a wide range of strategies to comprehend, interpret, evaluate, and appreciate texts. They draw on their prior experience, their interactions with other readers and writers, their knowledge of word meaning and of other texts, their word identification strategies, and their understanding of textual features (e.g., sound-letter correspondence, sentence structure, context, graphics).

4.  Students adjust their use of spoken, written, and visual language (e.g., conventions, style, vocabulary) to communicate effectively with a variety of audiences and for different purposes.

6.  Students apply knowledge of language structure, language conventions (e.g., spelling and punctuation), media techniques, figurative language, and genre to create, critique, and discuss print and nonprint texts.

12. Students use spoken, written, and visual language to accomplish their own purposes (e.g., for learning, enjoyment, persuasion, and the exchange of information).

---

## USING BOOK TALKS

*When to use the strategy:* Book Talks may be used effectively before reading or after reading by teachers and students. For example, teachers use Book Talks as a prereading strategy to motivate students to engage in reading the story. After reading, they may use Book Talks to summarize, interpret, and reflect on the story. Students engage in Book Talks after reading to share their reading experiences with their peers and to encourage them to read the book.

*Strategy modifications for grade levels:* For younger children, teachers engage students in a Book Talk by using the elements of the book to capture their attention—the title and illustrations on the cover as well as the pictures that are part of the story. For older students, Book Talks may be more complex as the teachers compare personal experiences with those of the character, use book language to focus on various story elements, and compare the book with stories that students have read.

### IMPLEMENTING THE BOOK TALK STRATEGY: STEP BY STEP

The Book Talk is conducted by the teacher and students using the same procedure. Their purpose is the same, to motivate and entice others to read and enjoy the book. Teachers use Book Talks to encourage students to read books from the school and classroom libraries and to introduce books that will be part of a curriculum unit or that they will read for literature circles or reading workshops. When Book Talks are frequent and become part of the literary routines within the classrooms, students learn from teacher demonstrations. Once familiar with the practice of Book Talks, students enjoy talking about and sharing the stories they read.

**Book Talks Conducted by Teachers and Students**

1. **Select a piece of children's literature.** The book selected should be appropriate for a Book Talk and for sharing with other students. Although teachers have specific curricular purposes for selecting and talking about books that are different from the purposes of students who use Book Talks to share a story with their peers, their intentions are similar: Teachers and students aspire to entice others to read their books.

2. **Preparation for conducting Book Talks is essential.** To engage students in a Book Talk, it is important to read the book. Prepare a presentation that will motivate students to read the book. Motivational devices include helping students connect with the characters or experiences within the book, comparing books that are familiar to students, and reading a short part of the story expressively. Select a short part of the story for reading. The selected passage should expand on the Book Talk, be 1 to 2 minutes in length, and be read with a great deal of expression and emotion. An important tip to remember when preparing for the Book Talk is not to give the story away. Unlike storytelling where listeners hear the whole story, in a Book Talk, only part of the story is told to entice others to read the book.

**Teachers Support Students in Preparing for Book Talks**

a. Provide demonstrations of Book Talks that are well-developed and carefully presented. Help students engage in presenting a Book Talk by providing them with good models of Book Talks.
b. Offer students a structured approach to planning for a Book Talk by explaining the following: (1) the purpose of the Book Talk, (2) selecting a book, (3) the steps in preparing to talk about a book, and (4) the importance of practicing fluent reading of a passage from the book.
c. Provide students with a list of questions to serve as guides for planning the Book Talk. Students may use one or two of the questions, such as those in Figure 23.1, to guide their Book Talk or they may develop their own questions.

| Figure 23.1 | Questions to Guide the Preparation of a Book Talk |
| --- | --- |

✓ Who is the main character, and how have you made a personal connection with this story character?

✓ Is the story setting described? Where does the story take place? When did it happen? How do you know this if the author does not make it clear?

✓ Why did the author write this book?

✓ Could this story ever happen today? Could the main character be your classmate? Your friend? Why?

✓ Why do you think this story is considered a tale, fantasy, science fiction, historical fiction, or realistic fiction?

✓ Did you ever read a book like this one? How was it the same or different?

✓ Why do you wish to share this book?

✓ Why do you think others should read this book?

3. **Conduct the Book Talk presentation.** A significant prop that should be used is the book. Show the cover of the book, read the title and author, and present the planned Book Talk, including the reading of a passage from the book.

## Applying the Book Talk Strategy: Third-Grade Lesson

The third-grade students read picture storybooks appropriate for the early primary grades to prepare Book Talks for children in kindergarten and grades 1 and 2. Small groups of three children worked together, reading and preparing Book Talks for the assigned classes. Their purpose was to persuade the younger children to read the books they presented.

One group of students assigned to first-grade students read and prepared a Book Talk of *The Ugly Duckling,* retold and illustrated by Rachel Isadora (2009). Within this interpretation of the Hans Christian Andersen fairy tale, Rachel Isadora uses Africa as the setting of the story. Students introduced the book by reading the title and the author, and they described their character, Ugly Duckling, to their audience. They also talked about the setting of the story. Their Book Talk was accompanied by their own descriptive drawings, which were similar to the illustrations in the book. Students talked about and showed through their pictures some of the challenging events Ugly Duckling experienced as he ran away from loneliness. As with all good Book Talks, the students did not give away the most important part of the story; rather, they encouraged the first-graders to read the book to find out how it ended.

Source: International Reading Association and National Council of Teachers of English (1996).

### IRA/NCTE Standards for English Language Arts

10. Students whose first language is not English make use of their first language to develop competency in the English language arts and to develop understanding of content across the curriculum.

## Differentiating Instruction for English Language Learners

Providing English language learners with appropriate children's literature will facilitate their language development and promote comprehension for narrative text. Students in classrooms where books are accessible read more (Krashen, 1998; Morrow, 2003). Such access to children's literature is especially significant to English language learners, but when the books are selected for their interest, relevance, and readability it furthers their acquisition of the new language they are learning and increases their understanding of text (Hadaway, Vardell, & Young, 2002). In selecting books that are appropriate for English language learners, Vardell, Hadaway, and Young (2006) suggest that teachers consider the following criteria:

1. *Content accessibility*: The themes and content of fiction should support students who are adjusting to language differences while offering important basic information.

2. *Language accessibility*: The language of the story should be simple, offering students a bridge between their native and new language. Many books written for young children have predictable language with repetitive vocabulary.

3. *Visual accessibility*: There are so many picture storybooks that receive awards for their illustrations. Books with pictures that support and clarify the meanings of ideas and concepts within the text provide a scaffold for language development.

4. *Cultural accessibility*: Stories must appeal to their readers. For English language learners, such books are those that connect to the students' lives.

## DIFFERENTIATING INSTRUCTION FOR STUDENTS WITH SPECIAL NEEDS

Students with special needs are often reluctant to engage in Book Talks and need additional support that may be given through teacher modeling and demonstrations, a structured procedure to engage in an effective Book Talk, as well as props that serve as a scaffold for the student when presenting the book. The teacher modifies the steps for the appropriate levels and needs of the students and, using those steps, demonstrates how to conduct a Book Talk. During the Book Talk, the teacher shows how artifacts that represent different story parts may be used in the presentation of a book. For example, an action figure or a small puppet may be used to represent the character, and miniature figures representing the story setting may be used to talk about where the story takes place. After modeling the process, the students engage in Book Talks and are given the appropriate assistance from the teacher.

## REFERENCES

Fischbaugh, R. (2004). Using book talks to promote high-level questioning skills. *The Reading Teacher, 58*(3), 296–299.

Hadaway, N. L., Vardell, S. M., & Young, T. A. (2002). *Literature-based instruction with English language learners, K–12.* Boston: Allyn & Bacon.

International Reading Association and National Council of Teachers of English. (1996). *Standards for the English language arts.* Newark, DE: International Reading Association and Urbana, IL: National Council of Teachers of English.

Krashen, S. (1998). Bridging inequity with books. *Educational Leadership, 55*(4), 18–22.

Morrow, L. M. (2003). Motivating lifelong voluntary readers. In J. Flood, D. Lapp, J. R. Squire, & J. M. Jensen (Eds.), *Handbook of research on teaching the English language arts* (pp. 857–867). Mahwah, NJ: Erlbaum.

Rasinski, T. V. (2003). *The fluent reader: Oral reading strategies for building word recognition, fluency, and comprehension.* New York: Scholastic.

Tompkins, G. E. (2006). *Literacy for the 21st century: A balanced approach* (4th ed.). Upper Saddle River, NJ: Merrill Prentice Hall.

Vardell, S. M., Hadaway, N. L., & Young, T. A. (2006). Matching books and readers: Selecting literature for English learners. *The Reading Teacher, 59*(8), 734–741.

## CHILDREN'S LITERATURE CITED

Isadora, R. (2009). *The ugly duckling.* New York: Putnam.

# Strategy
# 24

# Character Mapping

## SPEAKING BRIEFLY: AN OVERVIEW OF THE LITERACY STRATEGY

The characters in a story are the most important part of the narrative. As we read a book, we get to know the characters through their actions, intentions, emotions, relationships with other characters, how they solve story problems, and even their looks. Without characters, how will the problem be solved? The characters within a story have the power to teach values, entertain, create new world experiences, befriend, and help readers comprehend the story they are reading. "Authors bring characters to life in many ways: through metaphor, simile, and naming; through the actions they take and the thoughts they have; through what they say and what others say to and about them; through the reaction that others have to them and those they have to others; and through narration" (Eeds & Peterson, 1995, p. 14). When characters become the life and heart of a story, we follow them through the plot, "reflecting on their traits, mulling their relationships, gauging their development, or even weighing their goals—we find ourselves reading more deeply" (Roser, Martinez, Fuhrken, & McDonald, 2007, p. 548). Therefore, for readers to understand a story profoundly, they need to know the story characters.

The purpose of the *Character Mapping* strategy is to help students comprehend stories by learning about the traits of the main characters. Students will be trained to study characters through the story plot as they begin to understand their desires, feelings, values, and intentions. As students track the characters through the story events, they cannot help being influenced by the protagonist. Researchers describe the mental model that we use in comprehending a narrative. Bower and Morrow (1990) explain that to understand a story, we draw on the characters within the story, including their traits, relationships with other characters, desires, and occupations. Further, they argue that to comprehend the actions of storybook characters, readers use those of everyday characters that they know. Studies (Noh & Stine-Morrow, 2009; Zwaan & Rapp, 2006) demonstrate that to understand a narrative, students must be able to track characters through the plot. Such ability for constructing meaning from stories develops over time and is dependent on the reader's ability to engage in character analysis. Therefore, effective teaching of comprehension of narrative text must include the students' development in understanding story schema and their use of personal experiences and prior knowledge to interpret characters' traits and actions within a story. Helping students become proficient in analysis of story characters begins with the process of developing the concept of *character trait* and building their vocabularies to assist in describing story characters. Discussions of stories from class read-alouds, guided reading, Book Talks, and independent reading frequently focus on the story characters, their actions, and their traits (Manyak, 2007).

*Source:* International Reading Association and National Council of Teachers of English (1996).

## IRA/NCTE Standards for English Language Arts

3. Students apply a wide range of strategies to comprehend, interpret, evaluate, and appreciate texts. They draw on their prior experience, their interactions with other readers and writers, their knowledge of word meaning and of other texts, their word identification strategies, and their understanding of textual features (e.g., sound-letter correspondence, sentence structure, context, graphics).

4. Students adjust their use of spoken, written, and visual language (e.g., conventions, style, vocabulary) to communicate effectively with a variety of audiences and for different purposes.

6. Students apply knowledge of language structure, language conventions (e.g., spelling and punctuation), media techniques, figurative language, and genre to create, critique, and discuss print and nonprint texts.

12. Students use spoken, written, and visual language to accomplish their own purposes (e.g., for learning, enjoyment, persuasion, and the exchange of information).

# USING CHARACTER MAPPING

*When to use the strategy:* Students may be engaged in character analysis before, during, and after they read the story. For example, before reading, the teacher discusses the characters' traits and how they affect their actions; during reading, students may be focused on identifying and analyzing the character as they read; and after reading, students go back to the story to gather evidence to confirm and validate their initial analysis of the character.

*Strategy modification for grade levels:* Younger children in primary grades need to identify the most important traits of the story character. As students read more stories, they will be able to identify and discuss the character traits and their relationship to the story events. Older students with more story experiences will be able to infer and analyze the character's intentions as well as discuss the character's viewpoint and perspective on issues that were raised within the story.

## IMPLEMENTING THE CHARACTER MAPPING STRATEGY: STEP BY STEP

To teach the students how to analyze the traits of the story character, engage them in a read-aloud of a picture storybook. Work with the whole class to develop the concept of *character trait*, to build a character-trait vocabulary, and to learn the strategy for finding evidence within the text to confirm or reject assumptions about the story character.

1. **Introduce the concept of analyzing story characters through a guided discussion and a demonstration.**
   - Guide the discussion by facilitating the students' predictions about a character's traits. Explain that reading the book will tell more about the character. Include in the discussion how to study a character by (1) examining what the author has to say about the character, (2) finding out what the character says and thinks, (3) reading what other characters in the story have to say about the main character, and (4) examining the character's actions.

- Read aloud one or two short passages containing the character's dialogue, a description of the character, or an account of the character's actions, and ask the students what they now know about the character from listening to the passage.
- Write their responses on the chalkboard.
- Demonstrate how to use the text and illustrations to confirm or reject responses.

2. **Engage students in character analysis through a read-aloud.** The selected book may be a short picture storybook or a chapter in a longer book. Read the story to the students without stopping to ask questions or make comments.

3. **Return to the book to demonstrate how to follow a character through the story to learn about his/her character traits.** Select parts of the book—from its beginning, middle, and end—that tell about the character.
   - Model to students how to use the text to learn about the main character through a think-aloud by posing questions that apply to selected parts of the book. Sample questions used to explore the character's traits are provided below:
     o What do the words of the character tell us?
     o Does the picture tell us more about the character?
     o What do we learn from other characters about the main character?
     o What is the author telling us about the story character?
   - Answer the questions aloud and validate your response from the text or illustrations.
   - Encourage students to further respond and elaborate, and ask for evidence from the text.
   - Ask students whether there is anything they would like to learn about the character and how and where they can find this information.

4. **Use the character map to further the study of the story character.** Provide students with the graphic shown in Figure 24.1 to facilitate their study of story character. The teacher may use the graphic with intermediate and middle-grade students to discuss generic character traits and may direct them to complete the graphic. With primary-grade students, the teacher models the use of the character map and encourages them to use their own as they work on the map together.

## Applying the Character Mapping Strategy: Sixth-Grade Lesson

The sixth-grade students were reading the Newberry Honor book *Hatchet* by Gary Paulsen (1987). *Hatchet* is the story of Brian Robeson, whose thoughts and emotions are swirling around his mother's secret and his parents' divorce. Brian is the only passenger on a small plane headed for the oil fields of Canada, where he is to spend the summer with his father. When the plane crashes in the rugged wilderness of upstate New York, Brian is alone. For 54 days, Brian learns to survive physically and emotionally.

The teacher chose *Hatchet* to teach the students about character analysis. After students read Chapters 1 through 4, they broke into groups to revisit Brian's character. Each group was asked to explore Brian's traits based on what the main character said or thought, what the author had to say about the main character, what other characters said about the main character, and the actions of the main character. After assigning each group to one of the four areas of character study, the teacher explained the task and distributed the character maps. When the small groups completed their section, they were asked to present to the class their responses on their assigned area as the teacher

**Figure 24.1** Character Mapping

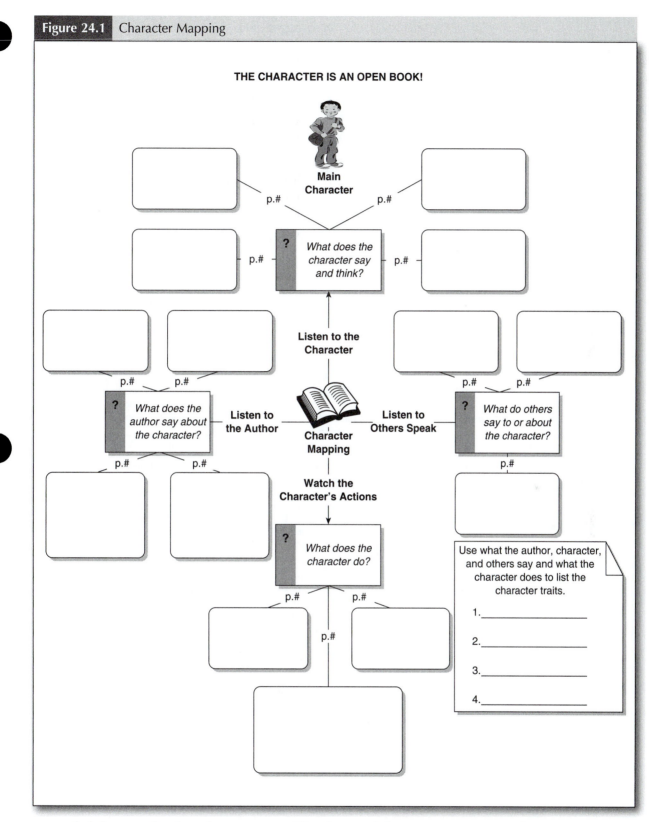

recorded them on the class character map. The class used the group responses to determine Brian's character traits, which were written on the class character map. Figure 24.2 illustrates the class character map for Brian as he was revealed in Chapters 1 through 4.

**Figure 24.2**    Character Map of the Main Character Brian in *Hatchet* by Gary Paulsen

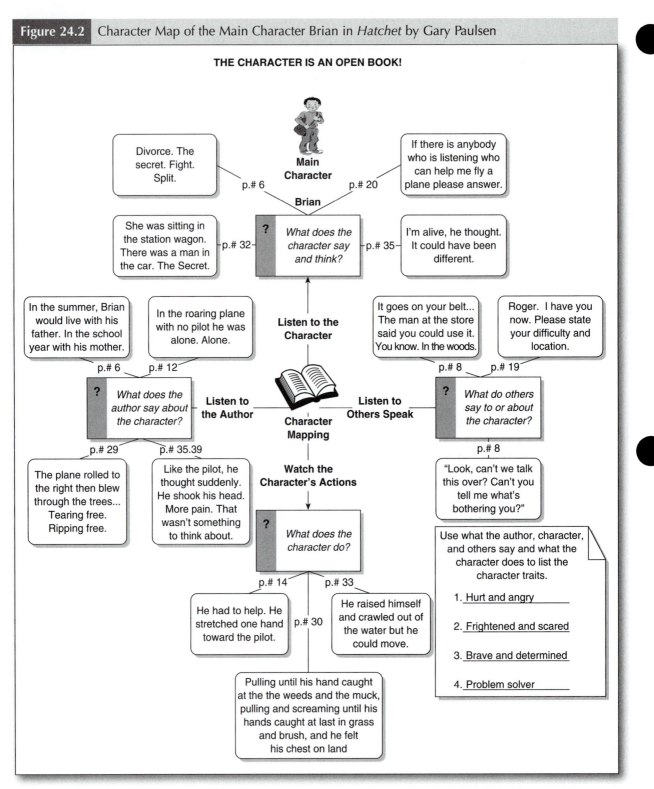

**THE CHARACTER IS AN OPEN BOOK!**

**Main Character**

**Brian**

Divorce. The secret. Fight. Split.

p.# 6

If there is anybody who is listening who can help me fly a plane please answer.

p.# 20

She was sitting in the station wagon. There was a man in the car. The Secret.

p.# 32

**?** *What does the character say and think?*

p.# 35

I'm alive, he thought. It could have been different.

**Listen to the Character**

In the summer, Brian would live with his father. In the school year with his mother.

p.# 6

In the roaring plane with no pilot he was alone. Alone.

p.# 12

It goes on your belt... The man at the store said you could use it. You know. In the woods.

p.# 8

Roger. I have you now. Please state your difficulty and location.

p.# 19

**?** *What does the author say about the character?*

**Listen to the Author**

**Character Mapping**

**Listen to Others Speak**

**?** *What do others say to or about the character?*

p.# 29

p.# 35.39

The plane rolled to the right then blew through the trees... Tearing free. Ripping free.

Like the pilot, he thought suddenly. He shook his head. More pain. That wasn't something to think about.

p.# 8

"Look, can't we talk this over? Can't you tell me what's bothering you?"

**Watch the Character's Actions**

**?** *What does the character do?*

p.# 14

p.# 33

He had to help. He stretched one hand toward the pilot.

p.# 30

He raised himself and crawled out of the water but he could move.

Pulling until his hand caught at the the weeds and the muck, pulling and screaming until his hands caught at last in grass and brush, and he felt his chest on land

Use what the author, character, and others say and what the character does to list the character traits.

1. Hurt and angry

2. Frightened and scared

3. Brave and determined

4. Problem solver

*Source:* International Reading Association and National Council of Teachers of English (1996).

> ### IRA/NCTE Standards for English Language Arts
>
> 10. Students whose first language is not English make use of their first language to develop competency in the English language arts and to develop understanding of content across the curriculum.

## DIFFERENTIATING INSTRUCTION FOR ENGLISH LANGUAGE LEARNERS

All readers may learn about literary concepts such as character traits from illustrations, but for English language learners, pictures play a central role in understanding text. Therefore, when English language learners are engaged in discussions on the study of character, use the illustrations that explicitly depict the story character's traits to support their understanding. During the guided discussion, the teacher should direct questions to English language learners about what they think of a specific character trait and whether they agree with another student's response. When another student's response is too complex for the English language learner, the teacher should rephrase it for understanding.

## DIFFERENTIATING INSTRUCTION FOR STUDENTS WITH SPECIAL NEEDS

Students experiencing comprehension problems often find it difficult to make inferences. Character maps require students to infer the character's traits from text. The instructional strategy requires students to examine the words of the author and the character, as well as the character's actions, to determine the character's traits. Therefore, the teacher needs to provide small-group instruction to help students understand the relationship between character traits and what they say and do.

## REFERENCES

Bower, G. H., & Morrow, D. G. (1990). Mental models in narrative comprehension. *Science, 247,* 44–48.

Eeds, M., & Peterson, R. L. (1995). What teachers need to know about the literacy craft. In N. L. Roser & M. G. Martinez (Eds.), *Book talk and beyond: Children and teachers respond to literature* (pp. 10–23). Newark, DE: International Reading Association.

International Reading Association and National Council of Teachers of English. (1996). *Standards for the English language arts.* Newark, DE: International Reading Association and Urbana, IL: National Council of Teachers of English.

Manyak, P. (2007). Character trait vocabulary: A schoolwide approach. *The Reading Teacher, 60*(6), 574–577.

Noh, S. R., & Stine-Morrow, E. A. L. (2009). Age differences in tracking characters during narrative comprehension. *Memory and Cognition, 37,* 769–778.

Roser, N., Martinez, M., Fuhrken, C., & McDonald, K. (2007). Characters as guides to meaning. *The Reading Teacher, 60*(6), 548–559.

Zwaan, R. A., & Rapp, D. N. (2006). Discourse comprehension. In M. A. Gernsbacher & M. A. Traxler (Eds.), *Handbook of psycholinguistics* (2nd ed., pp. 725–764). San Diego, CA: Academic Press.

## CHILDREN'S LITERATURE CITED

Paulsen, G. (1987). *Hatchet.* New York: Atheneum Books for Young Readers.

# Strategy

# 25

# Double-Entry Journals

## SPEAKING BRIEFLY: AN OVERVIEW OF THE LITERACY STRATEGY

The *Double-Entry Journal* strategy provides students with an opportunity to engage in written responses to the literature they have read. After students read a story, they write their responses in a journal. In the Double-Entry Journal, the page has two columns. In the first column, students write the text that that they will explore, and in the column next to it, they record their written responses. When students reflect on and respond to their readings, they put themselves in the story or text (Lindfors, 1995). Being placed in the context of a story, students process the text at deeper levels as they connect to the story in different ways.

Proficient readers know that responding to stories is not quite the same as reading and comprehending informational text. Louise Rosenblatt (1994) distinguishes between two types of reading. When reading a story, students may take an *aesthetic* stance; whereas when reading a textbook, they take an *efferent* stance. Adopting an aesthetic stance suggests that readers construct their own interpretations of the story based on their "lived-through experiences" with the story or poem. Using personal experiences, readers make connections to story characters and events to interpret the text. When readers adopt an efferent stance, they focus on the information within the text and work to construct meaning by using their prior knowledge. Rosenblatt (1991) emphasized that readers do not take an exclusively aesthetic or efferent stance while reading; rather, their approach is to read text with a predominantly aesthetic or efferent stance. Competent readers are flexible in their reading approach. At times, they focus on interpreting text through their own experiences, and at other times, they read to gain information. Too often, teachers' questions and activities that follow students' reading promote an efferent stance. As a result, when students read literature—informational or fictional—they lack the flexibility to respond aesthetically as they search for the one right answer. Therefore, teachers need to help students be flexible when reading: At times, they need to read and interpret the text based on their own "lived-through experiences," and at other times, they need to take an efferent stance where they read for information.

For the second entry, teachers should encourage students to reflect on their readings and respond aesthetically and efferently. Students need to be flexible in their types of responses. As they interpret the story for meanings, they should develop their responses through the use of personal experiences, thoughts, and feelings. For example, students' responses should reveal how the text made them feel and why they experienced such feelings, how they personally relate to a character or story event, what they wish they could change in the story, etc. Such responses are frequently based on meanings and interpretations of the text.

### IRA/NCTE Standards for English Language Arts

1. Students read a wide range of print and nonprint texts to build an understanding of texts, of themselves, and of the cultures of the United States and the world; to acquire new information; to respond to the needs and demands of society and the workplace; and for personal fulfillment. Among these texts are fiction and nonfiction, classic and contemporary works.

2. Students read a wide range of literature from many periods in many genres to build an understanding of the many dimensions (e.g., philosophical, ethical, aesthetic) of human experience.

3. Students apply a wide range of strategies to comprehend, interpret, evaluate, and appreciate texts. They draw on their prior experience, their interactions with other readers and writers, their knowledge of word meaning and of other texts, their word identification strategies, and their understanding of textual features (e.g., sound-letter correspondence, sentence structure, context, graphics).

4. Students adjust their use of spoken, written, and visual language (e.g., conventions, style, vocabulary) to communicate effectively with a variety of audiences and for different purposes.

9. Students develop an understanding of and respect for diversity in language use, patterns, and dialects across cultures, ethnic groups, geographic regions, and social roles.

11. Students participate as knowledgeable, reflective, creative, and critical members of a variety of literacy communities.

12. Students use spoken, written, and visual language to accomplish their own purposes (e.g., for learning, enjoyment, persuasion, and the exchange of information).

*Source:* International Reading Association and National Council of Teachers of English (1996).

## USING DOUBLE-ENTRY JOURNALS

*When to use the strategy:* Double-Entry Journals are typically used after reading and begin with engaging students in discussions. Classroom environments that lead to reflective responses are created through text talk that may be led by the teacher or students within their small literature circles. Listening to other students engage in discussions of interpretations, personal reflections, and novel ideas will result in deeper personal meanings and responses.

*Strategy modifications for grade levels:* The strategy may be modified for all grade levels. For very young children who are at the beginning stages of writing, teachers may record children's responses made during a discussion of the book or students may draw their responses in a journal. For students who are learning to use journals to respond, teachers demonstrate different types of reflective responses and provide prompts to help students get started. For middle school students, teachers provide a guide to help them think deeper into the story.

## IMPLEMENTING THE DOUBLE-ENTRY JOURNAL STRATEGY: STEP BY STEP

1. **Direct students to set up their journal pages for double entries.** Students divide their journal pages into two columns. On the top of the left column, they write the heading "Author's Words," and on the top of the right column, they write the heading "My Response."

2. **Demonstrate how a reader responds to a story.** Read an appealing short picture storybook that evokes many different responses from the readers. After the reading, engage students in a brief discussion that is guided by the prompts. On a large piece of chart paper designed like a Double-Entry Journal page, write the author's words on the left side and the students' responses next to the text on the right side. Explain to students that they can respond to and interpret the story in much the same way the class did by using the prompts to think carefully about the story.

3. **Provide different ways for a reader to respond to stories.** Show students the range of prompts that are appropriate to their reading and grade level, making them visible for use after reading. See Figure 25.1 for examples.

---

**Figure 25.1** Ways to Respond to Stories

Tell how this part makes you feel.

Visualize what you have read. What did you see? Draw and describe it.

Explain why you think this happened.

Did anything like this ever happen to you or a friend?

Describe what may happen next.

If you could talk to the character, what would you say?

How would you have ended the story?

---

4. **Read silently.** Students engage in reading their books. They may be reading a piece of literature as part of reading workshop, guided reading, literature circles, a whole-class read-aloud, or independent reading.

5. **Write passages, quotes, references with a page number in their journals.** After reading, students select quotes, passages, or use a page number to reference the text, and they write it in the left column. Within their discussion group, each student explains why they have selected the text and discusses that aspect of the story with the group.

6. **Respond to the quote.** Students use their prompts and select the most appropriate way to respond to the text. They write their responses in their journals in the right column next to the selected text. Students may share their responses with their small group or the class.

## APPLYING THE DOUBLE-ENTRY JOURNAL STRATEGY: SIXTH-GRADE LESSON ON THE HOLOCAUST

Sixth-grade students in social studies were studying the Holocaust. During an integrated English language arts and social studies unit, all students were reading Lois Lowry's (1989) Newberry Award-winning book, *Number the Stars*. To assist students in responding to the story, the teacher used Double-Entry Journals with the students and provided a time for sharing in small groups as well as large class discussions. After conducting a brief introduction of the book, the teacher demonstrated how to respond to a specific part of the text through writing in a Double-Entry Journal. Using the prompts shown in Figure 25.1, the teacher selected a short piece of text and wrote it in the journal in the left column, selected a prompt that related to the text, responded to the text through a think-aloud, and wrote the response in the right column next to the text. The students read the first chapter of the text, responded to a selected piece of text, and wrote their responses in their Double-Entry Journals. Figure 25.2 shows a sample entry made by a student. After completing their responses, the teacher directed the students to share them with their learning partners.

| **Figure 25.2** | Student's Journal Entries for *Number the Stars* |

| My Journal Entries<br><br>***Number the Stars***<br>by<br>**Lois Lowry** | | |
|---|---|---|
| **Date** | **Text** | **My Response** |
| *4/1/2009* | Chapter 1: pp. 1–10 "Annemarie stared up. There were two of them. That meant two helmets, two sets of cold eyes glaring at her, and four tall shiny boots planted firmly on the sidewalk, blocking her path to home" p. 2. | *I can't imagine living like that. The German soldiers were so mean. And everyone was frightened of them. They didn't belong in Denmark and they gave orders like they owned the country. When the tall soldier who Annemarie and Ellen called "the Giraffe" poked his rifle in Annemarie's backpack, it made her tremble. Could that ever happen here in the U.S.? Soldiers watching everything you do. Telling you what to do—don't race it makes you look like hoodlums when you run! Go home and study. They give orders to everyone. Even Annemarie's and Ellen's mothers were frightened, talking in low voices in their own homes.* |
| *4/1/2009* | Chapter 2: pp. 11–17 "It is true. Any Danish citizen would die for King Christian, to protect him." | *King Christian was the ruler of Denmark during the Nazi takeover. All the people of the country loved him, because he was kind and good. When the German soldiers asked a boy where his bodyguard was, he said that he didn't need one; all the people of the country will protect him. The small countries around Germany could not protect themselves. Germany had so many soldiers! I can't think of myself living like that, in fear every day, not being able to say what is on your mind, not being free. This story is helping me understand how important freedom is.* |

## IRA/NCTE Standards for English Language Arts

10. Students whose first language is not English make use of their first language to develop competency in the English language arts and to develop understanding of content across the curriculum.

*Source:* International Reading Association and National Council of Teachers of English (1996).

## DIFFERENTIATING INSTRUCTION FOR ENGLISH LANGUAGE LEARNERS

Many English language learners have difficulty comprehending and responding to text in personal ways. When requesting that students use their own experiences to interpret and respond to their readings, teachers need to anticipate that the English language learners will have difficulty understanding what is expected of them. Therefore, modify instruction for English language learners by creating scaffolds to work through the process of writing personal responses in their Double-Entry Journals. First, work with students to identify a piece of text that will elicit a personal response. After reading the text, discuss its meaning with the students. Then teach students to use their personal experiences to make a response by helping them recall similar experiences in their own lives or experiences that they have read about in other stories. The use of well-crafted questions works well to facilitate students' activation of background knowledge and personal experiences to make a response. Finally, using a think-aloud, demonstrate how to respond and connect to text using a personal experience.

## DIFFERENTIATING INSTRUCTION FOR STUDENTS WITH SPECIAL NEEDS

Students with special needs frequently have difficulty in story comprehension and also experience similar difficulties in writing personal responses to the text. Before students make written entries in their journals, engage them in discussions about their selected text. Following their discussion, have them talk through their written response, providing feedback and asking for an elaboration when necessary. Provide them with assistance during their writing. One way to help is by sharing the pen, having them write part of the response and completing the sentence for them.

## REFERENCES

International Reading Association and National Council of Teachers of English. (1996). *Standards for the English language arts.* Newark, DE: International Reading Association and Urbana, IL: National Council of Teachers of English.

Lindfors, J. W. (1995). "Playing the part of my ownself": Connecting life with literature through dialogue journals. In N. L. Roser & M. G. Martinez (Eds.), *Book talk and beyond: Children and teachers respond to literature* (pp. 208–216). Newark, DE: International Reading Association.

Rosenblatt, L. (1991). Literature—S. O. S.! *Language Arts, 68,* 444–448.

Rosenblatt, L. (1994). *The reader, the text, the poem: The transactional theory of the literary work.* Carbondale, IL: Southern Illinois University Press.

## CHILDREN'S LITERATURE CITED

Lowry, L. (1989). *Number the stars.* Boston: Houghton Mifflin.

# SECTION VI

# Essential Strategies for Teaching Comprehension of Informational Text

As we complete the first decade of the 21st century, society is experiencing the explosion of the information age as we surf the Internet to gather news, compare products, purchase items, or conduct banking. In order to prepare students for this digital age, teachers are seeking methods for teaching informational text across the grades, from early childhood through adolescence. This section discusses current research on best practices for teaching comprehension of informational text and explores instructional strategies.

## A BRIEF OVERVIEW OF COMPREHENSION OF INFORMATIONAL TEXT

*Comprehension* is the essence of reading, and effective comprehension instruction enables readers to construct meaning from text, connect new concepts to prior knowledge, and formulate ideas (Block & Pressley, 2007). Research indicates that expert readers stay active during reading by making predictions, activating prior knowledge, generating questions, and summarizing information (Duke & Pearson, 2002). In order to expertly comprehend, prerequisite skills such as strategic word identification, adequate vocabulary, and prior knowledge are necessary (Rasinski, Padak, & Fawcett, 2010).

Comprehension of informational text is especially challenging for the majority of students. In fact, teachers often point to the "fourth-grade slump" that occurs when students are required to read content-area textbooks. According to Chall, Jacobs, and Baldwin (1990), the "fourth-grade slump" occurs because students are not given enough exposure to expository text in early childhood. For many years, there was a debate in the literacy field as to whether primary-grade children could read and write informational text. However, recent research confirms that students need to be exposed to informational text as early as possible so that they can develop an awareness of text structure and vocabulary (Duke, 2000). When students are explicitly taught informational text structures and strategies to understand cognitively rich passages, their ability to read and write expository text improves (Duke, Bennett-Armistead, & Roberts, 2003). What are the critical comprehension strategies students need to understand informational text? Students should be able to

- activate prior knowledge and tap strategies to decode unknown words and derive meanings;

- preview text by scanning visual aids, titles, captions, and text features;

- generate, confirm, or change predictions during reading;

- set a purpose for reading and generate questions while reading;

- connect new concepts or ideas to prior knowledge or experiences; and

- summarize the text and reflect on new concepts (Block & Pressley, 2007).

The National Reading Panel (2000) recommended that these comprehension strategies be directly modeled, scaffolded, and practiced in order for readers to develop automaticity of their performance while reading.

## Instruction for Comprehension of Informational Text

In 2002, the RAND Reading Study Group reported that the explosion of information due to the Internet demanded increased instruction in expository text. Yet research indicates that primary-grade classrooms may spend as little as 3.6 minutes per day on informational text (Duke, 2000). In addition, 38% of passages on standardized tests are expository texts (Moss, 2004). It is increasingly apparent that the digital age and the accountability movement are generating the need to explicitly teach comprehension strategies for informational text.

Many teachers mistakenly believe that by simply reading aloud informational text, students will acquire the skills necessary to understand it (Gregg & Sekeres, 2006). It is evident that informational trade books are ideal vehicles for instruction (Moss, 2004). However, teachers need to explicitly demonstrate how to activate prior knowledge, identify expository text structure, interpret it, and connect new ideas to prior concepts (Dymock, 2005).

Recent research indicates that when students are exposed at an early age to strategic reading, the internalization of the comprehension process can take less time than previously believed (Block & Pressley, 2007). In fact, effective comprehension instruction emphasizes the use of multiple comprehension strategies in one reading performance, such as activating prior knowledge, visualizing images, or questioning the author (Block & Pressley, 2007; Duke & Pearson, 2002).

## Guidelines for Teaching Comprehension of Informational Text

The National Reading Panel (2000) and recent research have confirmed that direct, explicit teaching of comprehension strategies for informational text will improve reading performance. The following guidelines provide the framework for comprehension instruction of informational text:

1. Assessment of students' knowledge before comprehension instruction enables the teacher to fill any conceptual gaps (Gregg & Sekeres, 2006).

2. Effective comprehension instruction provides modeling, scaffolding, and support of strategic reading (Duke & Pearson, 2002).

3. Best practices in comprehension instruction of informational text emphasize activation of prior knowledge, interpretation of text, summarization, and reflection on new concepts (Block & Pressley, 2007).

4. Primary-grade children, English language learners, and striving readers are especially in need of direct instruction in constructing meaning from informational text (Moss, 2004).

5. Effective comprehension instruction models how to use multiple strategies to process text while reading (Block & Pressley, 2007; Duke & Pearson, 2002).

## A STRATEGY FOR ASSESSING COMPREHENSION SKILLS

Research indicates students need multiple strategies to comprehend informational text (Block & Pressley, 2007; Duke & Pearson, 2002). In order to develop strategic readers, teachers need to monitor students' progress on core comprehension skills and strategies. The "Assessment of Comprehension of Informational Text" shown in Figure VI.1 may be used as a formative or summative rubric to inform instruction. Teachers may also modify the rubric to address different components at the emergent, early, or fluent stage of literacy. The assessment is designed to provide teachers with data on the strategies students are using before, during, and after reading informational text. After data analysis, teachers may use the information to conference with struggling students or to provide targeted intervention for selected components.

## A GUIDE FOR USING RESPONSE TO INTERVENTION FOR COMPREHENSION OF INFORMATIONAL TEXT

The "Assessment of Comprehension of Informational Text" (see Figure VI.1) will alert instructors to students struggling with comprehension of informational text. Students scored as "developing" on the rubric may be selected for further intervention. Using data from the assessment, teachers focus the intervention on a specific comprehension skill, such as synthesizing information or selecting the main idea. Once a focal point for instructional support has been selected, the instructor may adapt the Scaffolding Academic Reading activity for a small-group intervention. During the think-aloud component of the strategy, instructors may provide a detailed coaching prompt such as, "I look at the pictures, graphs, and maps to get an idea of the topic." Students assessed at the lower end of the continuum will need more detailed prompts and explicit instruction in modeling and demonstration of comprehension skills.

In this section, "Essential Strategies for Comprehension of Informational Text," five instructional strategies are presented for use in explicit demonstrations of strategic

| Figure VI.1 | Assessment of Comprehension of Informational Text | | | |
|---|---|---|---|---|
| | | **Advanced (3)** | **Target (2)** | **Developing (1)** |
| **Before Reading** | **Analyzes text features** | Analyzes text features and uses charts, graphs, and headings to set purpose for reading | Analyzes _some_ text features and uses charts, graphs, and headings to set purpose for reading | _Rarely_ analyzes text features and does not use charts, graphs, and headings to set purpose for reading |
| | **Taps prior knowledge** | Uses text features to connect information with prior knowledge | _Partially_ uses text features to connect information with prior knowledge | _Rarely_ uses text features to connect information with prior knowledge |
| | **Sets purpose** | Sets purpose for reading text | _Sometimes_ sets purpose for reading text | _Rarely_ sets purpose for reading text |
| **During Reading** | **Questions the author** | Generates questions while reading | _Partially_ generates questions while reading | _Rarely_ generates questions while reading |
| | **Identifies key vocabulary** | Identifies and defines key vocabulary | _Sometimes_ identifies and defines key vocabulary | _Rarely_ identifies and defines key vocabulary |
| | **Synthesis** | Synthesizes information and makes connections | _Partially_ synthesizes information and makes connections | _Rarely_ synthesizes information and makes connections |
| **After Reading** | **Identifies main idea** | Summarizes content and provides main idea | _Sometimes_ summarizes content and provides main idea | _Rarely_ summarizes content and provides main idea |
| | **Organizes knowledge** | Organizes new concepts in categories or representation | _Partially_ organizes new concepts in categories or representation | _Rarely_ organizes new concepts in categories or representation |
| | **Reflects on reading** | Self-monitors performance and corrects errors | _Sometimes_ self-monitors performance and corrects errors | _Rarely_ self-monitors performance and corrects errors |

Advanced = 27–19 points

Target = 18–10 points

Developing = 9–1 points

reading. The instructional activities are presented as guides for teachers to use based on their data analysis of student needs.

## PROFESSIONAL RESOURCES

Grant, M., & Fisher, D. (2010). _Reading and writing in science: Tools to develop disciplinary literacy._ Thousand Oaks, CA: Sage.

Hoyt, L. (2002). _Make it real: Strategies for success with informational text._ Portsmouth, NH: Heinemann.

Neubert, G., & Wilkins, E. (2003). *Putting it all together: The directed reading lesson in the secondary content classroom.* Boston: Allyn & Bacon.

Tovani, C. (2000). *I read it but I don't get it: Comprehension strategies for adolescent readers.* Portland, ME: Stenhouse.

## REFERENCES

Block, C., & Pressley, M. (2007). Best practices in teaching comprehension. In L. Gambrell, L. M. Morrow, & M. Pressley (Eds.), *Best practices in literacy instruction* (pp. 220–242*)*. New York: Guilford.

Chall, J., Jacobs, V., & Baldwin, L. (1990). *The reading crisis: Why poor children fall behind.* Cambridge, MA: Harvard University Press.

Duke, N. (2000). 3.6 minutes per day: The scarcity of informational texts in first grade. *Reading Research Quarterly, 35,* 202–224.

Duke, N., Bennett-Armistead, V. S., & Roberts, E. M. (2003). Bridging the gap between learning to read and reading to learn. In D. M. Barone & L. M. Morrow (Eds.), *Literacy and young children: Research-based practices* (pp. 226–243). New York: Guilford.

Duke, N., & Pearson, P. D. (2002). Effective practices for developing reading comprehension. In A. E. Farstup & S. J. Samuels (Eds.), *What research has to say about reading instruction* (pp. 205–242). Newark, DE: International Reading Association.

Dymock, S. (2005). Teaching expository text awareness. *The Reading Teacher, 59,* 177–182.

Gregg, M., & Sekeres, D. (2006). Supporting children's reading of expository text in the geography classroom. *The Reading Teacher, 60,* 102–110.

Moss, B. (2004). Teaching expository text structures through information trade book retellings. *The Reading Teacher, 57,* 710–719.

National Reading Panel. (2000). *Teaching children to read: An evidence-based assessment of the scientific research literature on reading and its implications for reading instruction.* Washington, DC: National Institute of Child Health and Human Development, National Institutes of Health.

RAND Reading Study Group. (2002). *Reading for understanding: Toward an R&D program in reading comprehension.* Santa Monica, CA: Author.

Rasinski, T., Padak, N., & Fawcett, G. (2010). *Teaching children who find reading difficult.* Boston: Allyn & Bacon.

# Strategy
# 26

# Visualize It!

## SPEAKING BRIEFLY: AN OVERVIEW OF THE LITERACY STRATEGY

*Visualize It* is an instructional strategy that facilitates comprehension of informational text through the use of imagery. Proficient readers create "movies in their heads" as they read to construct meaning (Keene & Zimmerman, 2007). In order to visualize while reading, students need to tap multiple sources of information such as collaboration with others (Kress & Van Leeuwen, 2001).

The primary purpose for implementing the Visualize It instructional strategy is to explicitly teach striving readers and English language learners how to use imagery to understand. Reading aloud to students from early childhood through adolescence is the perfect introduction to visualization of informational text (Romano, 2006). As students share the images they generated from the read-aloud, all readers elaborate and deepen their conceptual understanding of the text (Romano, 2006; Schroder, 2008).

*Source:* International Reading Association and National Council of Teachers of English (1996).

### IRA/NCTE Standards for English Language Arts

1. Students read a wide range of print and nonprint texts to build an understanding of texts, of themselves, and of the cultures of the United States and the world; to acquire new information; to respond to the needs and demands of society and the workplace; and for personal fulfillment. Among these texts are fiction and nonfiction, classic and contemporary works.

11. Students participate as knowledgeable, reflective, creative, and critical members of a variety of literacy communities.

## USING VISUALIZE IT

*When to use the strategy:* Visualize It focuses on facilitating students' conceptual framework in order to comprehend text. It is best suited as a preparatory activity when a theme is introduced or before beginning a new unit in a textbook.

*Strategy modifications for grade levels:* This strategy may also be used as an intervention activity for striving readers attempting to understand content-area materials.

## IMPLEMENTING THE VISUALIZE IT STRATEGY: STEP BY STEP

1. **Introduce the topic to the students.** Teachers present the topic of study through a brainstorming activity such as a descriptive web.

2. **Model analysis of text features.** Teachers conduct a text walk before the read-aloud, noting maps, visual aids, and chapter headings. Selected key vocabulary words are presented in context and discussed.

3. **Read aloud selected passage.** Teachers read aloud the selected passage and direct students to sketch their ideas while listening.

4. **Discuss versions of illustrations.** Students share their images of the passage and discuss variations among them. Teachers ask students to note patterns across images such as scenes, objects, and emotions.

5. **Facilitate students' application to text.** Teachers ask students to write a summary of the passage based on the discussion. Students continue to read the text and use the visualization strategy to process the information.

## APPLYING THE VISUALIZE IT STRATEGY: FOURTH-GRADE LESSON ON EPIDEMICS

Students have been studying health and nutrition. At the midpoint of the unit, the teacher presents the trade book *Epidemics and Plagues* by Richard Walker (2006). The text uses photographs and diagrams to define epidemics and how to prevent them. The students are directed to the section that focuses on colds and flu pandemics. Before using the Visualize It graphic organizer shown in Figure 26.1, the teacher directs students to do the following:

- Write down prior knowledge of epidemics and disease in the first box of the graphic organizer.

- Define key vocabulary words and collaborate on setting a purpose for reading.

- Illustrate their summary of the passage on their graphic organizer and describe it to their partner.

- Work in dyads to compare summaries of passage and to reach consensus on the main idea.

After they have completed their illustrations of the section on colds and the flu, students work independently on epidemics related to food, such as famine and obesity. Students use a new graphic organizer for each section and discuss their work with their reading partner.

---

### IRA/NCTE Standards for English Language Arts

10. Students whose first language is not English make use of their first language to develop competency in the English language arts and to develop understanding of content across the curriculum.

*Source:* International Reading Association and National Council of Teachers of English (1996).

**Figure 26.1** Visualize It!

| What do I know about it? | What are key words? |
|---|---|
| | |

**What do I see?**

**Summary:**

**Main Idea:**

## DIFFERENTIATING INSTRUCTION FOR ENGLISH LANGUAGE LEARNERS

It is increasingly apparent that visualizing while reading is especially important for English language learners (Keene & Zimmerman, 2007). One modification for second-language learners is to pair them with a native, proficient speaker for this activity (Herrera, Perez, & Escamilla, 2010). After the teacher has modeled the strategy, the English language learner collaborates with the native speaker on generating images while they read informational text. The dyad's diverse experiences and culture will enable both students to expand their conceptual frameworks and comprehend on a higher level.

## DIFFERENTIATING INSTRUCTION FOR STUDENTS WITH SPECIAL NEEDS

Students with special needs often struggle with informational text due to their limited background knowledge on certain topics (Hirsch, 2003). An adaptation for students with special needs is to prepare them for the visualization strategy by preloading their conceptual framework. Before the teacher conducts the read-aloud, students with special needs may be given podcasts on the topic or bookmarked sites to view on the Internet. Prior exposure to the topic enables students with special needs to construct a cognitive framework in order to generate imagery from informational text.

## REFERENCES

Herrera, S., Perez, D., & Escamilla, K. (2010). *Teaching reading to English language learners: Differentiated instruction*. Boston: Allyn & Bacon.

Hirsch, E. D. (2003). Reading comprehension requires knowledge of words and the world. *American Educator, 27,* 10–13.

International Reading Association and National Council of Teachers of English. (1996). *Standards for the English language arts*. Newark, DE: International Reading Association and Urbana, IL: National Council of Teachers of English.

Keene, E., & Zimmerman, S. (2007). *Mosaic of thought* (2nd ed.). Portsmouth, NH: Heinemann.

Kress, G., & Van Leeuwen, T. (2001). *Multimodal discourse: The modes and media of contemporary communication*. New York: Oxford University Press.

Romano, T. (2006). Picturing meaning. *Journal of Adult and Adolescent Literacy, 49,* 374–378.

Schroder, M. (2008). Reading is thinking, Part II: Modeling comprehension strategies with picture books. *Book Links, 17,* 20–22.

## CHILDREN'S LITERATURE CITED

Walker, R. (2006). *Epidemics and plagues*. Boston: Kingfisher.

# Strategy
# 27

# Discussion Circles

## SPEAKING BRIEFLY: AN OVERVIEW OF THE LITERACY STRATEGY

*Discussion Circles* use oral language and collaborative inquiry to facilitate "deep processing" of expository text (Beck, McKeown, & Kucan, 2002). Recent research has determined that oral language is a powerful vehicle for engaging students in academic discourse that immerses them in informational text (Zehr, 2009). At-risk students and English language learners have smaller vocabularies and less background knowledge relevant to informational text (August, Francis, Hsu, & Snow, 2006). In addition, elementary school students have limited exposure to expository text and grapple with the genre (Moss, 2004). When all students collaborate on retellings of informational text and discuss its framework, they are gradually introduced to its demanding text structure (Moss, 2004).

Elementary school teachers are often reluctant to approach expository text structure due to its complex nature. However, multiple forms of the genre, such as narrative nonfiction (biographies or autobiographies), are especially suited for elementary school students (Williams, 2009). Discussion Circles provide students of varying levels with scaffolded practice in academic discourse. As students engage in retellings or informational text, they use academic vocabulary and build the necessary prior knowledge to comprehend.

*Source:* International Reading Association and National Council of Teachers of English (1996).

### IRA/NCTE Standards for English Language Arts

1. Students read a wide range of print and nonprint texts to build an understanding of texts, of themselves, and of the cultures of the United States and the world; to acquire new information; to respond to the needs and demands of society and the workplace; and for personal fulfillment. Among these texts are fiction and nonfiction, classic and contemporary works.

3. Students apply a wide range of strategies to comprehend, interpret, evaluate, and appreciate texts. They draw on their prior experience, their interactions with other readers and writers, their knowledge of word meaning and of other texts, their word identification strategies, and their understanding of textual features (e.g., sound-letter correspondence, sentence structure, context, graphics).

# USING DISCUSSION CIRCLES

*When to use the strategy:* Discussion Circles are best implemented as a whole-class activity. However, the strategy may be modified for a small guided-reading group lesson or as an intervention for English language learners.

*Strategy modifications for grade levels:* Teachers of primary grade students may implement this activity with several days of modeling Discussion Circles and visual responses.

## IMPLEMENTING THE DISCUSSION CIRCLES STRATEGY: STEP BY STEP

1. **Assess background knowledge.** Teachers use a descriptive web to assess students' background knowledge on the topic of the text. Students discuss terms they are unfamiliar with and provide their own definitions.

2. **Select discussion questions.** Teachers select discussion focus questions to guide students' reading and set a purpose.

3. **Scaffold guided reading.** Teachers introduce vocabulary words that may impede comprehension before students begin reading the text. Students are instructed to write notes on Post-its while they read and to record unfamiliar vocabulary words or questions they raise while engaged with the text.

4. **Write response to text.** Teachers direct students to write a quick answer to the focus question in preparation for the discussion. Striving readers or English language learners may also draw their response.

5. **Discuss retelling.** Teachers lead students in a discussion by first asking for their response to the focus questions. Teachers place students in groups of three to create Discussion Circles. During the discussion, students share the questions they raised during their reading and any unfamiliar vocabulary words.

6. **Summarize discussion.** Teachers revisit the descriptive web and ask students to add information based on their reading and the discussion.

## APPLYING THE DISCUSSION CIRCLES STRATEGY:
## FIFTH-GRADE LESSON ON CHARLES DARWIN

Students have completed a unit on the environment, and the teacher has selected the text *Animals Charles Darwin Saw: An Around-the-World Adventure* (Markle, 2009) to anchor their discussion. The teacher assesses students' knowledge on the topic by asking them to complete a concept map on ecosystems. Before distributing the text, the teacher shows illustrations of the Galapagos Islands and Charles Darwin. Using the "Discussion Circles Guide" shown in Figure 27.1, the teacher directs students to complete the following:

- Focus their reading on the following discussion question: How did Darwin's voyage change his view of animal species and their environment?

- Use sticky notes to jot down their questions while reading and to identify new vocabulary words.

- Write their response to the focus question immediately after reading.

- Share their responses to the focus question in Discussion Circles and collaborate on definitions for new vocabulary words.

When the Discussion Circles have completed their conversations, the teacher gathers students together again. Leaders from each circle report out their collaborative response to the focus question. The teacher leads a discussion on questions that were raised during the reading. Each Discussion Circle chooses a question to follow up and research for

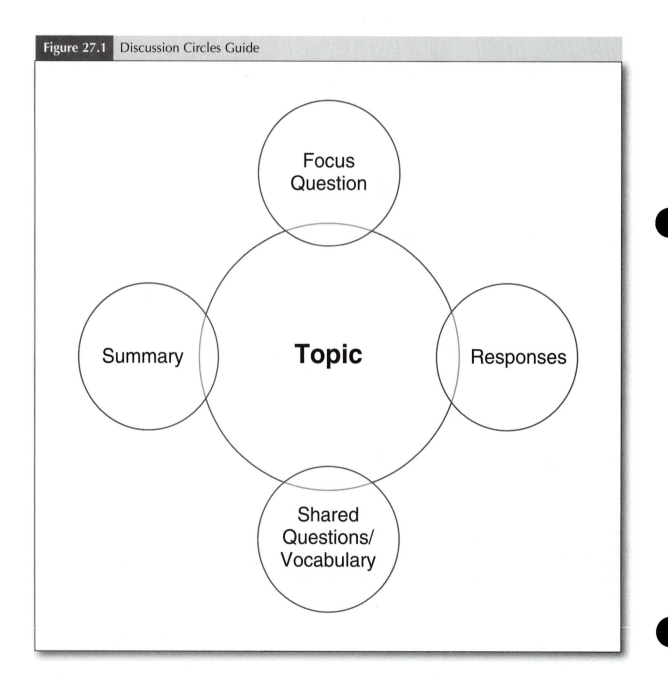

**Figure 27.1**    Discussion Circles Guide

> ## IRA/NCTE Standards for English Language Arts
>
> 10. Students whose first language is not English make use of their first language to develop competency in the English language arts and to develop understanding of content across the curriculum.

*Source:* International Reading Association and National Council of Teachers of English (1996).

homework. The session is concluded with students revisiting their concept map on ecosystems in order to apply their new knowledge.

## DIFFERENTIATING INSTRUCTION FOR ENGLISH LANGUAGE LEARNERS

English language learners may not be familiar with the background knowledge needed to process informational text, and therefore, their comprehension is impaired (August et al., 2006). One modification for English language learners is to prepare before this instructional strategy so that they can fully engage with the text and participate in the discussion. Teachers may provide students with a webquest of bookmarked links on the topic a few days before the unit is introduced. When English language learners are paired with native speakers, they are also exposed to different discourse patterns for deep processing of text (Beck et al., 2002).

## DIFFERENTIATING INSTRUCTION FOR STUDENTS WITH SPECIAL NEEDS

Students with special needs especially benefit from oral language enrichment activities that focus on informational text (Zehr, 2009). As students with special needs participate in Discussion Circles, they are immersed in academic discourse and concepts. As a preparation for the instructional strategy, students with special needs may create a "visual thesaurus" on the computer that uses clip art or photographs to illustrate the academic vocabulary selected by the teacher. Students print their visual thesaurus and share it with their Discussion Circle partners.

## REFERENCES

August, D., Francis, D., Hsu, H., & Snow, C. (2006). Assessing reading comprehension in bilinguals. *Elementary School Journal, 107,* 221–239.

Beck, I., McKeown, M. G., & Kucan, I. (2002). *Bringing words to life: Robust vocabulary instruction.* New York: Guilford.

International Reading Association and National Council of Teachers of English. (1996). *Standards for the English language arts.* Newark, DE: International Reading Association and Urbana, IL: National Council of Teachers of English.

Moss, B. (2004). Teaching expository text structures through information trade book retellings. *The Reading Teacher, 57,* 710–719.

Williams, T. (2009). A framework for nonfiction in the elementary grades. *Literacy Research and Instruction, 48,* 247–254.

Zehr, M. (2009, October 21). Oral language skills for English learners focus of research. *Education Week, 29*(8), 8.

## Children's Literature Cited

Markle, S. (2009). *Animals Charles Darwin saw: An around-the-world adventure.* Z. Saunders (Illus.). San Francisco: Chronicle.

# Scaffolding
# Academic Reading

# Strategy
# 28

Elementary school students are naturally curious about their world and how objects work. This strategy builds on their sense of wonder to facilitate comprehension of informational text (Webster, 2009). In this information age, it is critically important that expository text gain prominence in the curriculum (Santoro, Chard, Howard, & Baker, 2008).

*Scaffolding Academic Reading* provides elementary school students with "text talk" for informational text (Beck & McKeown, 2001). As students dialogue on a topic, their conceptual knowledge is deepened and their vocabulary is expanded (Santoro et al., 2008). Comprehension is scaffolded as teachers guide students in connecting new ideas to prior knowledge, querying the author, and identifying the main idea.

---

### IRA/NCTE Standards for English Language Arts

1. Students read a wide range of print and nonprint texts to build an understanding of texts, of themselves, and of the cultures of the United States and the world; to acquire new information; to respond to the needs and demands of society and the workplace; and for personal fulfillment. Among these texts are fiction and nonfiction, classic and contemporary works.

3. Students apply a wide range of strategies to comprehend, interpret, evaluate, and appreciate texts. They draw on their prior experience, their interactions with other readers and writers, their knowledge of word meaning and of other texts, their word identification strategies, and their understanding of textual features (e.g., sound-letter correspondence, sentence structure, context, graphics).

*Source:* International Reading Association and National Council of Teachers of English (1996).

---

## USING SCAFFOLDING ACADEMIC READING

*When to use the strategy:* This strategy is designed for whole-class instruction and can be modified for English language learners or students with special needs. In order to increase motivation, teachers may survey students to identify topics of interest such as space exploration or the presidency. It is critical that teachers present the informational read-aloud as a collaborative conversation rather than a "grand inquisition." Students need to feel that their voices are validated in order to participate in the discussion.

*Strategy modifications for grade levels:* Intermediate-grade teachers may use their content-area textbooks to implement this strategy in order to model and practice scaffolded academic reading.

## IMPLEMENTING THE SCAFFOLDING ACADEMIC READING STRATEGY: STEP BY STEP

1. **Select appropriate text.** Prior to the lesson's implementation, teachers select an informational text to be read aloud that is slightly challenging for the students.

2. **Assess prior knowledge.** Teachers use a descriptive web to assess students' concepts and identify academic vocabulary they already know.

3. **Set a purpose for reading.** Teachers use the book cover and graphics to conduct a "picture walk" of the text. Students then generate "I wonder" questions to post on a chart.

4. **Create mental images.** Teachers model creating mental images while reading informational text by thinking aloud during the read-aloud. Teachers encourage students to share their mental images as well.

5. **Summarize main points.** After the read-aloud, students generate a summary of the main points of the text and provide supporting details. Teachers jot down their responses on chart paper to model note taking.

6. **Directed look-backs.** Teachers facilitate directed look-backs (Webster, 2009) to aid students' research regarding their "I wonder" questions.

7. **Return to descriptive web.** Teachers direct students' attention to the descriptive web that was created. Students add new concepts and vocabulary to the web and verbalize how their knowledge base has expanded.

## APPLYING THE SCAFFOLDING ACADEMIC READING STRATEGY: SECOND-GRADE LESSON ON AFRICA

The whole school has been participating in a theme study of the African continent. The teacher has selected the picture book *14 Cows for America* by Carmen A. Deedy (2009). The book tells the true story of the Maasai tribe in Kenya and their gift of 14 cows to the people of the United States to express their sorrow after the events of September 11, 2001. Students are shown a map of the African continent with Kenya highlighted. The teacher asks students to share what they know about tribal life. Key vocabulary words such as *Maasai*, *elders*, and *village* are discussed. Before conducting a picture walk, the teacher focuses students' attention on the cover and then does the following:

- The teacher directs students to describe the village and its people from the cover and the illustrations. Then students generate their "I wonder" questions based on the picture walk. The teacher lists the questions on chart paper.

- The teacher then models for the class how to create a mental image while reading. After modeling, the teacher selects a few students to share their imagery for various passages.

- After the read-aloud, the teacher leads a retelling of the story. Students collaborate on a summary of the story, which is written on chart paper. The teacher asks students to identify the main idea and to write down supporting details from the text.

- Students' questions are revisited, and the teacher uses directed look-backs to model searching the text for answers.

- The teacher returns to the map of Africa and asks students to post sticky notes with new knowledge about Kenya and the Maasai tribe.

When selected students have posted their new concepts regarding Kenya, the teacher leads a discussion on how the text changed their view of Africa. Students are directed to the book's website for further exploration of the topic.

---

### IRA/NCTE Standards for English Language Arts

10. Students whose first language is not English make use of their first language to develop competency in the English language arts and to develop understanding of content across the curriculum.

*Source:* International Reading Association and National Council of Teachers of English (1996).

---

## DIFFERENTIATING INSTRUCTION FOR ENGLISH LANGUAGE LEARNERS

Research indicates that dialogic read-alouds of informational text are effective in building English language learners' vocabulary and comprehension (Hickman, Pollard-Durodola, & Vaughn, 2004). One modification for English language learners is to provide a podcast of the text for repeated readings. The podcast will enable second-language learners to revisit the complex syntax and academic vocabulary of informational text and therefore build fluency.

## DIFFERENTIATING INSTRUCTION FOR STUDENTS WITH SPECIAL NEEDS

Similarly to second-language learners, students with special needs need repeated practice with academic discourse. As students with special needs participate in text talk regarding informational text, they are immersed in the academic vocabulary and sentence structure (Beck & McKeown, 2001). Teachers may provide students with special needs with a scaffolded note-taking activity for repeated practice with informational text (Santoro et al., 2008). In this activity, teachers pair students with special needs with a more fluent reading partner. Working collaboratively, students reread the notes generated by the class and use the text to jot down additional concepts and supporting details. On completion, the dyad shares their work with the whole class.

## REFERENCES

Beck, I., & McKeown, M. G. (2001). Text to talk: Capturing the benefits of read-aloud experiences for young children. *The Reading Teacher, 55,* 10–20.

Hickman, P., Pollard-Durodola, S., & Vaughn, S. (2004). Storybook reading: Improving vocabulary and comprehension for English language learners. *The Reading Teacher, 57,* 720–731.

International Reading Association and National Council of Teachers of English. (1996). *Standards for the English language arts.* Newark, DE: International Reading Association and Urbana, IL: National Council of Teachers of English.

Santoro, L., Chard, D., Howard, L., & Baker, S. (2008). Making the very most of classroom read-alouds to promote comprehension and vocabulary. *The Reading Teacher, 61,* 396–408.

Webster, P. (2009). Exploring the literature of fact. *The Reading Teacher, 62,* 662–671.

## CHILDREN'S LITERATURE CITED

Deedy, C. A. (2009). *14 cows for America.* T. Gonzalez (Illus.). Atlanta, GA: Peachtree.

# Strategy
# 29

# Connect It

*Connect It* focuses on students' prior knowledge on a topic and enables them to make connections while they read. Recent research indicates that when we direct students' attention to informational content and help them make connections while they read, integration of concepts and processing of text is improved (McKeown, Beck, & Blake, 2009b).

The primary purpose for implementing the Connect It activity is to facilitate readers' ability to integrate their prior knowledge with new concepts gained from informational text (McKeown, Beck, & Blake, 2009a). As students share their prior knowledge on a topic and collaborate on making connections, they are scaffolding one another's comprehension of informational text.

---

### IRA/NCTE Standards for English Language Arts

1. Students read a wide range of print and nonprint texts to build an understanding of texts, of themselves, and of the cultures of the United States and the world; to acquire new information; to respond to the needs and demands of society and the workplace; and for personal fulfillment. Among these texts are fiction and nonfiction, classic and contemporary works.

11. Students participate as knowledgeable, reflective, creative, and critical members of a variety of literacy communities.

*Source: International Reading Association and National Council of Teachers of English (1996).*

---

## USING CONNECT IT

*When to use the strategy:* Connect It is primarily used for guided-reading groups or intervention tutorial sessions. Teachers may use the strategy in content-area lessons to model the process of making connections while reading informational text.

*Strategy modifications for grade levels:* Primary-grade teachers may use picture books on the topic to provide background knowledge before implementing this strategy.

## Implementing the Connect It Strategy: Step by Step

1. **Present the topic.** Teachers present the graphic organizer shown in Figure 29.1 and provide a video or photos on the topic.

2. **Assess prior knowledge.** Teachers ask students what they already know concerning the topic. Student responses are written in the "What I Already Know" component of the graphic organizer.

3. **Pair students to read text.** Students read the text with a partner. As they read, students discuss how new information in the text can be integrated with their prior knowledge. They jot down these connections on the graphic organizer in the "Making Connections" section.

4. **Summarize content.** Teachers ask students to report out their summaries of the text. Teachers guide students in making connections among the concepts presented in the text and facilitate their processing of the main idea.

5. **Identify new learning.** After discussing the main idea, students write new concepts they have learned in the center of the graphic organizer.

## Applying the Connect It Strategy: Third-Grade Lesson on Civil Rights

It is January and the second grade is preparing for the celebration of Dr. King's birthday by studying the civil rights movement. The teacher has chosen the trade book *When Marian Sang* by Pam Munoz Ryan (2002) to implement this strategy. The teacher shows a YouTube clip that depicts Marian Anderson singing at the Lincoln Memorial. The teacher asks students if they know the woman and why she is so famous. Students write down their prior knowledge regarding Marian Anderson and her struggle for equality in the "What I Already Know" component of the graphic organizer shown in Figure 29.1. The teacher directs students to do the following:

- Read the text with a partner and write down any connections with Dr. King or the civil rights movement.

- Retell the story to the partner and collaborate on a written summary.

- Explain to the partner how they now understand civil rights after reading the text.

After they have completed their activity, the teacher leads a discussion on the main idea. Students then revisit their graphic organizers and complete the "New Concept" section using what they learned.

*Source:* International Reading Association and National Council of Teachers of English (1996).

### IRA/NCTE Standards for English Language Arts

10. Students whose first language is not English make use of their first language to develop competency in the English language arts and to develop understanding of content across the curriculum.

| Figure 29.1 | Connect It |
| --- | --- |

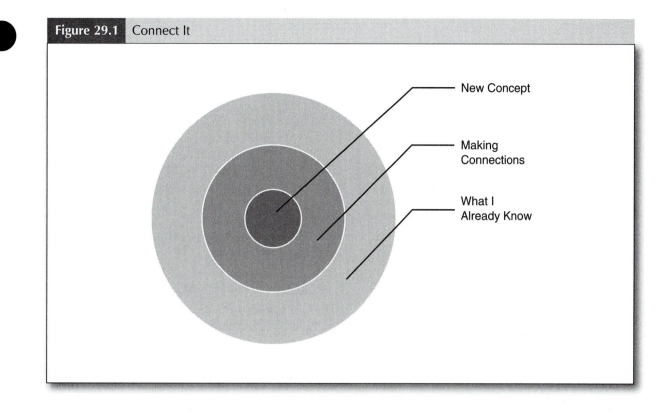

## DIFFERENTIATING INSTRUCTION FOR ENGLISH LANGUAGE LEARNERS

Visual representations are critically important for English language learners. Imagery enables second-language learners to anchor their concepts in concrete symbols and discuss them. An adaptation of this strategy for English language learners is to upgrade their prior knowledge by supplementing the instructional materials (McKeown et al., 2009b). For example, teachers may supply second-language learners with a topic "book bag." In the bag are photos, vocabulary cards, and additional books for them to explore with a reading partner. As they discuss these materials and read the text with their partner, their prior knowledge is upgraded and expanded for deeper processing of informational text.

## DIFFERENTIATING INSTRUCTION FOR STUDENTS WITH SPECIAL NEEDS

Students with special needs often struggle with limited background knowledge in regard to informational topics (Zehr, 2009). The collaborative nature of Connect It enables students with special needs to expand their knowledge base through dialogue. In order to retain the information, students with special needs need to be able to define the concept and explain why it is important to them (Webster, 2009). One adaptation for students with special needs is a follow-up activity where they work with their reading partner to create their own "My Book About" on the topic. Students with special needs use the academic concepts and vocabulary to put the information in their own words and to make connections with their prior knowledge and new learning. On completion, the book is placed in the classroom library for all students to read and enjoy.

## REFERENCES

McKeown, M., Beck, I., & Blake, R. (2009a). Reading comprehension instruction: Focus on content or strategies? *Perspectives on Language & Literacy, 35,* 28–33.

McKeown, M., Beck, I., & Blake, R. (2009b). Rethinking reading comprehension instruction: A comparison of instruction for strategies and content approaches. *Reading Research Quarterly, 44,* 218–253.

International Reading Association and National Council of Teachers of English. (1996). *Standards for the English language arts.* Newark, DE: International Reading Association and Urbana, IL: National Council of Teachers of English.

Webster, P. (2009). Exploring the literature of fact. *The Reading Teacher, 62,* 662–671.

Zehr, M. (2009, October 21). Oral language skills for English learners focus of research. *Education Week, 29*(8), 8.

## CHILDREN'S LITERATURE CITED

Ryan, P. M. (2002). *When Marian sang.* B. Selznick (Illus.). New York: Scholastic.

# Keys to Understanding

## SPEAKING BRIEFLY: AN OVERVIEW OF THE LITERACY STRATEGY

*Keys to Understanding* is an instructional strategy that focuses on identifying the main idea while reading expository text. Elementary school students often struggle with the myriad facts contained in informational text and are unable to grasp the "big idea" (Keene & Zimmerman, 2007). In order to support students in the processing of informational text, it is critical to provide readers with strategies to focus on important points, supporting details, and summaries (Block & Pressley, 2007). Readers are also more likely to process and retain information when they generate summaries and visual representations of text (Duke & Pearson, 2002).

The focus of this strategy is to facilitate readers' understanding of informational text as they discuss their prior knowledge and connect it to new concepts. Partners work collaboratively to focus on the main points in the text and identify supporting details. As they dialogue and cooperatively comprehend text, readers begin to internalize the necessary strategies to analyze and process informational text.

---

### IRA/NCTE Standards for English Language Arts

1. Students read a wide range of print and nonprint texts to build an understanding of texts, of themselves, and of the cultures of the United States and the world; to acquire new information; to respond to the needs and demands of society and the workplace; and for personal fulfillment. Among these texts are fiction and nonfiction, classic and contemporary works.

3. Students apply a wide range of strategies to comprehend, interpret, evaluate, and appreciate texts. They draw on their prior experience, their interactions with other readers and writers, their knowledge of word meaning and of other texts, their word identification strategies, and their understanding of textual features (e.g., sound-letter correspondence, sentence structure, context, graphics).

*Source:* International Reading Association and National Council of Teachers of English (1996).

# Using Keys to Understanding

*When to use the strategy:* Keys to Understanding is used after teachers have modeled it during a whole-class session. Students are then placed in dyads with a reading partner who is on a moderately higher reading level. The strategy can also be modified for use as an intervention, with the teacher taking the place of the partner.

*Strategy modifications for grade levels:* The strategy may be introduced with an informational trade book and then modified for textbook chapters.

## Implementing the Keys to Understanding Strategy: Step by Step

1. **Assess prior knowledge.** Teachers conduct a picture walk of the informational text, focusing attention on the illustrations, charts, and subheadings. Students' predictions and comments on the text are charted.

2. **Highlight vocabulary words and text.** Students use a pink highlighter to identify key vocabulary words and a yellow marker to note important sentences or phrases.

3. **Summarize passage.** Students reread the highlighted sentences and phrases. They then discuss a summary of the passage and write a statement together on the graphic organizer, similar to the one shown in Figure 30.1.

4. **Identify main idea.** Students use their summary statement to identify the main idea and write it on the graphic organizer.

5. **Find supporting details.** Using a blue highlighter, students reread the text to identify supporting details for the main idea and write them on the sheet.

6. **Reflect on the process.** Students discuss any problems they had with the activity and note how they can improve their performance.

## Applying the Keys to Understanding Strategy: Fifth-Grade Lesson on Apollo 11

The fifth grade has begun a unit on discovery. The teacher has chosen the trade book *Moonshot: The Flight of Apollo 11* by Brian Floca (2009) to focus on space exploration. The teacher begins the picture walk with the quote from President Kennedy on America's choice to go to the moon. After the picture walk, the teacher charts students' predictions and notes their comments. Students are placed in dyads and are given copies of the text with blue, yellow, and pink highlighters. Using their Keys to Understanding graphic organizer, the teacher directs students to do the following:

- Highlight key vocabulary words in pink and key sentences in yellow.

- Reread their highlighted sentences and use them to write a summary on the graphic organizer.

- Use the summary statement to generate the main idea; students select the blue highlighter to find supporting details in the text.

- Reflect on their performance and jot down how they solved any comprehension problems while reading

When students have finished their reading, the teacher gathers the whole class together for a debriefing session. Students share their summary statements and any comprehension problems they had while reading. The teacher lists the strategies they used to gain understanding on chart paper for use as a reference during independent reading time.

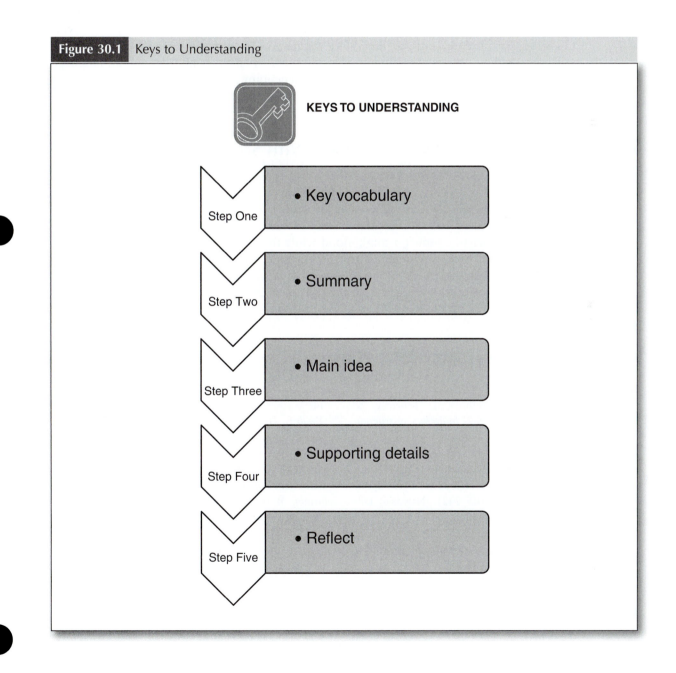

**Figure 30.1** Keys to Understanding

KEYS TO UNDERSTANDING

Step One — • Key vocabulary

Step Two — • Summary

Step Three — • Main idea

Step Four — • Supporting details

Step Five — • Reflect

*Source:* International Reading Association and National Council of Teachers of English (1996).

### IRA/NCTE Standards for English Language Arts

10. Students whose first language is not English make use of their first language to develop competency in the English language arts and to develop understanding of content across the curriculum.

## DIFFERENTIATING INSTRUCTION FOR ENGLISH LANGUAGE LEARNERS

English language learners can become overwhelmed by the amount of informational text (Herrera, Perez, & Escamilla, 2010). Teachers can diminish their anxiety by providing support before, during, and after reading of informational text. The Keys to Understanding strategy facilitates this support by partnering the second-language learner with a proficient reader. However, depending on the proficiency level of the English language learner, teachers may need to implement this strategy as a small guided-reading group to increase support.

## DIFFERENTIATING INSTRUCTION FOR STUDENTS WITH SPECIAL NEEDS

Students with special needs may struggle with summarizing informational text after reading (Schirmer, 2010). One adaptation for students with special needs is to ask their reading partner to conduct a think-aloud while they summarize the text. Teachers may need to model this component during the whole class demonstration session. When students with special needs are given an explicit model of how to connect textual information with prior knowledge to paraphrase, their comprehension is enhanced.

## REFERENCES

Block, C., & Pressley, M. (2007). Best practices in teaching comprehension. In L. Gambrell, L. Morrow, & M. Pressley (Eds.), *Best practices in literacy instruction* (pp. 220–242). New York: Guilford.

Duke, N., & Pearson, P. D. (2002). Effective practices for developing reading comprehension. In A. E. Farstup & S. J. Samuels (Eds.), *What research has to say about reading instruction* (pp. 205–242). Newark, DE: International Reading Association.

Herrera, S., Perez, D., & Escamilla, K. (2010). *Teaching reading to English language learners: Differentiated instruction.* Boston: Allyn & Bacon.

International Reading Association and National Council of Teachers of English. (1996). *Standards for the English language arts.* Newark, DE: International Reading Association and Urbana, IL: National Council of Teachers of English.

Keene, E., & Zimmerman, S. (2007). *Mosaic of thought* (2nd ed.). Portsmouth, NH: Heinemann.

Schirmer, B. (2010). *Teaching the struggling reader.* Boston: Pearson.

## CHILDREN'S LITERATURE CITED

Floca, B. (2009). *Moonshot: The flight of Apollo 11.* New York: Atheneum.

# SECTION VII

# Essential Strategies for Teaching Questioning for Understanding

Ohe of the primary purposes of education is to provide students with the necessary tools to engage in self-inquiry. This chapter presents the research on best practices for teaching questioning for understanding and will explore its use for new literacies.

## A BRIEF OVERVIEW OF QUESTIONING FOR UNDERSTANDING

Our concept of what it means to "understand" text has undergone a radical transformation with the advent of new literacies (Dalton & Proctor, 2009). New literacies—or digital/online text—are nonlinear, multimodal, visually oriented, and often confusing as to authorship (Coiro & Dobler, 2007). Today's students will spend the majority of their lives reading and interacting with digital text and therefore need specific strategies to navigate their comprehension of it. Despite its revolutionary nature, the same process of scaffolded support of comprehension strategies, such as questioning, is vital for understanding digital text (Dalton & Proctor, 2009). The transactional strategy approach provides teachers with a framework for supporting students' use of questioning to dissect digital or printed text (Pressley & McDonald, 2006).

Transactional strategy instruction focuses on explicit teacher modeling and explanation of strategies. Students are then given scaffolded support in shared reading or small guided-reading groups while they practice the strategy (Collins-Block & Pressley, 2007). As students are encouraged to query one another and themselves on the author's purpose, the quality/authenticity of content, literary elements, and interpretations of text, their level of engagement and comprehension is improved (Mills, 2009/2010). The process of querying text provokes students to identify key ideas, make connections with prior knowledge or previous texts, and comprehend (Ciardiello, 1998). Research confirms that question generation is one of the most effective self-monitoring strategies for comprehension (Gunning, 2008).

Research also indicates that the types of questions asked by the teacher or by students themselves directly impact their level of comprehension (Duke & Pearson, 2002). For example, if students are asked only literal questions, their reading of text will focus on the main idea rather than an interpretive stance. In order to gain proficiency, students must be exposed to varying levels of questioning from teachers and their peers, such as the following:

- *Locate and Retell:* Readers query the main idea or factual information.

- *Integrate and Interpret:* Questions in this category focus on establishing relationships between ideas or prior knowledge.

- *Connections:* Readers query the text to see patterns between prior knowledge, previously read texts, and world knowledge.

- *Critique and Evaluate:* The highest level of questioning focuses on making a judgment regarding the quality or message of the text. (Gunning, 2008)

In order to attain proficiency, students must be explicitly told that reading a text straight through without questioning is passive reading (Collins-Block & Pressley, 2007). It is through systematic, explicit modeling and support of inquiry reading that readers begin to transform into strategic consumers of both digital and printed texts.

## INSTRUCTION IN QUESTIONING FOR UNDERSTANDING

The RAND Reading Study Group (2002) defined comprehension as a process of active construction of meaning involving the reader, text, task, and context. Proficient readers are metacognitive and self-regulate their understanding as they query the text (Coiro & Dobler, 2007). As more students are immersed in digital text, it is vital that students learn to query informational text as well as narrative forms (Dalton & Proctor, 2009). Research confirms that even young children can conduct rich, elaborative discussions regarding informational text if they are provided support in dissecting them (Duke, Bennett-Armistead, & Roberts, 2003).

What are the instructional methods to support this deeper level of processing text? Best practices in teaching for understanding emphasize explicit modeling and scaffolding of strategic reading such as questioning (Duke & Pearson, 2002). When teachers conduct a think-aloud to demonstrate how to ask both literal and inferential questions while reading, students' understanding of text is strengthened (Taboada & Guthrie, 2006). As readers practice querying text during shared or guided reading, their internalization of this powerful strategy occurs (Keene, 2008). However, this transformation will not occur unless questioning is included as a routine component of the reading process rather than a special event (Collins-Block & Pressley, 2007). This chapter presents several instructional strategies that use guidelines formed from research on best practice to instruct students in questioning for understanding.

## GUIDELINES FOR DEVELOPING QUESTIONING FOR UNDERSTANDING

The National Reading Panel (2000) determined that questioning was an effective strategy to gain understanding while reading. The following guidelines provide the framework for instruction in developing inquiry-based reading:

1. Effective instruction in questioning for understanding focuses on modeling, explanation, and guided practice of querying while reading (Pressley & McDonald, 2006).

2. Proficient readers use questioning to clarify meaning, demonstrate a critical stance, determine the author's intent, and interpret content (Keene, 2008).

3. Best practices in teaching for understanding use myriad types of text, such as digital and printed materials, to develop "cognitive flexibility" (Coiro & Dobler, 2007).

4. Students' active engagement in querying text involves asking "Why" questions such as, "Did this make sense with what I know about the topic?" (Collins-Block & Pressley, 2007).

5. Effective instruction in teaching recognizes that students need to be exposed to levels of questions in order to process text at a deeper level (Gunning, 2008).

| Figure VII.1 | Self-Assessment of Inquiry-Based Reading |
|---|---|

**MY CHECKLIST OF INQUIRY-BASED READING** 🔍

| PREPARE | ✓ Did I preview the text and make predictions?<br>✓ Did I set a purpose for reading?<br><br>**My Response:** | ➢ How can I improve in this area next time?<br><br>**My Response:** |
|---|---|---|
| QUESTION | ✓ Did I ask questions that were "right there" in the text?<br>✓ Did I ask questions that were "think and search"?<br>✓ Did I use "author and you" questions?<br><br>**My Response:** | ➢ How can I improve in this area next time?<br><br><br><br>**My Response:** |
| ANSWER | ✓ Did I locate information in the text to find answers?<br>✓ Did I integrate the text and my prior knowledge to find answers?<br><br>**My Response:** | ➢ How can I improve in this area next time?<br><br><br>**My Response:** |
| REPAIR | ✓ How did I fix problems I had while reading?<br><br>**My Response:** | ➢ How can I improve in this area?<br><br>**My Response:** |

***SUMMARY OF MY PERFORMANCE:***

## A STRATEGY FOR ASSESSING QUESTIONING FOR UNDERSTANDING

The National Reading Panel (2000) confirmed that self-monitoring of comprehension was critical to understanding text. In order to facilitate engagement and motivation for processing complex material, teachers may use the inquiry-based reading checklist shown in Figure VII.1 with the students. The purpose of the checklist is to encourage readers to self-assess their abilities to actively process and query text in both digital and print formats. Teachers may also use the data to monitor students' progress toward critical reading to inform their instruction. It is also a great tool to inform parents of how they can help their children comprehend digital media at home.

## A GUIDE FOR USING RESPONSE TO INTERVENTION FOR QUESTIONING FOR UNDERSTANDING

The inquiry-based reading checklist (see Figure VII.1) is designed as a self-assessment for students to gauge their skills in querying text. However, it may also be adapted for instructors to assess students' skills in questioning for understanding. Students in need of intervention may note on the checklist that they struggle with repairing their reading performance if they cannot comprehend text. Teachers may also use their observational data or running records for further progress monitoring in this area. The Question-Answer Relationship strategy (Raphael, 1986) in this section may be selected for striving readers requiring intervention. Due to the instructor's explicit modeling and demonstration, striving readers are provided with prompts to use while reading. Effective intervention should focus on one area of questioning at a time, such as "Think and Search," which is determined by assessment data.

In this section, "Essential Strategies for Teaching Questioning for Understanding," five instructional strategies are presented for use in developing querying of text. The strategies are presented as guides for teachers to use based on their ongoing assessment data.

## PROFESSIONAL RESOURCES

Beck, I., & McKeown, M. (2006). *Improving comprehension with questioning the author*. New York: Scholastic.

Ciardiello, A. V. (2006). *Puzzle them first: Motivating adolescent learners with question finding*. Newark, DE: International Reading Association.

International Reading Association and National Council of Teachers of English. (2010). *Read/Write/Think*.

Retrieved February 15, 2010, from http://www.read writethink.org

Raphael, T. (2006). *QAR now: A powerful and practical framework that develops comprehension and higher level thinking in all students*. New York: Scholastic.

Silver, H., Reilly, E., & Perini, M. (2010). *The thoughtful education guide to reading for meaning*. Thousand Oaks, CA: Sage.

# REFERENCES

Ciardiello, A. V. (1998). Did you ask a good question today? Alternative cognitive and metacognitive strategies. *Journal of Adolescent and Adult Literacy, 42,* 210–219.

Coiro, J., & Dobler, E. (2007). Exploring the online reading comprehension strategies used by sixth-grade skilled readers to search for and locate information on the Internet. *Reading Research Quarterly, 42,* 214–259.

Collins-Block, C., & Pressley, M. (2007). Best practices in teaching comprehension. In L. Gambrell, L. Mandel-Morrow, & M. Pressley (Eds.), *Best practices in literacy instruction* (pp. 220–243). New York: Guilford.

Dalton, B., & Proctor, C. P. (2009). The changing landscape of text and comprehension in the age of new literacies. In J. Coiro, M. Knobel, C. Lankshear, & D. Leu (Eds.), *Handbook of research on new literacies* (pp. 297–325). New York: Routledge.

Duke, N., Bennett-Armistead, V. S., & Roberts, E. M. (2003). Bridging the gap between learning to read and reading to learn. In D. M. Barone & L. M. Morrow (Eds.), *Literacy and young children: Research-based practices*(pp. 226–243). New York: Guilford.

Duke, N., & Pearson, P. D. (2002). Effective practices for developing reading comprehension. In A. E. Farstup & S. J. Samuels (Eds.), *What research has to say about reading instruction* (pp. 205–242). Newark, DE: International Reading Association.

Gunning, T. (2008). *Developing higher level literacy in all students: Building reading, reasoning, and responding.* Boston: Allyn & Bacon.

Keene, E. (2008). *To understand: New horizons in reading comprehension.* Portsmouth, NH: Heinemann.

Mills, K. (2009/2010). Floating on a sea of talk: Reading comprehension through speaking and listening. *The Reading Teacher, 63,* 325–329.

National Reading Panel. (2000). *Report of the National Reading Panel: Teaching children to read: An evidence-based assessment of the scientific research literature on reading and its implications for reading instruction.* Washington, DC: National Institute of Child Health & Human Development, National Institutes of Health.

Pressley, M., & McDonald, R. (2006). The need for increased comprehension instruction. In M. Pressley (Ed.), *Reading instruction that works: The case for balanced instruction* (3rd ed., pp. 293–347). New York: Guilford.

RAND Reading Study Group. (2002). *Reading for understanding: Toward an R&D program in reading comprehension.* Santa Monica, CA: Author.

Raphael, T. (1986). Teaching Question-Answer Relationships revisited. *The Reading Teacher, 39,* 516–522.

Taboada, A., & Guthrie, J. (2006). Contributions of student questioning and prior knowledge to construction of knowledge from reading informational text. *Journal of Literacy Research, 38,* 1–38.

# Strategy
# 31

# Questioning the Author

## SPEAKING BRIEFLY: AN OVERVIEW OF THE LITERACY STRATEGY

*Questioning the Author* is a content-focused approach to comprehension that requires readers to activate their prior knowledge and integrate it with textual information (McKeown, Beck, & Blake, 2009). It allows readers to see the process of comprehension as a challenge rather than a chore (Beck & McKeown, 2002). The teacher's role is one of guide or facilitator as students collaborate with one another to gain understanding (Beck, McKeown, Hamilton, & Kucan, 1997).

The primary purpose for Questioning the Author is to explicitly model, explain, and scaffold inquiry-based reading to develop self-regulated learners (Blachowicz & Ogle, 2008). This strategy was designed for informational text; however, it can be adapted for narrative structures. It is also well suited for scaffolding students' understanding of digital text.

*Source:* International Reading Association and National Council of Teachers of English (1996).

### IRA/NCTE Standards for English Language Arts

1. Students read a wide range of print and nonprint texts to build an understanding of texts, of themselves, and of the cultures of the United States and the world; to acquire new information; to respond to the needs and demands of society and the workplace; and for personal fulfillment. Among these texts are fiction and nonfiction, classic, and contemporary works.

3. Students apply a wide range of strategies to comprehend, interpret, evaluate, and appreciate texts. They draw on their prior experience, their interactions with other readers and writers, their knowledge of word meaning and of other texts, their word identification strategies, and their understanding of textual features (e.g., sound-letter correspondence, sentence structure, context, graphics).

# USING QUESTIONING THE AUTHOR

*When to use the strategy:* Questioning the Author may be used as a whole-class or guided-reading lesson. Effective implementation of this strategy is dependent on careful planning. Teachers must carefully choose texts that will provide good discussions and that will focus on key understandings for their students. Teachers must also explicitly state that students are allowed to question the author of any text and to query their credentials for authorship.

*Strategy modifications for grade levels:* Teachers may adopt this strategy for specific grades by selecting texts that are on students' instructional reading levels.

## IMPLEMENTING THE QUESTIONING THE AUTHOR STRATEGY: STEP BY STEP

1. **Select key understandings for reading.** Teachers identify key goals for understanding as the first phase of the planning process. Goals focus on making connections and interpreting ideas rather than focusing solely on factual information.

2. **Segment the text and think about roadblocks to understanding.** Teachers examine the text and select where to stop and query the author. They also use assessment data to determine possible roadblocks to comprehension, such as lack of prior knowledge, and how these might be circumvented.

3. **Prepare queries.** Teachers prepare questions for the session as well as follow-up queries. Examples of initiating queries are "What is the author talking about?" or "What is the author trying to say?" Examples of follow-up queries are "What did the author mean here?" or "How does this connect to what we know about the topic?" or "What did the author not tell us?" (Beck et al., 1997). Students are provided with the query sheet shown in Figure 31.1 to use as a guide.

4. **Model with think-aloud.** Give students a copy of the text to follow along as teachers stop at designated segments and question the author. Explicitly demonstrate how confusing sections of the text are processed.

5. **Discuss inquiry.** After the think-aloud, focus discussion on what the author wrote, why he or she wrote it, and why it is important. Teachers may use discussion movers such as the following to facilitate the discussion: turning back (reviewing text to clarify information), recasting students' comments to aid expressions, and annotating (providing information that was not supplied by the author; Beck et al., 1997).

6. **Review the session.** Teachers ask students to review the session and list the problems they encountered while reading and how they were solved.

7. **Application of strategy.** Teachers place students in dyads for guided practice of Questioning the Author in follow-up sessions or in guided-reading groups.

## APPLYING THE QUESTIONING THE AUTHOR STRATEGY: SIXTH-GRADE LESSON

The teacher has selected *Three Cups of Tea: One Man's Journey to Change the World . . . One Child at a Time* (Thomson, Mortenson, & Relin, 2009) to focus on cultural differences and the purpose of education. The teacher examines the book for

| Figure 31.1 | Query Sheet |

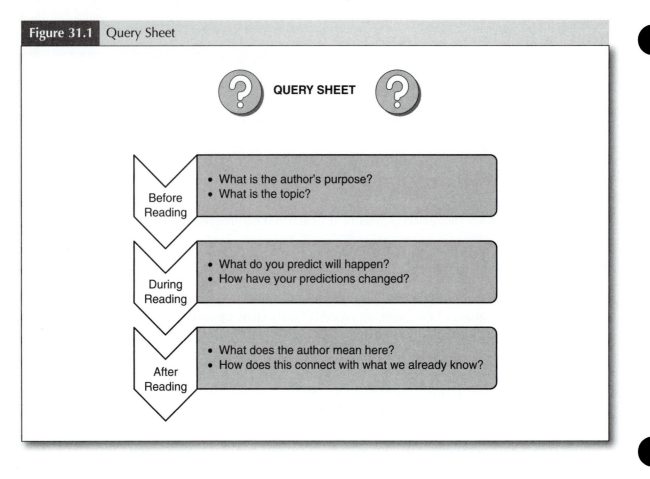

various segments to stop and pose questions. In preparing for the session, the teacher realized that a possible roadblock to comprehension might be students' lack of knowledge about Pakistan. In order to solve this problem, the teacher shows the class a video on YouTube about life in the villages of Pakistan. After distributing the query sheet shown in Figure 31.1, the teacher introduces the Questioning the Author strategy with the following steps:

- Begin the session with the initiating query, "What is the author trying to say about Pakistan?" As students voice their ideas, integrate their answers with the information provided in the video about village life in Pakistan.

- Use the title of the text to query students during the reading of the text: "Why did the author choose the title of the story, *Three Cups of Tea?*" Use the "turn-back" discussion mover to encourage students to consult the text in seeking answers to challenging questions.

- Discuss the message in the story by posing follow-up queries such as, "What message is the author trying to convey?" or "How would building a school in a poor area of America differ from the one in Pakistan?" or "What information did the author leave out about Pakistan?" Use the annotating discussion technique to provide students with additional information about Pakistan to expand their understanding.

After the session, the teacher asks students to jot down any problems they had in comprehending the text and how they were resolved. After a 2-minute quick-write, the teacher asks students to report out the strategies they used to answer the questions that were raised and to share any remaining queries they may have about cultural differences.

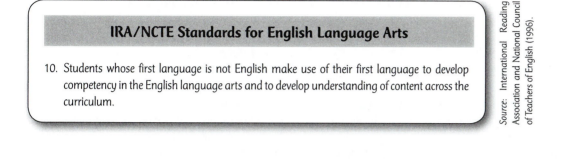

### IRA/NCTE Standards for English Language Arts

10. Students whose first language is not English make use of their first language to develop competency in the English language arts and to develop understanding of content across the curriculum.

*Source:* International Reading Association and National Council of Teachers of English (1996).

## DIFFERENTIATING INSTRUCTION FOR ENGLISH LANGUAGE LEARNERS

Research indicates that English learners may comprehend more than they are able to communicate and can often tackle more difficult text than they are typically given (Manyak & Bauer, 2008). Questioning the Author provides second-language learners with the support they need to tackle more challenging text. One modification for English language learners is to provide them with a question bookmark, as shown in Figure 31.2, making available to them possible locations for finding an answer to their queries. Second-language learners may work with a more proficient reader to implement the strategy during independent reading time.

| Figure 31.2 | Question Bookmark |
| --- | --- |

**Directions:** *Use the question bookmark to help find the answers to questions about texts you've read.*

| Question | Notes |
| --- | --- |
| ➢ **What is the author's purpose?** | |
| **Look** | |
| ○ **at the topic sentence or first paragraph of text.** | |
| **Question** | |
| ➢ **What is the text about?** | |
| **Look** | |
| ○ **at the Table of Contents and chapter headings.** | |

## DIFFERENTIATING INSTRUCTION FOR STUDENTS WITH SPECIAL NEEDS

Students with special needs may need additional supports to implement this strategy for understanding. One modification may be to partner students with special needs with a more proficient partner to implement the strategy using digital text. The visual orientation of online texts and support features such as pronunciations of unknown words enable students with special needs to focus on the process of querying.

## REFERENCES

Beck, I., & McKeown, M. (2002). Questioning the author: Making sense of social studies. *Educational Leadership, 60,* 44–48.

Beck, I., McKeown, M., Hamilton, R., & Kucan, L. (1997). *Questioning the author: An approach for enhancing student engagement with text.* Newark, DE: International Reading Association.

Blachowicz, C., & Ogle, D. (2008). *Reading comprehension strategies for independent learners.* New York: Guilford.

International Reading Association and National Council of Teachers of English. (1996). *Standards for the English language arts.* Newark, DE: International Reading Association and Urbana, IL: National Council of Teachers of English.

Manyak, P., & Bauer, E. (2008). Explicit code and comprehension instruction for English learners. *Reading Research Quarterly, 61,* 432–435.

McKeown, M., Beck, I., & Blake, R. (2009). Rethinking reading comprehension instruction: A comparison of instruction for strategies and content approaches. *Reading Research Quarterly, 44,* 218–254.

## CHILDREN'S LITERATURE CITED

Thomson, S., Mortenson, G., & Relin, D. O. (2009). *Three cups of tea: One man's journey to change the world . . . one child at a time.* New York: Puffin.

## SPEAKING BRIEFLY: AN OVERVIEW OF THE LITERACY STRATEGY

The National Reading Panel (2000) confirmed the value of generating and asking questions while reading to monitor comprehension and facilitate active engagement with text. Graphic organizers were also mentioned in the report as effective tools to enable readers to see relationships among concepts and to focus on text structure.

The purpose of *My Web of Questions* is to facilitate students' comprehension of text through question generation. My Web of Questions provides students with a graphic organizer to guide them through the process of strategic reading and specifically the strategy of inquiry-based reading.

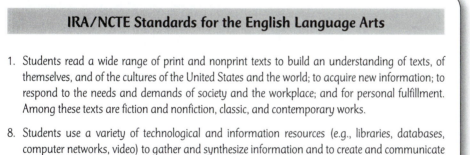

**IRA/NCTE Standards for the English Language Arts**

1. Students read a wide range of print and nonprint texts to build an understanding of texts, of themselves, and of the cultures of the United States and the world; to acquire new information; to respond to the needs and demands of society and the workplace; and for personal fulfillment. Among these texts are fiction and nonfiction, classic, and contemporary works.

8. Students use a variety of technological and information resources (e.g., libraries, databases, computer networks, video) to gather and synthesize information and to create and communicate knowledge.

*Source:* International Reading Association and National Council of Teachers of English (1996).

## USING MY WEB OF QUESTIONS

*When to use the strategy:* My Web of Questions is designed for intervention lessons and is best used with narrative text structures. It may also be used in guided-reading sessions or for literacy center activities. However, students must receive explicit modeling of the strategy before it is placed in the literacy center.

*Strategy modifications for grade levels:* Teachers may modify this lesson for younger students by placing them in dyads with more advanced readers to scaffold the activity.

## IMPLEMENTING THE MY WEB OF QUESTIONS STRATEGY: STEP BY STEP

1. **Select appropriate text.** Teachers select text that is on students' instructional reading level and is slightly challenging.

2. **Conduct a picture walk.** Teachers lead students in a picture walk to set a purpose for reading and to make predictions based on the cover and illustrations.

3. **Demonstrate using the web.** Teachers conduct a think-aloud and demonstrate how to generate questions on the web illustrated in Figure 32.1.

4. **Discuss answers to queries.** Teachers demonstrate strategies such as rereading the text or making an inference to answer the questions previously generated.

5. **Summarize story content.** Using the web graphic organizers, teachers model how to summarize the main idea and important details in the story.

6. **Make connections.** Teachers demonstrate how to make connections to prior knowledge, other texts, or world knowledge and how to record it on the web graphic organizer.

7. **Critique the text.** As the final step, teachers model how to evaluate the story based on their knowledge of narrative genre and other stories with similar plots.

## APPLYING THE MY WEB OF QUESTIONS STRATEGY: SEVENTH-GRADE LESSON

The teacher begins the lesson by showing a map of Korea on Google Earth and discussing what students know about the country. Using the My Web of Questions graphic organizer, shown in Figure 32.1, the teacher demonstrates how to use *A Single Shard* (Park, 2001), its title, front, and blurb to generate questions:

- What would be our purpose for reading this story? Do we know what life was like in 12th-century Korea?

- What do you think the title *A Single Shard* means? From the cover we can infer it relates to pottery, yet we don't know how that impacts the story; so let's generate a question such as, "How does pottery impact Tree-ear's life?"

- What should be our final question? Let's return to the summary on the back, where it mentions a dangerous journey. Do we know where and why Tree-ear travels? Let's record that as our fourth question.

Students use Figure 32.1 to jot down their responses as they read the corresponding chapters. Since the book contains 13 chapters, students may be assigned to read a few as homework or over several class sessions. When the text is completed, students work with a partner to share their responses to the questions on the graphic organizer and to record their summaries. The teacher asks each dyad to report out their work, and the class generates a descriptive web to summarize their new knowledge about life in Korea during the 12th century and to make connections with their modern world.

**Figure 32.1** My Web of Questions

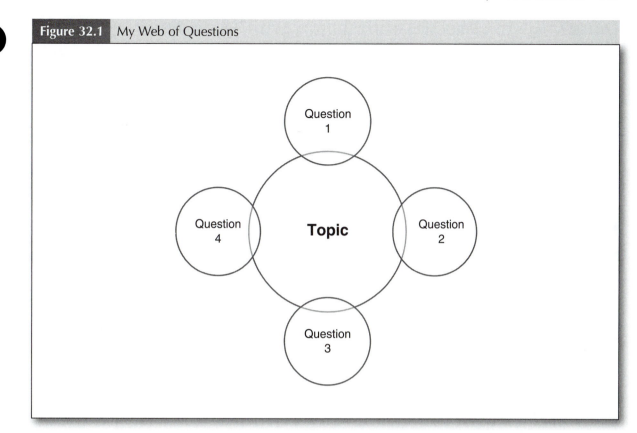

### IRA/NCTE Standards for English Language Arts

10. *Students whose first language is not English make use of their first language to develop competency in the English language arts and to develop understanding of content across the curriculum.*

## DIFFERENTIATING INSTRUCTION FOR ENGLISH LANGUAGE LEARNERS

It is critical that all learners develop strategies to self-monitor their comprehension while reading (Blachowicz & Ogle, 2008). English language learners need additional support to communicate their understanding as they actively process text and monitor their reading. One method for providing support is to allow second-language learners to illustrate their answers to the questions before writing their responses. English learners can then use their oral explanations of the illustrations to dictate their answers to a more proficient partner acting as scribe.

## Differentiating Instruction for Students With Special Needs

Research indicates that scaffolded discussion assists students' deep processing of text (Mills, 2009/2010). One adaptation of this strategy for students with special needs is to first guide them in a discussion of their responses to the questions. Through elaboration and recasting of student responses, teachers guide and support students with special needs as they attempt to answer the questions they generated. If students experience comprehension problems, teachers may intervene with suggested strategies to tackle their roadblocks to understanding.

## References

Blachowicz, C., & Ogle, D. (2008). *Reading comprehension strategies for independent learners.* New York: Guilford.

International Reading Association and National Council of Teachers of English. (1996). *Standards for the English language arts.* Newark, DE: International Reading Association and Urbana, IL: National Council of Teachers of English.

Mills, K. (2009/2010). Floating on a sea of talk: Reading comprehension through speaking and listening. *The Reading Teacher, 63,* 325–329.

National Reading Panel. (2000). *Report of the National Reading Panel. Teaching children to read: An evidence-based assessment of the scientific research literature on reading and its implications for reading instruction.* Washington, DC: National Institute of Child Health & Human Development, National Institutes of Health.

## Children's Literature Cited

Park, L. S. (2001). *A single shard.* New York: Dell Yearling.

# Scaffolding Reading Comprehension Through Student Questioning

# Strategy 33

## SPEAKING BRIEFLY: AN OVERVIEW OF THE LITERACY STRATEGY

*Scaffolding Reading Comprehension Through Student Questioning* provides all learners with explicit modeling and guided practice in self-monitoring and metacognition (Manyak & Bauer, 2008). The purpose of the strategy is to engage learners in collaborative strategic reading (Klinger & Vaughn, 1999) to cooperatively process content-area text.

Research confirms that all learners benefit from authentic literacy events that facilitate discussion and attention to the features and structures of specific genres (Purcell-Gates, Duke, & Martineau, 2007). In this strategy, support is embedded as readers work with a partner to identify new vocabulary words and assimilate new concepts.

---

### IRA/NCTE Standards for English Language Arts

1. Students read a wide range of print and nonprint texts to build an understanding of texts, of themselves, and of the cultures of the United States and the world; to acquire new information; to respond to the needs and demands of society and the workplace; and for personal fulfillment. Among these texts are fiction and nonfiction, classic, and contemporary works.

11. Students participate as knowledgeable, reflective, creative, and critical members of a variety of literacy communities.

*Source:* International Reading Association and National Council of Teachers of English (1996).

# USING SCAFFOLDING READING COMPREHENSION THROUGH STUDENT QUESTIONING

*When to use the strategy:* Scaffolding Reading Comprehension Through Student Questioning is designed for a whole-class session using content-area text. The teacher may follow up the session with guided reading lessons that provide further scaffolding of the targeted skill or strategy.

*Strategy modifications for grade levels:* Teachers may modify this lesson for younger students by using informational picture books to implement the activity.

## IMPLEMENTING THE SCAFFOLDING READING COMPREHENSION THROUGH STUDENT QUESTIONING STRATEGY: STEP BY STEP

1. **Select text for targeted instruction.** Using assessment data, teachers select a content-area text or informational book for students to read. Teachers segment the text and select sections to stop and pose questions.

2. **Preview text and tap prior knowledge.** Before reading the text, teachers lead students on an "informational tour" of the text using subheadings and illustrations or charts to tap prior knowledge. Teachers direct students to "turn and talk" with their partner about what they think the text is about and to record questions about it.

3. **Identify new vocabulary and concepts.** Teachers ask students to identify words they do not recognize and record any new concepts in the graphic organizer (shown in Figure 33.1).

4. **Read text and discuss.** Students collaborate on strategically reading the text, stopping to ask questions such as, "What does this mean here? How is this connected to what we already know about the topic? What is the main idea?"

5. **Summarize the text.** After reading the text, students work with their partners to orally summarize the main idea and supporting details of the text. After discussing it, they return to the graphic organizer shown in Figure 33.1 and record their summary and any new concepts they learned through their reading. Students review new vocabulary words and record their definitions. Teachers ask students to report out their work and to generate new questions on the topic for follow-up research projects.

## APPLYING THE SCAFFOLDING READING COMPREHENSION THROUGH STUDENT QUESTIONING STRATEGY: FIFTH-GRADE LESSON ON TRADE

The fifth grade is beginning a new unit of study on trade. The teacher introduces the concept with the picture book *The Silk Route: 7,000 Miles of History* by John S. Major (1995). The teacher begins the lesson with a picture walk discussing the beautiful illustrations of places along the Silk Route, such as China, India, and Baghdad. Students discuss how people are dressed in the various scenes and their modes of travel across the Silk Route. After distributing student copies of the text, the teacher directs students to survey the book and then turn and talk with their partners about their predictions.

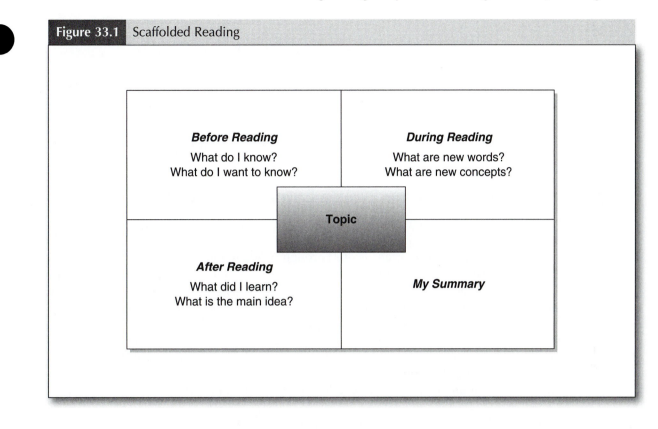

**Figure 33.1**   Scaffolded Reading

***Before Reading***
What do I know?
What do I want to know?

***During Reading***
What are new words?
What are new concepts?

**Topic**

***After Reading***
What did I learn?
What is the main idea?

***My Summary***

Students record their questions about the text on the "Before Reading" section of the graphic organizer shown in Figure 33.1. Before reading the text, the teacher directs students to do the following:

- "Now that you have generated your questions about the text, jot down any new vocabulary words on the next section of the graphic organizer while you are reading. From the title of the text, what can we predict the people in the book are trading?" The teacher uses their responses to discuss why silk was traded and why it was valuable to the ancient world.

- The teacher directs students to stop at the midpoint and discuss with their partners if their predictions were correct. They are also instructed to talk about how the text is connected to what they already know about trading.

- After the text is completed, students discuss their new concepts and vocabulary words. The teacher records them on a thematic word wall for the unit of study. Students share their knowledge of the Silk Route and how it compares with trading in today's world.

- After the discussion, students write their summaries in the final component of the graphic organizer. The teacher uses their summaries to assess initial concepts of trading and how to adapt further lessons on the topic.

At the conclusion of the session, dyads are given commodities such as salt, oil, and codfish to study and report on to their class.

*Source:* International Reading Association and National Council of Teachers of English (1996).

> ### IRA/NCTE Standards for English Language Arts
>
> 10. Students whose first language is not English make use of their first language to develop competency in the English language arts and to develop understanding of content across the curriculum.

## DIFFERENTIATING INSTRUCTION FOR ENGLISH LANGUAGE LEARNERS

Scaffolding Reading Comprehension Through Student Questioning provides English language learners with embedded support to tackle complex concepts and vocabulary (Manyak & Bauer, 2008). In order to increase their engagement and motivation, one adaptation for second-language learners is to "preload" their conceptual understanding of the topic by creating a webquest. A webquest is a series of bookmarked websites with accompanying questions and activities. English learners may work with a native speaker on the webquest to gain background knowledge on the topic before the class is introduced to the text. Preparatory work, such as webquests, allows English learners to feel more confident and engaged in discussions on informational text.

## DIFFERENTIATING INSTRUCTION FOR STUDENTS WITH SPECIAL NEEDS

Similarly to English language learners, students with special needs may lack the necessary background knowledge to process informational text. One adaptation for students with special needs is to create a book bag of lower level books on the same topic that they may use to prepare for the activity. After reading lower level texts on the topic, students with special needs will be more familiar with the academic vocabulary and concepts.

## REFERENCES

International Reading Association and National Council of Teachers of English. (1996). *Standards for the English language arts*. Newark, DE: International Reading Association and Urbana, IL: National Council of Teachers of English.

Klinger, J., & Vaughn, S. (1999). Promoting reading comprehension, content learning, and English acquisition through Collaborative Strategic Reading (CSR). *The Reading Teacher, 52,* 738–747.

Manyak, P., & Bauer, E. (2008). Explicit code and comprehension instruction for English learners. *Reading Research Quarterly, 61,* 432–435.

Purcell-Gates, V., Duke, N., & Martineau, J. (2007). Learning to read and write generic specific text: Roles of authentic experience and explicit teaching. *Reading Research Quarterly, 42,* 8–45.

## CHILDREN'S LITERATURE CITED

Major, J. S. (1995). *The Silk Route: 7,000 miles of history*. S. Fieser (Illus.). New York: HarperCollins.

# Question-Answer Relationships

# Strategy
# 34

## SPEAKING BRIEFLY: AN OVERVIEW OF THE LITERACY STRATEGY

*Question-Answer Relationships (QAR)* is a technique to help students differentiate the types of questions they can ask of text (Raphael, 1986). Research confirms that QAR is an effective method for developing self-efficacy and confidence in readers as they grapple with processing text (Duke & Pearson, 2002).

This modified version of QAR is designed to be used with pictures (Cortese, 2003). Visual imagery is a key component of digital text, and the ability to make an inference from a picture is a critical skill in the new literacies (Dalton & Proctor, 2009). As students construct the main idea and generate inferences using visual images, they are internalizing critical strategies to also process printed text.

---

### IRA/NCTE Standards for English Language Arts

1. Students read a wide range of print and nonprint texts to build an understanding of texts, of themselves, and of the cultures of the United States and the world; to acquire new information; to respond to the needs and demands of society and the workplace; and for personal fulfillment. Among these texts are fiction and nonfiction, classic, and contemporary works.

3. Students apply a wide range of strategies to comprehend, interpret, evaluate, and appreciate texts. They draw on their prior experience, their interactions with other readers and writers, their knowledge of word meaning and of other texts, their word identification strategies, and their understanding of textual features (e.g., sound-letter correspondence, sentence structure, context, graphics).

*Source:* International Reading Association and National Council of Teachers of English (1996).

# Using Question-Answer Relationships

*When to use the strategy:* QAR is designed for whole-class or small guided-reading lessons. In order to implement this instructional activity, the teacher will need to find an illustration or photograph that will generate inferences. It is best to begin with a print of a painting or illustration before moving on to photographs. Norman Rockwell's illustrations are particularly well suited for introducing the process, as they often generate ideas for stories. It is also important to model only one strategy at a time; so it will take several sessions to complete all four components of QAR.

*Strategy modifications for grade levels:* Teachers may modify this lesson for primary-grade students by using wordless picture books to implement the activity.

### Implementing the Question-Answer Relationships Strategy: Step by Step

1. **Explain the process.** Teachers state that answers to questions either come from the text or from our knowledge on the topic. Explain that a process for creating and answering questions is called Question-Answer Relationships, or QAR.

2. **Display poster of components.** Teachers display a poster that illustrates the four categories of questions:

   - *Right There:* Answer is explicitly stated in the text or in the picture.
   - *Think and Search:* Question requires information from different parts of the picture or different sections of the text.
   - *On My Own:* Answer is generated from your prior knowledge and not from the picture or text.
   - *Artist/Author and Me:* Answer is not explicitly in the text. You create the answer by thinking about what you already know and what the artist/author is telling you.

3. **Distribute illustration.** Teachers distribute the illustration for the activity and explain that they will learn the QAR process by using pictures first and then moving to text in later sessions.

4. **Model "Right There."** Teachers write examples of "Right There" questions on the graphic organizer shown in Figure 34.1. Teachers model how to find the answer to the questions by studying the illustration and recording the answer on the graphic organizer.

5. **Guided practice.** Teachers place students in dyads to try to generate "Right There" questions. After generating questions, the whole class answers a selected few and records them on the graphic organizer.

6. **Reflect on the process.** Teachers lead students in a discussion of their implementation of QAR. Students share problems they encountered and discuss possible solutions to comprehension roadblocks.

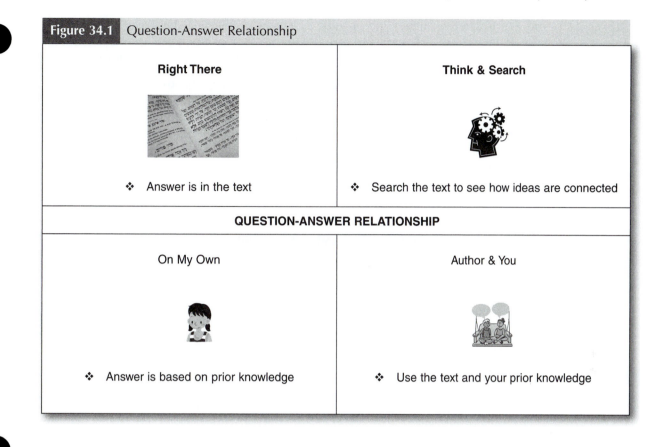

**Figure 34.1** | Question-Answer Relationship

**Right There**

❖ Answer is in the text

**Think & Search**

❖ Search the text to see how ideas are connected

**QUESTION-ANSWER RELATIONSHIP**

On My Own

❖ Answer is based on prior knowledge

Author & You

❖ Use the text and your prior knowledge

## APPLYING THE QUESTION-ANSWER RELATIONSHIPS STRATEGY: SECOND-GRADE LESSON

The teacher gathers students in the meeting area to introduce the QAR strategy. A poster is displayed with the four components, and the teacher explains that they can use it to categorize questions in order to answer them. Using the graphic organizer (see Figure 34.1), the teacher directs students to do the following:

- "Yesterday, we finished reading *Henry's Freedom Box* (Levine, 2007) about the underground railway. Today, we're going to use what we know from the story to practice our new strategy. Let's look at the first component, 'Right There.' This category means the answer is right in the text. One example of a 'Right There' question is, 'Who was Henry?' I can answer this by rereading the text. Can you think of any other 'Right There' types of questions?" The teacher records their factual questions and answers in the first box on the poster.

- The teacher guides students in a similar way through the next component, "Think and Search": "This type of question requires us to put several pieces of information from the story together to answer it. One example of this question is, 'Why was Nancy worried that her master had lost a lot of money?' How would we answer that question?"

- The teacher continues to explicitly demonstrate the final two components, "On My Own" and "Author and You." After all four components are demonstrated, the teacher leads students in a discussion of when they can use the strategy.

- Students are given the graphic organizer and a new text to apply the first two components of the strategy with a partner. After feedback from the teacher on their work, students complete the graphic organizer for homework.

The teacher continues to use the QAR strategy in guided-reading groups for several weeks to aid students' mastery of it.

*Source:* International Reading Association and National Council of Teachers of English (1996).

### IRA/NCTE Standards for English Language Arts

10. Students whose first language is not English make use of their first language to develop competency in the English language arts and to develop understanding of content across the curriculum.

## DIFFERENTIATING INSTRUCTION FOR ENGLISH LANGUAGE LEARNERS

The use of visual imagery to aid comprehension is especially helpful for English language learners. One adaptation of the QAR technique is to provide English learners with a symbol for each of the components. Since the heading for each component might be confusing for second-language learners, a symbol to associate with each component will ensure that they perform the correct strategy. Teachers may encourage second-language learners to create their own symbols to further aid association with the component.

## DIFFERENTIATING INSTRUCTION FOR STUDENTS WITH SPECIAL NEEDS

Research indicates that students with special needs especially need explicit instruction in comprehension strategies (Collins-Block & Pressley, 2007). When teachers segue from pictures to text for QAR, students with special needs may need to first use picture books as a support mechanism. Picture books will provide a scaffold for them to use the strategies they learn and gradually transfer them to printed text. As students with special needs become more adept at QAR, the teacher may gradually wean them off picture books and move them toward print-only texts.

## REFERENCES

Collins-Block, C., & Pressley, M. (2007). Best practices in teaching comprehension. In L. Gambrell, L. Mandel-Morrow, & M. Pressley (Eds.), *Best practices in literacy instruction* (pp. 220–243). New York: Guilford.

Cortese, E. (2003). The application of Question-Answer Relationship strategies to pictures. *The Reading Teacher, 57,* 374–380.

Dalton, B., & Proctor, C. P. (2009). The changing landscape of text and comprehension in the age of new literacies. In J. Coiro, M. Knobel, C. Lankshear, & D. Leu (Eds.), *Handbook of research on new literacies* (pp. 297–325). New York: Routledge.

Duke, N., & Pearson, P. D. (2002). Effective practices for developing reading comprehension. In A. E. Farstup & S. J. Samuels (Eds.), *What research has to say about reading instruction* (pp. 205–242). Newark, DE: International Reading Association.

International Reading Association and National Council of Teachers of English. (1996). *Standards for the English language arts.* Newark, DE: International Reading Association and Urbana, IL: National Council of Teachers of English.

Raphael, T. (1986). Teaching Question-Answer Relationships revisited. *The Reading Teacher, 39,* 516–522.

## CHILDREN'S LITERATURE CITED

Levine, E. (2007). *Henry's freedom box.* K. Nelson (Illus.). New York: Scholastic.

# Strategy
# 35

# ReQuest

## SPEAKING BRIEFLY: AN OVERVIEW OF THE LITERACY STRATEGY

*ReQuest* is an instructional strategy that explicitly models how to construct questions while reading and how to process text (Manzo, Manzo, & Estes, 2004). During the strategy, teachers and students take turns querying one another and supporting their responses with evidence from the text. Research confirms that explicit modeling and guided practice in querying text improves comprehension (Duke & Pearson, 2002). However, teachers must ensure that students vary their types of questions so that they do not focus only on literal queries (Pressley & McDonald, 2006).

The purpose of the ReQuest strategy is to facilitate readers' engagement with text through questioning. As students attempt to answer the questions that are generated, the teacher acts as facilitator to guide them in referencing the text and using prior knowledge to comprehend.

*Source:* International Reading Association and National Council of Teachers of English (1996).

---

### IRA/NCTE Standards for English Language Arts

8. Students use a variety of technological and information resources (e.g., libraries, databases, computer networks, video) to gather and synthesize information and to create and communicate knowledge.

11. Students participate as knowledgeable, reflective, creative, and critical members of a variety of literacy communities.

---

## USING REQUEST

*When to use the strategy:* ReQuest was designed for small guided-reading groups; however, it is easily adapted for whole-class sessions. This version of ReQuest has been designed for use with digital text to strengthen students' comprehension of online materials.

Teachers will need laptops for students to view web documents and a SMART Board to display the full website and to highlight text.

*Strategy modifications for grade levels:* Teachers may modify this lesson for primary-grade students by using informational picture books to implement the activity.

## IMPLEMENTING THE REQUEST STRATEGY: STEP BY STEP

1. **Select the digital text.** Teachers may choose an online document or news article that is slightly challenging. It must be long enough to be segmented for turn taking. After selecting the digital text, the teacher decides where to segment the article for questioning.

2. **Explain the strategy.** Teachers describe the ReQuest strategy and remind students that in order to be active readers, they must generate questions while they read.

3. **Tap prior knowledge.** Teachers direct students' attention to the website. Students are asked to identify the author of the article and to ascertain if it is a credible site.

4. **Read segmented text.** Teachers and students read the first section of the article and think of questions to ask while reading.

5. **Invite students to generate questions.** Teachers ask students to "act as teachers" and pose questions to stump their teacher. In order to model processing of digital text, teachers use hyperlinks or digital images on the website to answer questions.

6. **Reverse roles.** Teachers direct students to read the next passage and to reverse roles with them. After students finish reading the selection, teachers pose questions to students while carefully modeling higher level types of questions that require elaborate answers.

7. **Repeat process.** Teachers and students repeat the process until a purpose for reading can be set. It should not take longer than 10 minutes.

8. **Categorize questions.** After students have completed the activity, ask them to categorize the types of questions that were generated as either lower or higher level thinking. Discuss why it is important to generate higher level questions while reading.

## APPLYING THE REQUEST STRATEGY: FOURTH-GRADE LESSON ON ABRAHAM LINCOLN

The fourth grade is completing a unit on Abraham Lincoln. The teacher uses the SMART Board to connect to the American Memory website from the Library of Congress (2009). The teacher uses the print image of Presidents Washington and Lincoln to review students' knowledge about both figures. The teacher uses the digital image to explain the ReQuest process and directs students to do the following:

• "Work with your partner to generate questions based on the print. Remember to create questions that represent higher level thinking, such as, 'What is the message of this image?'"

• When dyads have generated their questions, they take turns trying to "stump" the teacher with them. The teacher then reverses roles and models higher level thinking by asking students questions that require elaborate answers. All questions are recorded on the SMART Board.

- After both sides have taken turns posing questions, the teacher displays Figure 35.1 and asks students to categorize their questions as either higher level or lower level.

When students have completed the activity, they discuss the importance of asking higher level questions while they read or during discussions in class.

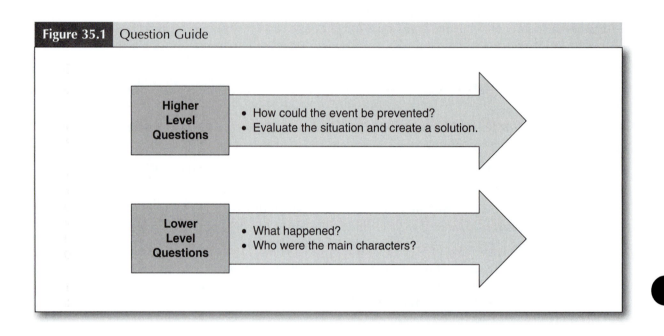

**Figure 35.1**   Question Guide

Higher Level Questions
- How could the event be prevented?
- Evaluate the situation and create a solution.

Lower Level Questions
- What happened?
- Who were the main characters?

*Source:* International Reading Association and National Council of Teachers of English (1996).

### IRA/NCTE Standards for the English Language Arts

10. Students whose first language is not English make use of their first language to develop competency in the English language arts and to develop understanding of content across the curriculum.

## DIFFERENTIATING INSTRUCTION FOR ENGLISH LANGUAGE LEARNERS

Digital text can be especially confusing for English language learners if they are not provided with support. One modification of this strategy for second-language learners is to use the "translate" icon on Google so that they can understand some of the online content in their native language. This modification will not work if students are unable to read in their first language. If that is the case, teachers may use other bilingual students who are more proficient in English to translate the main concepts of the digital text as a support. Once students are more knowledgeable about the content of the digital text, they can work with a native speaker on the ReQuest process.

## DIFFERENTIATING INSTRUCTION FOR STUDENTS WITH SPECIAL NEEDS

Research confirms that students with special needs often need more than an explicit model of questioning (Walker, 2005). One way to adapt ReQuest for students with special needs is to provide them with a graphic organizer that gives examples of higher/lower level questions (see Figure 35.1). Students with special needs use the sheet to write their own versions of the sample questions as they work with their partners. Collaboratively with their partners, they use hyperlinks and search engines to answer any questions that are not readily answered from the bookmarked website.

## REFERENCES

Duke, N., & Pearson, P. D. (2002). Effective practices for developing reading comprehension. In A. E. Farstup & S. J. Samuels (Eds.), *What research has to say about reading instruction* (pp. 205–242). Newark, DE: International Reading Association.

International Reading Association and National Council of Teachers of English. (1996). *Standards for the English language arts*. Newark, DE: International Reading Association and Urbana, IL: National Council of Teachers of English.

Manzo, A. V., Manzo, V. C., & Estes, T. H. (2004). *Content-area literacy: Interactive teaching for active learning* (3rd ed.). New York: Wiley.

Pressley, M., & McDonald, R. (2006). The need for increased comprehension instruction. In M. Pressley (Ed.), *Reading instruction that works: The case for balanced instruction* (3rd ed., pp. 293–347). New York: Guilford.

U.S. Library of Congress. (2009). "Washington and Lincoln: The father and the saviour of our country." *American Memory*. Retrieved January 31, 2010, from http://memory.loc.gov/cgi-bin/ampage?collId=lprbscsm &fileName=scsm0405/lprbscsmscsm0405.b&rec Num=0&itemLink=r?ammem/scsmbib:@field (DOCID +@lit(scsm 000405))

Walker, B. (2005). Thinking aloud: Struggling readers often require more than a model. *The Reading Teacher, 58*, 688–693.

# SECTION VIII

# Essential Strategies for Teaching Discussion for Understanding

## A Brief Overview of Discussion for Understanding

The purpose of Section VIII is to provide teachers with instructional strategies that use discussion as the central tool for student understanding and learning. We have included discussion as a separate section because of its value in promoting higher level thinking and acquiring academic language. Theories and research have supported the role of classroom talk in cognitive and literacy development. Using Vygotsky's (1978) perspective, literacy learning occurs from *socially meaningful activities* that are mediated through language. Teachers who support social constructivism believe that literacy is learned and developed in classroom environments where authentic dialogue is supported and encouraged. Such authentic dialogue is quite different from teacher-led discussions where they pose the questions and students work to provide the expected responses. Authentic dialogue is promoted through student-led discussions when teachers create strategies that are designed with language working as the medium through which learning takes place (Wells & Chang-Wells, 1992).

For all students, especially young children, the teacher needs to be concerned about language development. The dialogic episodes that occur around good literature before, during, and after reading ensure language learning as well as construction of knowledge. Clearly, the nature of language use by teachers and children determines the quality of student learning. Wolf, Crosson, and Resnick (2006) studied classroom talk in elementary and middle school classrooms. Their results indicate that high student participation in classroom discussion results in academic rigor. Such academic rigor relates to (1) participation, (2) teachers and students linking ideas, (3) asking for and providing knowledge, and (4) asking for and providing critical thinking. Clearly, their research demonstrates that the teachers are responsible for rigorous student learning through making students accountable for classroom talk.

When children are not experienced in peer-led discussions, teachers need to provide a framework through modeling and demonstrations, offer instructional strategies where discussion is central to the activity, and guide students' participation and responses to ensure such academic rigor. Modeling high-quality book conversations or discussions does not occur without teacher planning. To help students engage in effective literature discussions, McGee (1995) suggests the following: (1) Select a good piece of children's literature that is appropriate for the students and will stimulate lively book conversations. Prepare for the discussion by prereading the book and developing a few thought-provoking questions. (2) Establish guidelines for students for listening and reading during book discussions. Such guidelines should include appropriate behaviors while listening or reading the story as well as students' active participation in the discussion. (3) Provide an extension or follow-up activity for students after the book discussion.

Discussion groups led by students increase their enjoyment of reading literature (Long & Gove, 2003–2004). However, such discussions are typically focused on surface retellings of the text. To engage students in "grand conversations" where they make a range of connections with the text that lead to deep comprehension and the construction of knowledge, it is important that they learn to use the most effective strategies for understanding text. These include summarizing, analyzing the author's craft, posing questions, connecting to the text, and looking back (Clark & Byrne, 2006).

For English language learners, language-rich classrooms provide the opportunity for academic literacy development. Hill and Flynn (2006, p. 56) emphasize that small-group discussions led by peers are especially beneficial to English language learners because such classroom talk offers them (1) repetition of key words and phrases, (2) functional speech that is context relevant, (3) practice of academic vocabulary and book language, (4) rich feedback, and (5) reduced anxiety.

## GUIDELINES FOR TEACHING DISCUSSION FOR UNDERSTANDING

When teachers engage students in discussion of text, their major goal is to assist and guide them in comprehending the text and constructing knowledge within a social context (Blanton, Wood, & Taylor, 2010). Effective peer-led discussion groups that lead to student learning take time, practice, and teacher guidance toward successful learning outcomes. The following are guidelines for helping students engage in authentic classroom dialogue:

- Provide clear expectations to students regarding the discussion activity and the task.

- Model effective discussion strategies.

- Monitor students' discussions so they become accountable for their talk.

- Use research-based approaches that are appropriate for the grade and literacy development level of the students.

## A STRATEGY FOR ASSESSING DISCUSSION FOR UNDERSTANDING

Teachers who embrace a constructivist theory of learning use discussion as a critical teaching and learning tool. Students who benefit from small-group and classroom discussions are those who develop related performance behaviors that lead to meaning-ful discussions. Effective teachers monitor students' progress in the development of discussion skills; align their assessments to instruction; link instruction and assessment to accountability standards, such as the English language arts standards developed by the International Reading Association and National Council of Teachers of English (1996) and the state standards; and use assessment results to inform their instruction (Reutzel & Cooter, 2005). One of the tools that teachers may use for monitoring students' progress in developing discussion skills is a rubric provided in Figure VIII.1.

| **Figure VIII.1** Rubric for Assessing Students' Performances During Discussion | | | |
|---|---|---|---|
| **Performance Criterion** | **Developing (1–0 Points)** | **Proficient (2–3 Points)** | **Advanced (4–5 Points)** |
| **Participates** | Rarely participates in the discussion and does not move the discussion to initiate higher levels of thinking | Actively participates in the discussion sometimes and at times moves the discussion to initiate higher levels of thinking | Actively participates in the discussion at all times and frequently moves the discussion to initiate higher levels of thinking |
| **Listens** | Rarely demonstrates effective listening behaviors through appropriate responses and behaviors | Sometimes demonstrates effective listening behaviors through appropriate responses and behaviors | Always demonstrates effective listening behaviors through appropriate responses and behaviors |
| **Responds to questions** | Rarely makes responses to questions that are analytical and lead to meaningful discussions | At times makes responses to questions that are analytical and lead to meaningful discussions | Frequently makes responses to questions that are analytical and lead to meaningful discussions |
| **Poses questions** | Rarely asks insightful and appropriate questions related to the topic that result in critical thinking | Sometimes asks insightful and appropriate questions related to the topic that result in critical thinking | Frequently asks insightful and appropriate questions related to the topic that result in critical thinking |
| **OVERALL SCORES FOR PERFORMANCE LEVELS** Advanced: 4–0 points Proficient: 12–5 points Developing: 20–13 points | | | |

## A GUIDE FOR USING RESPONSE TO INTERVENTION FOR DISCUSSION FOR UNDERSTANDING

Students' engagement in meaningful discussions develops their understanding of the topic. Effective teachers work to improve students' discussion skills and evaluate their develop-ment. Third-grade students with special needs were discussing a story that they had com-pleted during a shared read-aloud session. During the discussion, the teacher used the "Assessing Students' Performances During Discussion" rubric shown in Figure VIII.1 to guide her evaluation of each student's engagement in the conversation around the story. Her observations revealed that this small group of students responded with brief phrases and even one-word responses. Using the assessment results, the teacher targeted the students for an intervention and selected a strategy to develop and expand their responses during a discussion of the story. The teacher used Dialogic Reading for the purpose of engaging the students in a discussion and facilitating their efforts to expand their responses to teacher-posed questions.

## PROFESSIONAL RESOURCES

Adler, M., & Rougle, E. (2005). *Building literacy through classroom discussion: Research-based strategies for developing critical readers and thoughtful writers in middle school.* New York: Scholastic.

Spiegel, D. L. (2005). *Classroom discussion: Strategies for engaging all students, building higher level thinking skills, and strengthening reading and writing across the curriculum.* New York: Scholastic.

## REFERENCES

Blanton, W. E., Wood, K. D., & Taylor, D. B. (2010). Rethinking middle school reading instruction: A basic activity. In M. Cappello & B. Moss (Eds.), *Contemporary readings in literacy education* (pp. 213–222). Thousand Oaks, CA: Sage.

Clark, K. F., & Byrne, J. (2006). *Sentence starters.* Paper presented at the International Reading Association annual convention, Chicago.

Hill, J. D., & Flynn, K. M. (2006). *Classroom instruction that works with English language learners.* Alexandria, VA: Association for Supervision and Curriculum Development.

International Reading Association and National Council of Teachers of English. (1996). *Standards for the English language arts.* Newark, DE: International Reading Association and Urbana, IL: National Council of Teachers of English.

Long, T. W., & Gove, M. K. (2003–2004). How engagement strategies and literature circles promote critical response in a fourth-grade, urban classroom. *The Reading Teacher, 57,* 350–361.

McGee, L. M. (1995). Talking about books with young children. In N. L. Roser & M. G. Martinez (Eds.), *Book talk and beyond: Children and teachers respond to literature* (pp. 105–115). Newark, DE: International Reading Association.

Reutzel, D. R., & Cooter, R. B. (2005). *The essentials of teaching children to read: What every teacher needs to know.* Upper Saddle River, NJ: Merrill Prentice Hall.

Wells, G., & Chang-Wells, G. L. (1992). *Constructing knowledge together: Classrooms as centers of inquiry and literacy.* Portsmouth, NH: Heinemann.

Wolf, M. K., Crosson, A. C., & Resnick, L. B. (2006). *Accountable talk in reading comprehension and instruction* (Center for the Study of Evaluation Technical Report 670). Los Angeles: National Center for Research on Evaluation, Standards, and Student Testing.

Vygotsky, L. S. (1978). *Mind in society.* Cambridge, MA: Harvard University Press.

# Strategy

# Anticipation Guides

# 36

---

The *Anticipation Guide* strategy is an effective instructional technique that assists students in surveying the text, activating prior knowledge, making predictions about the text, analyzing their understandings of ideas and beliefs, setting a purpose for reading, and confronting and clarifying their misconceptions of concepts and beliefs (Gunning, 2008). Discussion is central to this instructional strategy and promises to facilitate students' active participation in their learning. Students' discussion is motivated and deepened through their response to the debatable statements.

The Anticipation Guide includes a set of statements that relates to the readings with the purpose of promoting student discussion as they respond to the statements. As students talk through each statement, they agree or disagree based on their point of view and their knowledge of the underlying ideas. Readence, Bean, and Baldwin (2004) suggest that meaningful discussions that result in learning are achieved in small groups or cooperative learning pairs. Students' collaborative discussion of each of the statements activates their prior knowledge and establishes a purpose for reading the text. Anticipation Guides may be used with informational books as well as fictional stories. As students read the text, they check their knowledge and beliefs. Post-reading discussions result in students confirming and developing their conceptual knowledge or identifying erroneous information and misconceptions. One extension of the Anticipation Guide suggested by Head and Readence (1986) includes students finding evidence from the text to confirm their initial stance. Duffelmeyer and Baum (1992) further suggest that students find the text that offers a confirmation or fails to validate their beliefs, summarize it, and then record it on their graphic. One important role that the teacher plays in facilitating student learning is monitoring their use of Anticipation Guides. Students need to know that they may disagree with the text or with their peers. However, it is important for teachers to help them confront their own misconceptions to further their learning.

An important aspect of the strategy is the statement to which students respond to engage in discussion and learn from text. Tompkins (2004) suggests that the statements should be "general enough to stimulate discussion and useful for clarifying misconceptions" (p. 410). Duffelmeyer (1994) emphasizes that "anticipation guides are only as effective as the statements composing them" (p. 52) and offers the following attributes of statements that lead to learning from text: "(1) Effective statements convey a sense of the major ideas students will encounter; (2) effective statements activate and draw upon students' prior experience; (3) effective statements are general rather than specific; and (4) effective statements challenge students' beliefs" (pp. 455–456).

*Source:* International Reading Association and National Council of Teachers of English (1996).

---

### IRA/NCTE Standards for English Language Arts

1. Students apply a wide range of strategies to comprehend, interpret, evaluate, and appreciate texts. They draw on their prior experience, their interactions with other readers and writers, their knowledge of word meaning and of other texts, their word identification strategies, and their understanding of textual features (e.g., sound-letter correspondence, sentence structure, context, graphics).

2. Students adjust their use of spoken, written, and visual language (e.g., conventions, style, vocabulary) to communicate effectively with a variety of audiences and for different purposes.

11. Students participate as knowledgeable, reflective, creative, and critical members of a variety of literacy communities.

12. Students use spoken, written, and visual language to accomplish their own purposes (e.g., for learning, enjoyment, persuasion, and the exchange of information).

---

## USING ANTICIPATION GUIDES

*When to use the strategy:* The Anticipation Guide is used before reading to activate prior knowledge and to set purposes for reading (Tierney & Readence, 2005). During and after reading, students engage in finding evidence from text to develop their conceptual knowledge or confront their misconceptions.

*Strategy modifications for grade levels:* Anticipation Guides may be used at all grade levels. Teachers in the primary grades work with students using modeling techniques and guided group discussions. For younger children, teachers begin by using one or two statements.

### IMPLEMENTING THE ANTICIPATION GUIDE STRATEGY: STEP BY STEP

1. **Identify the major concepts to be learned.** Prepare by carefully reading the text to identify the major concepts or themes from the reading. Select the central concepts from the readings to be learned.

2. **Consider the students' backgrounds.** Effective planning takes into account the students' background knowledge, their literacy and age levels, their attitudes toward reading and learning, and their experiences and cultural backgrounds to determine the target concepts. Use the students' backgrounds to create the statements, determine the number to use, and decide on the level of scaffolding and assistance that students need.

3. **Write the statements.** Using the selected concepts to be learned and students' backgrounds, write an appropriate number of statements for the guide. Statements

should be open-ended, comprehensible, motivating, and relevant to the students. To promote student learning, each statement should include the central concepts to be learned; to foster lively discussions, statements should be motivating and meaningful.

4. **Create a graphic organizer.** The graphic should include the statements and a response option. For example, depending on the nature of the response and readings, create a response option from one of the following: (1) a "true" or "false" option; (2) a "yes," "no," or "maybe" option; (3) an "agree" or "disagree" option; or (4) a rating scale showing the level of agreement or disagreement. Figure 36.1 shows a sample graphic for an Anticipation Guide.

5. **Arrange students in small groups.** Separate students into small collaborative groups of three to five or into learning pairs. Small groupings will foster discussion and encourage participation from all students.

6. **Present students with the Anticipation Guide.** Before reading the text, direct students to respond to each statement and choose an option on the graphic organizer. After each statement, students within their groups discuss their responses and agree or disagree with their group's response. Encourage students to discuss their reason for choosing their response.

7. **Engage students in a class discussion before reading.** Have students from various groups share their responses and reasons for selecting the options with the class.

8. **Direct students to read the text or listen to the reading.** Help students establish a purpose for their reading by reading to find evidence for their choices on the debatable statements.

9. **After reading, direct students to return to their Anticipation Guide to check their responses.** Students revisit the statements and respond once again, using evidence from their readings. They find support from the text, summarize the evidence, and record it on their Anticipation Guides.

10. **Engage students in a post-reading discussion.** Students visit their small groups and discuss each statement. They compare the support from the text for their responses. The teacher conducts a final large-group discussion where students contribute evidence found in the text to support their responses. The teacher takes this opportunity to correct misconceptions or misinterpretations of the text.

## APPLYING THE ANTICIPATION GUIDE STRATEGY: FOURTH-GRADE LESSON

Fourth-graders are reading the Newbery Honor Award book *The Family Under the Bridge* by Natalie Savage Carlson (1958). The story is about an old man, Armand, who lives under the bridge in Paris. When a young woman with her three children tries to seek shelter, Armand first ignores them but later finds himself caring for the family by sharing his home under the bridge with them. To engage the students in their reading, the teacher begins a discussion on people who live on the street and how we should respond to them. Using the Anticipation Guide as shown in Figure 36.2, the teacher presents three statements to the students that will help them explore their own beliefs about poverty and homelessness prior to reading. After reading the story, they will revisit the statements and find evidence for validating or changing their beliefs.

**Figure 36.1** Anticipation Guide

| Before Reading | | Statement | After Reading | | Support From Text |
|---|---|---|---|---|---|
| Agree | Disagree | | Agree | Disagree | |
| | | 1. | | | |
| | | 2. | | | |
| | | 3. | | | |
| | | 4. | | | |
| | | 5. | | | |

**Figure 36.2** Anticipation Guide for Reading *The Family Under the Bridge*

| Before Reading | | Statement | After Reading | | Support From Text |
|---|---|---|---|---|---|
| Agree | Disagree | | Agree | Disagree | |
| | | 1. Most people live on the streets because they do not wish to work. | | | |
| | | 2. Totally ignore anyone on the street who is in need. | | | |
| | | 3. Most people who live on the street are not honest and would steal from you. | | | |

*Source:* International Reading Association and National Council of Teachers of English (1996).

### IRA/NCTE Standards for English Language Arts

10. Students whose first language is not English make use of their first language to develop competency in the English language arts and to develop understanding of content across the curriculum.

## DIFFERENTIATING INSTRUCTION FOR ENGLISH LANGUAGE LEARNERS

Anticipation Guides offer English language learners ways to improve comprehension through discussions and at the same time develop oral English proficiency. Goldenberg (2010) cites evidence from research on how teachers need to modify their instructional approaches to benefit English language learners' comprehension and language proficiency. First, provide scaffolds for the task of completing an Anticipation Guide by breaking down the process into small steps. Understand students' English language limitations and respond appropriately. For example, students may use nonverbal gestures and sometimes one or two words. Teachers may restate their response by elaborating on it, speaking slowly and clearly.

## DIFFERENTIATING INSTRUCTION FOR STUDENTS WITH SPECIAL NEEDS

An important aspect of using Anticipation Guides with students with special needs is assisting them in formulating a response to the statements. Students with special needs often need support in understanding the statements. Modify the guide by simplifying the statements on the Anticipation Guide, ensuring that they are understandable for the students before they begin to establish an opinion. Another way to modify the Anticipation Guide for students with special needs is to help them make a connection to each statement. In other words, "What does the statement mean to the student?" Engage students in a brief discussion of each statement to ensure their comprehension and help them make personal connections to the statement.

## REFERENCES

Duffelmeyer, F. A. (1994). Effective anticipation guide statements for learning from expository prose. *Journal of Reading, 37*(6), 452–457.

Duffelmeyer, F. A., & Baum, D. D. (1992). The extended anticipation guide revisited. *Journal of Reading, 35*(8) 654–656.

Goldenberg, C. (2010). Teaching English language learners: What the research does—and does not—say. In M. Cappello & B. Moss (Eds.), *Contemporary readings in literacy education* (pp. 271–295). Thousand Oaks, CA: Sage.

Gunning, T. G. (2008). *Creating literacy: Instruction for all students* (6th ed.). Boston: Allyn & Bacon.

Head, M. H., & Readence, J. E. (1986). Anticipation guides: Meaning through prediction. In E. K. Dishner, T. W. Bean, J. E. Readence, & D. W. Moore (Eds.),

*Reading in the content area* (2nd ed., pp. 229–234). Dubuque, IA: Kendall/Hunt.

International Reading Association and National Council of Teachers of English. (1996). *Standards for the English language arts.* Newark, DE: International Reading Association and Urbana, IL: National Council of Teachers of English.

Readence, J. E., Bean, T. W., & Baldwin, R. S. (2004). *Content area literacy: An integrated approach.* Dubuque, IA: Kendall/Hunt.

Tierney, R. J., & Readence, J. E. (2005). *Reading strategies and practices: A compendium* (6th ed.). Boston: Allyn & Bacon.

Tompkins, G. (2004). *50 literacy strategies: Step by step* (2nd ed.). Upper Saddle River, NJ: Merrill Prentice Hall.

## CHILDREN'S LITERATURE CITED

Carlson, N. S. (1958). *The family under the bridge.* New York: Harper Trophy.

# Strategy 37

# Dialogic Reading

## SPEAKING BRIEFLY: AN OVERVIEW OF THE LITERACY STRATEGY

The *Dialogic Reading* strategy offers children an opportunity to play an active role in reading picture storybooks. Children's participation and role in Dialogic Readings are dramatically different than in read-alouds (Biemiller, 2006). In the traditional story reading, the teacher reads and the child listens. In Dialogic Reading, the children are engaged as storytellers and the adult listens to them, asks questions, offers prompts, scaffolds children's answers, and encourages them to elaborate on their responses. The research-based strategy of Dialogic Reading is found in "the theory that practice in using language, feedback regarding language, and appropriately scaffolded adult-child interactions in the context of picture book reading all facilitate young children's language development" (Zevenbergen & Whitehurst, 2003, p. 171). Briefly, Dialogic Reading involves multiple readings and teacher-child conversations about the book, where children become dynamic players as they answer and respond to the strategic questions posed by the teachers (Doyle & Bramwell, 2006).

Research by Whitehurst and colleagues (1994, 1999) has shown the positive effects on young children's language development when they were active participants in the reading experience. Further, studies of Dialogic Reading showed positive effects on increasing content-area vocabulary of elementary students (Blachowicz & Obrochta, 2005). Numerous other studies have found beneficial effects of Dialogic Reading on the development of oral language and literacy skills for all young children, especially for young, at-risk children and those from diverse backgrounds.

The techniques for the Dialogic Reading strategy engage children in the reading experience through guided discussion of the story (Zevenbergen &Whitehurst, 2003). The procedure employs questions and statements from the teacher that are framed around specific prompts. Additionally, the teacher evaluates students' responses, requests that they expand a response for greater sophistication of language, and repeat a verbalization. Additionally, there is a rereading of the storybook so that children become the "storytellers" through their responses and interactive participation.

*Source:* International Reading Association and National Council of Teachers of English (1996).

## IRA/NCTE Standards for English Language Arts

4. Students adjust their use of spoken, written, and visual language (e.g., conventions, style, vocabulary) to communicate effectively with a variety of audiences and for different purposes.

11. Students participate as knowledgeable, reflective, creative, and critical members of a variety of literacy communities.

12. Students use spoken, written, and visual language to accomplish their own purposes (e.g., for learning, enjoyment, persuasion, and the exchange of information).

# USING DIALOGIC READING

*When to use the strategy:* To develop children's language, the strategy is used before, during, and after reading. Prior to reading, talking about the story helps students make text connections that will assist them in comprehension as well as motivate them to listen to and read the story; during the reading, discussion clarifies parts of the story, develops vocabulary, and makes clear new information; and after reading, dialogic text talk will stretch the students' minds as they return to the story for further explanations and interpretations.

*Strategy modifications for grade levels:* Dialogic Reading has been introduced as a reading strategy or intervention for young children and has been used successfully in kindergarten through grade 2. It may be modified for elementary and middle school students by using it as an interactive read-aloud where the teacher guides students' responses through prompts and questions for developing vocabulary and content knowledge.

## IMPLEMENTING THE DIALOGIC READING STRATEGY: STEP BY STEP

An important aspect of this strategy is the appropriate selection of literature for the students' language and literacy development. Throughout the instructional sequence, the students take the lead and the teacher follows their responses with prompts, repeating their answers to questions and statements. Another critical element is evaluation of students' responses and teacher feedback. Teachers encourage and praise accurate responses and gently correct responses that are incorrect.

1. **Prepare for Dialogic Reading.** The teacher prepares by selecting an engaging piece of literature. The book should contain one of the best models of language, include illustrations to promote responses, and provide interest and relevance to the students. Through the prereading of the picture story, the teacher becomes familiar with the content for preparing the prompts—questions and statements—that ensure students' engagement in the discussion. A sample of the types of prompts may be found in Figure 37.1.

2. **Introduce the book to the students.** Motivate students to engage in a participatory story reading through a stimulating book introduction. Showing the cover, read

| Figure 37.1 | Prompts for Dialogic Reading* |
|---|---|

**Guiding the Story Discussion Through Questions and Statements**

| Type of Prompt | Definition | Application to Story |
|---|---|---|
| **Completion prompt** | A prompt or question requiring filling in the blank or completing the sentence | |
| **Recall prompt** | A question that asks students to recall a detail or fact from the story | |
| **Open-ended prompt** | A statement that prompts a response about a specific part of the story | |
| **Wh- prompt** | Prompts that are *what, where,* and *why* questions | |
| **Distancing prompt** | Prompts that require students to go beyond or "outside" the story by making connections | |
| **Naming and talking prompt** | Prompts that encourage the students to name and talk about objects in the book | |
| **Evaluate** | Statements that evaluate a student's response by validating it when it is correct or correcting it when it is inaccurate | |
| **Expand** | Prompts that ask students to expand on a response by providing more information | |
| **Repeat** | Statements that require the students to repeat the teacher's response or another student's | |

*The descriptions of prompts are based on Zevenbergen and Whitehurst (2003).*

the title and the author of the book; then read one or two pages, showing the illustrations. Ask students to respond to the title and cover illustrations: "What do you think this story will be about?"

3. **Continue to read the story.** As each page is read, show the story illustrations to the students. Prompt students with an appropriate question or statement that will encourage discussion. For the first reading, the objective is to increase children's vocabulary, expanding their conceptual knowledge. Use prompts that apply to the first reading of the story with questions based on pictures as well as the text.

4. **Continue through the story until the book is finished.** During the reading of the story, encourage students' participation with prompts that help them focus on specific objects and ideas that represent new and interesting words to build and develop students' vocabulary. Teachers may include prompts that encourage

students to label and describe objects in pictures by asking them *what* questions. For example, "What is that in the picture? Can you name it?" In other words, questions or prompts are designed to help students understand the meanings of the words that will further their understanding of the story.

5. **Reread the book multiple times.** Revisit the book several times. As students participate in additional rereadings of the story, they will respond to prompts that deepen their understanding of the story. Prompts now focus on the story elements, including the characters, story events, the problem, and the story solution. The teacher guides students through the story conversation with questions that develop the students' understanding of the story.

6. **Focus final readings on students as active storytellers.** The goal of Dialogic Reading is to develop vocabulary and language through students' participation in reading. In the final readings of the picture story, the students' participation is heightened through becoming the storyteller. They have appropriated the language of the book and use it to retell the story and offer personal responses to it.

## APPLYING THE DIALOGIC READING STRATEGY: KINDERGARTEN LESSON ON BEARS

Students in kindergarten are studying about different types of bears, including the polar bear. They begin the study of the polar bear through their engagement in a Dialogic Reading of *Ice Bear: In the Steps of the Polar Bear* by Nicola Davies (2005). The teacher has selected this piece of literature because of the content—which was carefully researched by Nicola Davies, a zoologist and award-winning author of children's books—as well as the illustrations, which deliver the information with accuracy. The first reading of the book includes prompts for the purpose of developing students' vocabulary. During this first reading, the teacher and students discuss words such as *camouflage, cubs, Inuit, skin, toe pads,* and *Nanuk.* There are additional rereadings of the story, helping students focus on various aspects of the book. Throughout the readings, the teacher uses prompts, similar to the samples shown in Figure 37.2, to engage students in the readings.

| Figure 37.2 | Sample Prompts for Dialogic Reading of *Ice Bear: In the Steps of the Polar Bear* by Nicola Davies |
| --- | --- |

| PROMPTS FOR DIALOGIC READING* | | |
| --- | --- | --- |
| Sample Prompts for Kindergarten Children for *Ice Bear: In the Steps of the Polar Bear* by Nicola Davies | | |
| **Type of Prompt** | **Definition** | **Application to Story** |
| **Completion prompt** | A prompt or question requiring filling in the blank or completing the sentence | *The people of the Arctic are Inuit, and they called the polar bear____.* |
| **Recall prompt** | A question that asks students to recall a detail or fact from the story | *What were some ways that the polar bear used to keep warm?* |
| **Open-ended prompt** | A statement that prompts a response about a specific part of the story | *What are some ways that we can help the polar bear survive?* |

| Wh- prompt | Prompts that are *what, where,* and *why* questions | *Where do polar bears live? What do polar bears eat? Why do polar bears have webbed feet?* |
|---|---|---|
| Distancing prompt | Prompts that require students to go beyond or "outside" the story by making connections | *Do you think the polar bear is different from the black bear? Are they the same in any way?* |
| Naming and talking prompt | Prompts that encourage the students to name and talk about objects in the book | *Find the mother polar bear and the cubs in the snow den. Tell how she takes care of them and teaches them. How big are the cubs when they are born?* |
| Evaluate | Statements that evaluate a student's response by validating it when it is correct or correcting it when it is inaccurate | *You said that the polar bear moves fast. That is right! The author tells us that polar bears can run as fast as a snowmobile.* |
| Expand | Prompts that ask students to expand on a response by providing more information | *Can you tell more ways that we can help save the polar bears?* |
| Repeat | Statements that require the students to repeat the teacher's response or another student's | *Yes, Stephen said why global warming is dangerous. Tell us again. Polar bears need sea ice to live and global warming melts it.* |

*\*The descriptions of prompts are based on Zevenbergen and Whitehurst (2003).*

---

### IRA/NCTE Standards for English Language Arts

10. Students whose first language is not English make use of their first language to develop competency in the English language arts and to develop understanding of content across the curriculum.

*Source:* International Reading Association and National Council of Teachers of English (1996).

## DIFFERENTIATING INSTRUCTION FOR ENGLISH LANGUAGE LEARNERS

English language learners benefit from story conversations when the group is small and the dialogue includes gentle feedback and encouragement. Research suggests that Dialogic Reading conducted in a family setting yields positive benefits for children as well as parents (Jimenez, Filippini, & Gerber, 2006). They found that when Dialogic Reading occurs in Latino homes, there is an increased occurrence of home language. Further, parents develop their own comprehension skills while engaging in book conversations with their children. Children also have an opportunity for increasing their comprehension strategies, furthering their vocabulary, and developing a positive attitude toward books. Thus, literacy coaches should consider implementing a training program for parents in using dialogic strategies.

## DIFFERENTIATING INSTRUCTION FOR STUDENTS WITH SPECIAL NEEDS

Greater rewards from the Dialogic Reading strategy are offered to students with special needs when the strategy is used as an intervention for language and literacy skill development. During the intervention, the student works with the literacy coach or reading specialist on an individual basis. The selection of the picture story, the framing of the prompts, and the feedback to the student's answers become highly individualized. Thus, the teacher focuses on the specific language and literacy skills that the student needs.

## REFERENCES

Blachowicz, C. Z., & Obrochta, C. (2005). Vocabulary visits: Virtual field trips for content vocabulary development. *The Reading Teacher, 59*(3), 262–268.

Biemiller, A. (2006). Vocabulary development and instruction: A prerequisite for school learning. In D. K. Dickinson & S. B. Neuman (Eds.), *Handbook of early literacy research* (Vol. II, pp. 41–51). New York: Guilford.

Doyle, B., & Bramwell, W. (2006). Promoting emergent literacy and social-emotional learning through dialogic reading. *The Reading Teacher, 59*(6), 554–564.

International Reading Association and National Council of Teachers of English. (1996). *Standards for the English language arts.* Newark, DE: International Reading Association and Urbana, IL: National Council of Teachers of English.

Jimenez, T. C., Filippini, A. L., & Gerber, M. (2006). Shared reading with Latino families: An analysis of reading interactions and language use. *Bilingual Research Journal, 30*(22), 431–452.

Whitehurst, G. J., Epstein, J. N., Angell, A. L., Payne, A. C., Crone, D. A., & Fischel, J. E. (1994). Outcomes of an emergent literacy intervention program in Head Start. *Journal of Educational Psychology, 86,* 542–555.

Whitehurst, G. J., Zevenberg, A. A., Crone, D. A., Schultz, M. D., Velting, O. N., & Fischel, J. E. (1999). Outcomes of an emergent literacy intervention program in Head Start through second grade. *Journal of Educational Psychology, 91,* 261–272.

Zevenbergen, A. A., & Whitehurst, G. J. (2003). Dialogic reading: A shared picture book reading intervention for preschoolers. In A. van Kleeck, S. A. Stahl, & E. B. Bauer (Eds.), *On reading books to children: Parents and teachers* (pp. 171–202). Mahwah, NJ: Erlbaum.

## CHILDREN'S LITERATURE CITED

Davies, N. (2005). *Ice bear: In the steps of the polar bear.* Cambridge, MA: Candlewick.

# Strategy 38

# Discussion Web

---

The purpose of the *Discussion Web* strategy (Alvermann, 1991) is to engage students in peer-led, small-group conversations where they have an opportunity to explore issues and ideas through text talk. The Discussion Web strategy is central to helping students comprehend text at deeper levels. As students listen to other ideas and examine their own points of view, they are led to a critical analysis of the issues that are at the heart of their discussion.

The graphic organizer that is used with this strategy is a tool that helps students visualize the essential elements of the issue and identify similar and opposing points of view. Students use the graphic to structure their discussions as they record the issue, their own ideas, and their partner's, as well as draw conclusions. While the graphic serves as an organizer of ideas, it is discussion that is at the heart of learning; student talk is the medium for articulating thoughts, critically analyzing the sides of an issue, summarizing and drawing conclusions, and restructuring one's knowledge. Wells (2001) explains that dialogic inquiry serves to mediate knowledge. Dialogic inquiry is typically not achieved through large-group discussions; rather, dialogism occurs through face-to-face conversations between students asking authentic questions and seeking honest answers.

The Discussion Web strategy may be used with fiction or nonfiction literature and with any text that poses issues that may have different points of view. Alvermann (1991) has provided a five-step procedure that includes the following: (1) preparing students for reading the text, (2) discussing a central question, (3) regrouping for analyzing different points of view, (4) reaching consensus, and (5) sharing with the class. Although the procedure includes independent reading, discussing, and recording of ideas, steps may be modified for the primary grades by the teacher providing scaffolding and more guidance to the children.

*Source:* International Reading Association and National Council of Teachers of English (1996).

### IRA/NCTE Standards for English Language Arts

11. Students participate as knowledgeable, reflective, creative, and critical members of a variety of literacy communities.

12. Students use spoken, written, and visual language to accomplish their own purposes (e.g., for learning, enjoyment, persuasion, and the exchange of information).

# USING DISCUSSION WEBS

*When to use the strategy:* This strategy may be used as part of guided reading, literature circles, independent reading, or read-alouds, as well as for teaching literacy across the curriculum. One of the most effective uses of the Discussion Web strategy occurs when the teacher prepares students for reading the text and uses the strategy as a means to develop their critical thinking and deepen comprehension around central ideas within the text.

*Strategy modifications for grade levels:* Students at all grade levels will benefit from engaging in discussion with their peers by listening to their views on an issue and expressing their own ideas about an issue from their readings. The strategy may be modified for younger children who will be more dependent on the teacher's guidance during this process. Students in the middle grades may use this strategy when engaged in collaborative research on controversial issues or engaged in lively discussions during literature circles.

## IMPLEMENTING THE DISCUSSION WEB STRATEGY: STEP BY STEP

The Discussion Web strategy includes five essential elements that are used to guide students throughout their reading and discussion of issues from the text.

1. **Guide students in their reading of the text.** Select a piece of literature that poses a question resulting in the readers having different opinions. Prepare the students for reading by doing the following: (1) Lead a prereading discussion that helps students activate their prior knowledge required for understanding the text, (2) teach core vocabulary that students need to know for comprehending the text, (3) engage students in making predictions about the text, and (4) involve students in making personal and content connections to the readings.

2. **Pair students for discussion.** Select appropriate partners for each student for discussing the story, resulting in small groups of two. Distribute copies of the Discussion Web graphic prepared with the question to be discussed. Teach students how to use the Discussion Web, explaining how it will help them talk about the text. Further, explain that they will answer "yes" or "no" to the question, emphasizing that each partner should consider the pros as well as the cons. For each "yes" or "no" decision, students think of a reason and record it on the graphic in the appropriate box.

3. **Regroup students for further discussion to achieve consensus.** When students have responded to the discussion question, the teacher then regroups the students by putting two small groups together. The four students work together to reach consensus on the discussion question. The teacher clarifies the goal for each group— that is, to reach a group conclusion by reading or listening to all the answers and reasons for their decision, then finding the best one from the group. The teacher emphasizes that it is acceptable to disagree with the group's final conclusion but that open-mindedness about different reasons is very important. When some students find it difficult to reach consensus, the teacher reminds them that they will have an opportunity to voice their opinions individually during the whole-class discussion.

4. **Engage students in a whole-class discussion.** After each group has arrived at a group conclusion, they select a spokesperson that will represent the group to the whole class. Each spokesperson is given 3 minutes to discuss the reasons that best support the group's decision and conclusion. Dissenting viewpoints may be voiced at the time of the whole-class sharing.

5. **Each student writes an individual conclusion.** Engage students in the follow-up activity of writing their own conclusions. Encourage them to think about their readings, small-group and large-group discussions including different viewpoints, and their own personal views to come to individual conclusions. Students record their individual conclusions on the graphic.

## APPLYING THE DISCUSSION WEB STRATEGY: SEVENTH-GRADE LESSON ON CULTURAL DIFFERENCES

Students in the seventh-grade social studies class are reading and learning about the concept of culture and how it differs in many countries. The teacher introduced some of the cultural traditions of India and engaged students in a discussion on how the culture differs from the one they practice in the United States. To further students' understanding of cultural differences, the teacher used *Homeless Bird* by Gloria Whelan (2000) as an assigned reading—a piece of literature that has received a number of national awards, including the National Book Award, an ALA Notable Book award, a School Library Journal Best Book, and the International Reading Association Notable Book for a Global Society.

While students were engaged in reading an attractively written piece of literature, they learned about the cultural traditions that are poles apart from their own—as when Koly, the main character, enters into an arranged marriage that she does not want but cannot resist. The teacher began the lesson by conducting a book introduction, providing students with insights into the cultural traditions of India and foreshadowing their readings. After students read the first chapter, they identified the major question. The teacher wrote the question on the board and directed students to record it on their Discussion Web graphic, as shown in Figure 38.1. Students worked in small groups to discuss the guiding question: *Should Koly run away and not get married?* They wrote three reasons for answering "yes" and three for answering "no." Each group then stated their reasons as the teacher recorded them on the whiteboard for use during the whole-class discussion. The teacher directed the students to write their own conclusions based on the readings and discussion.

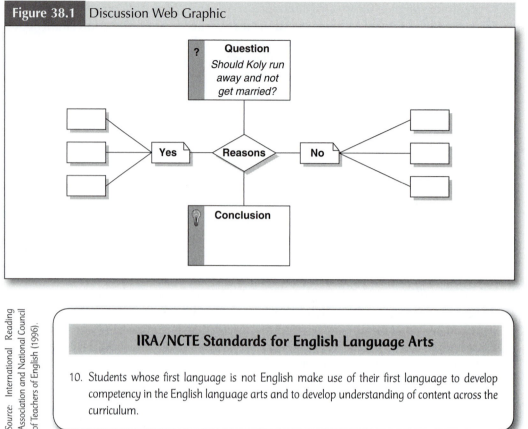

**Figure 38.1**   Discussion Web Graphic

*Source:* International Reading Association and National Council of Teachers of English (1996).

**IRA/NCTE Standards for English Language Arts**

10. Students whose first language is not English make use of their first language to develop competency in the English language arts and to develop understanding of content across the curriculum.

## DIFFERENTIATING INSTRUCTION FOR ENGLISH LANGUAGE LEARNERS

One of the major components of a framework for effective literacy instruction for English language learners is offering language-rich instruction. Oral language is essential to the Discussion Web strategy. Manyak (2007) emphasizes the importance of offering English language learners access to competent speakers and comprehensible input of the target language within a comfortable environment. Therefore, when designing groups for small-group discussion, the teacher needs to consider the needs of English language learners as well as the communication skills and attitudes of all group members. The teacher should monitor their discussion and provide thoughtful feedback and encouragement that will help develop their language use.

## DIFFERENTIATING INSTRUCTION FOR STUDENTS WITH SPECIAL NEEDS

For students who are experiencing severe reading difficulties, including listening and responding to others, provide a more structured and guided approach to discussion. The teacher may become part of the group and act as "discussion mover" by prompting students to take turns and encouraging students to respond to others in the group. Additionally, to make the procedure explicit to the students, a group Discussion Web graphic may be used with the teacher acting as scribe and recording students' reasons and conclusions. As students learn the process, they will become responsible for their own graphic.

## References

Alvermann, D. E. (1991). The discussion web: A graphic aid for learning across the curriculum. *The Reading Teacher, 45*(2), 92–98.

International Reading Association and National Council of Teachers of English. (1996). *Standards for the English language arts.* Newark, DE: International Reading Association and Urbana, IL: National Council of Teachers of English.

Manyak, P. C. (2007). A framework for robust literacy instruction for English learners. *The Reading Teacher, 6*(20), 197–199.

Wells, G. (2001). *Action, talk, and text: Learning and teaching through inquiry.* New York: Teachers College Press.

## Children's Literature Cited

Whelan, G. (2000). *Homeless bird.* New York: HarperCollins.

# Strategy

# 39

# Collaborative Language Charts

## SPEAKING BRIEFLY: AN OVERVIEW OF THE LITERACY STRATEGY

*Collaborative Language Charts* provide a record of children's literature and their discussions of the books. The strategy was developed for the purpose of promoting students' discussions of children's literature and displaying their responses to selected books on the chart (Roser & Hoffman, 1995). Collaborative book talks are at the heart of the strategy, while the public display of students' participation in collaborative literacy through the use of language charts is "testimony to the importance of the sharing and study of literature in the classroom" (p. 83).

Collaborative Language Charts began with a structured approach to students' reading of books selected for a specific unit. As teachers began to use the strategy, modifications to the approach based on students' literacy development, grade level, and curriculum were made. For example, one application of the strategy to a fifth-grade author study focused on the author's writing style. Third-grade students read different versions of *Cinderella* and used a literature chart to record the similarities and differences among the different versions of fairy tale (Antonacci & O'Callaghan, 2006). Other applications to using literature across the curriculum were made in middle-grade social studies and science classes.

In all the applications of the Collaborative Language Charts strategy, students read selected literature for a purpose, they engage in rich discussions that are guided by their purposes for reading as well as their own responses to the book, and the teacher and students record their discussion notes on the Collaborative Literature Chart. To serve as a guide for establishing student purposes for reading as well as for steering the discussion, essential questions are noted on the Collaborative Literature Chart as a reference for teachers and students during their readings and discussion. The benefits for using Collaborative Literature Charts are manifold: The strategy demonstrates to students the reading and writing connection; it serves as a reference to the literature that students read and discussed; it assists students in the discovery of themes and ideas occurring across literature; it serves as a record of book language, academic vocabulary, and conceptual knowledge warehoused in children's literature; and the collaborative use of language charts is a stimulus for personal and efferent responses to literature (Roser & Hoffman, 1995).

### IRA/NCTE Standards for English Language Arts

1. Students read a wide range of print and nonprint texts to build an understanding of texts, of themselves, and of the cultures of the United States and the world; to acquire new information; to respond to the needs and demands of society and the workplace; and for personal fulfillment. Among these texts are fiction and nonfiction, classic and contemporary works.

2. Students read a wide range of literature from many periods in many genres to build an understanding of the many dimensions (e.g., philosophical, ethical, aesthetic) of human experience.

11. Students participate as knowledgeable, reflective, creative, and critical members of a variety of literacy communities.

12. Students use spoken, written, and visual language to accomplish their own purposes (e.g., for learning, enjoyment, persuasion, and the exchange of information).

## USING COLLABORATIVE LANGUAGE CHARTS

*When to use the strategy:* After the reading, students engage in a discussion of the book. The teacher or the students record the students' responses on the chart. The discussion continues as the students compare their responses and answers with the questions about the books. Students are encouraged to continue the discussion by asking questions, offering personal responses, and adding ideas.

*Strategy modifications for grade levels:* The Collaborative Language Chart strategy may be used for all grade levels. Although an interactive approach is central to the strategy at all levels, in the primary grades, the teacher closely guides the discussion and serves as the scribe in recording students' responses. In the intermediate and middle grades, the teacher is more of a facilitator who assists students in focusing their discussion on the essential questions and themes.

### IMPLEMENTING THE COLLABORATIVE LANGUAGE CHART STRATEGY: STEP BY STEP

The format and design of Collaborative Language Charts are determined by their purpose. For example, when they are used across the curriculum and with nonfictional literature for the purpose of developing specific concepts and academic vocabulary in a content area, different kinds of questions and categories of information will be developed for students to discuss in comparison with the language chart used for fairy tales or author studies. Further, the focus of the charts also changes when used by students to record their responses to literature.

1. **Select appropriate children's literature based on the unit of study.** The teacher selects children's literature that fits into a theme, a unit of study, or a specific topic that is being studied in a content area or in the English language arts class. For example, students in the sixth grade are engaged in an author study of Patricia Reilly Giff. The teacher uses the following four books in which the main characters are experiencing

personal problems: *All the Way Home* (Giff, 2001), *Pictures of Hollis Woods* (Giff, 2002), *Lily's Crossing* (Giff, 1997), and *Willow Run* (Giff, 2005). Working in small groups, students collaborate to identify the elements of each of the stories and record them on the Collaborative Language Chart, as shown in Figure 39.1.

2. **Prepare the language chart with the children.** Using a matrix, write the titles of the books across the top of the chart. On the left side of the matrix in the vertical boxes, include important information, questions, and ideas about the book to be discussed. The language chart should be large enough so that it may be seen by all students. The teacher may leave some categories blank for student inquiries or to further develop the information after their readings.

3. **Prepare the students for reading by setting a purpose and introducing the books.** Using the categories and questions on the language chart, establish a purpose for reading; engage students in a brief book introduction for each selection, showing them how the readings are related to the theme or topic of study.

4. **Engage students in reading a selection.** Depending on the students' ages and reading levels, engage them in reading through a read-aloud, guided reading, literature circles, or independent reading. For younger children, books will be short and may be read in one sitting. Reading chapter books will take longer, and students may read in class or at home.

5. **Engage students in a book discussion.** After reading the book or a selection from a chapter book, engage students in a discussion. Guide the discussion by using the questions and categories on the language chart as well as the vocabulary, characters and their motivations or intentions, new ideas and concepts, the relation of the readings to the theme or topic of study, facts, and personal responses.

6. **Summarize the discussion and record ideas on the Collaborative Language Chart.** After the story is complete, the teacher and students work together to summarize the points that were discussed, which are then recorded on the language chart. The teacher acts as scribe for younger children in the early primary grades, and students in the intermediate and middle grades assume the responsibility for posting their responses on the chart.

## APPLYING THE COLLABORATIVE LANGUAGE CHART STRATEGY: THIRD-GRADE LESSON ON FAIRY TALES

Students in the third grade were learning about the elements that are common to fairy tales. The teacher used a study of the tales of Hans Christian Andersen. After students

| Figure 39.1 | Collaborative Language Chart for Author Study: Patricia Reilly Giff |
|---|---|

| LANGUAGE CHART FOR AN AUTHOR STUDY |
|---|
| *Patricia Reilly Giff* |

| Title | Author | Who Were the Main Characters? | Tell About Their Problems | What Did the Main Character Do to Solve the Problem? | How Did the Main Character Change? | What New Words Did You Learn From the Story? |
|---|---|---|---|---|---|---|
| *Pictures of Hollis Woods* | Patricia Reilly Giff | | | | | |

| Title | Author | Who Were the Main Characters? | Tell About Their Problems | What Did the Main Character Do to Solve the Problem? | How Did the Main Character Change? | What New Words Did You Learn From the Story? |
|---|---|---|---|---|---|---|
| *All the Way Home* | Patricia Reilly Giff | | | | | |
| *Lily's Crossing* | Patricia Reilly Giff | | | | | |
| *Willow Run* | Patricia Reilly Giff | | | | | |

listened to *The Little Match Girl,* adapted and illustrated by Jerry Pinkney (1999), they chose one of the following to read: *The Tinderbox,* retold by Stephen Mitchell (2008) and illustrated by Bagram Ibatoulline; *The Nightingale,* retold by Stephen Mitchell (2002) and illustrated by Bagram Ibatoulline; or *The Steadfast Tin Soldier,* retold by Tor Seidler (1997) and illustrated by Fred Marcellino. The Collaborative Language Chart strategy was used to identify and organize the elements of each tale. The students read their selected book, and the teacher engaged them in a lesson about the elements of a classic fairy tale. She then engaged students in a teacher-led discussion of *The Little Match Girl* that focused on identifying the elements of the fairy tale. As the students identified each element, they recorded it on their language charts. The teacher placed the students in small groups based on the tale they had chosen to read. Each group was directed to talk about the story, to identify the elements found in fairy tales, and to record them on their language charts. The teacher assisted each group in using the categories on the chart as a discussion point and in recording their responses. Using the groups' Collaborative Language Charts, a comparison of Hans Christian Andersen's fairy tales was made. The teacher directed each group to select a leader to share their language chart with the class and use the class chart to record each group's findings.

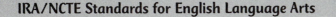

### IRA/NCTE Standards for English Language Arts

10. Students whose first language is not English make use of their first language to develop competency in the English language arts and to develop understanding of content across the curriculum.

*Source:* International Reading Association and National Council of Teachers of English (1996).

## DIFFERENTIATING INSTRUCTION FOR ENGLISH LANGUAGE LEARNERS

In the application for this strategy, students were studying Hans Christian Andersen's stories. The teacher selected a number of stories for students to compare and contrast.

An important aspect of differentiating instruction for English language learners is the selection of literature that they read to analyze and compare. English language learners will be able to make more connections to stories from their own culture, which will result in their learning and understanding about literature. Further, comparing the elements of four stories would be overwhelming for English language learners. To modify the strategy for them, the teacher should consider limiting the discussion to one story at a time and assisting them in identifying each element or category that is being discussed. The students would continue their study of literature, analyzing and comparing stories through discussion, one story at a time.

## DIFFERENTIATING INSTRUCTION FOR STUDENTS WITH SPECIAL NEEDS

Striving readers need additional instruction and scaffolds in using Collaborative Language Charts for understanding aspects of literature through small-group discussions. When teaching students to analyze literature, provide direct instruction and use modeling. Think-alouds work well when concepts and procedures are more complex. Discussion is the major focus of the strategy; therefore, provide scaffolds through guided questions and feedback. When introducing the strategy, select literature that is not complex and that is written at the students' reading levels.

## REFERENCES

Antonacci, P. A., & O'Callaghan, C. M. (2006). *A handbook for literacy instructional and assessment strategies, K–8*. Boston: Allyn & Bacon.

International Reading Association and National Council of Teachers of English. (1996). *Standards for the English language arts*. Newark, DE: International Reading Association and Urbana, IL: National Council of Teachers of English.

Roser, N. L., & Hoffman, J. V. (with Labbo, L. D., & Farest, C.). (1995). Language charts: A record of story time talk. In N. L. Roser & M. G. Martinez (Eds.), *Book talk and beyond: Children and teachers respond to literature* (pp. 80–89). Newark, DE: International Reading Association.

## CHILDREN'S LITERATURE CITED

Giff, P. R. (1997). *Lily's crossing*. New York: Dell Yearling.

Giff, P. R. (2001). *All the way home*. New York: Dell Yearling.

Giff, P. R. (2002). *Pictures of Hollis Woods*. New York: Dell Yearling.

Giff, P. R. (2005). *Willow run*. New York: Random House Children's Books.

Mitchell, S. (Adapted). (2002). *The nightingale*. B. Ibatoulline (Illus.). Somerville, MA: Candlewick.

Mitchell, S. (Adapted). (2008). *The tinderbox*. B. Ibatoulline (Illus.). London: Walker.

Pinkney, J. (Adapted). (1999).*The little match girl*. J. Pinkney (Illus.). New York: Dial.

Seidler, T. (Adapted). (1997). *The steadfast tin soldier*. F. Marcellino (Illus.). New York: HarperCollins.

# Save the Last Word for Me

# Strategy 40

## SPEAKING BRIEFLY: AN OVERVIEW OF THE LITERACY STRATEGY

*Save the Last Word for Me* provides students with the opportunity to interpret text within a collaborative context. Students select a sentence from the book they are reading, write it down, and provide a written response to their selected text. During the small-group discussion of the text, students listen as their classmates respond to their selected text. The student who selects the text for others to respond to is given the chance to have the last word by sharing his/her response with the group members (Short, Harste, & Burke, 1996).

The Save the Last Word for Me strategy promotes student responses and interpretations of readings through student-led discussions. Such book conversations facilitate students' understanding of text within a collaborative context as they explore and expand their initial responses to literature. Within small discussion groups, students are free to talk about their book and share their responses and interpretations of text with no "right" or "wrong" answers. These collaborative contexts for the construction of meaning have been called interpretive communities (Fish, 1980). Save the Last Word for Me is a strategy that is often used by teachers to help students think more deeply about the book they are reading (Short & Kauffman, 1995).

There are many advantages to using this strategy with students as they read. Buehl (2009, p. 152) explains that Save the Last Word for Me promotes a reflective stance to reading, more students are apt to participate in the discussions, the strategy provides the context for making personal connections to the text, and frequently, students may revise their interpretations and responses after listening to others. This strategy may be used with fiction as well as informational literature, and it is important that teachers monitor students' interpretations more closely when applying the strategy to informational texts that contain unfamiliar concepts and those that are especially difficult to understand.

*Source:* International Reading Association and National Council of Teachers of English (1996).

> ### IRA/NCTE Standards for English Language Arts
>
> 11. Students participate as knowledgeable, reflective, creative, and critical members of a variety of literacy communities.
>
> 12. Students use spoken, written, and visual language to accomplish their own purposes (e.g., for learning, enjoyment, persuasion, and the exchange of information).

## Using Save the Last Word for Me

*When to use the strategy:* Save the Last Word for Me is used during and after reading. As students read the book, they identify the text to which they wish to respond. After reading, they write a response, which is followed by a small-group discussion where responses are shared.

*Strategy modifications for grade levels:* The strategy may be used without modifications with elementary, intermediate, and middle school students. For primary-grade children in kindergarten and first grade not yet fluent in writing, the strategy may be modified so students dictate their responses to the teacher, who serves as a scribe. In this case, each student identifies a part of the text and reads it aloud and members of the group respond, saving the last word for the student who selected the text.

### Implementing the Save the Last Word for Me Strategy: Step by Step

1. **Select the literature.** Select a piece of literature that is appropriate for student-led discussions and creates a book introduction.

2. **Arrange students in small groups.** Place students in small groups of three or four, choosing students who work well together and who will engage in discussions.

3. **Distribute 3x5-inch cards to students.** Each student receives cards to write selected text and comments. Explain to students how they will use the cards while they read.

4. **Explain how to mark selected text and comment.** Explain to students that during the reading, they should identify sentences with a light pencil mark, such as a check, noting that they agree, disagree, or feel a strong response; after reading, they should write each sentence that they wish to respond to on one side of the card and write a comment on its reverse side. Model the process of identifying, selecting, and responding to text when students would benefit from that process.

5. **Conduct a book introduction and assign readings to students.** Present the assigned readings to students using a motivating book introduction. Assign the readings and have students read their text.

6. **After students complete their readings, guide them in responding to the text.** Provide students with time to write their selected text and comments on the cards.

7. **Group students for discussion.** Place students in small groups of three or four for the purposes of discussion.

8. **Begin the discussion.** Have students in each group select one member to begin the process. That group member begins by reading the selected text and calling for each group member to participate by commenting, explaining, agreeing, or disagreeing with the text that was read. Encourage all group members to comment on the text.

9. **Save the last word for me!** The student who read the text for others to comment on has the last word by reading his/her response or comment.

10. **Continue the discussion.** One by one, group members receive a turn to read their selected text, call on members within their group to respond or comment, and then have the last word or comment on their text.

## APPLYING THE SAVE THE LAST WORD FOR ME STRATEGY: FIFTH-GRADE LESSON

Within their literature groups, the fifth-grade teacher used the Save the Last Word for Me strategy to engage students in peer-led discussions. In one group, the assigned reading was *The Secret School* by Avi (2001), a renowned book that has won four different outstanding book awards. The teacher introduced the book, focusing on the setting of the story—a one-room schoolhouse in rural Colorado in 1925. After reading the assigned chapters, students selected text to comment on and used them to engage in peer-led discussions. An example of one student's Save the Last Word for Me card may be found in Figure 40.1.

**Figure 40.1**    Sample Selected Text and Comments for *The Secret School* by Avi

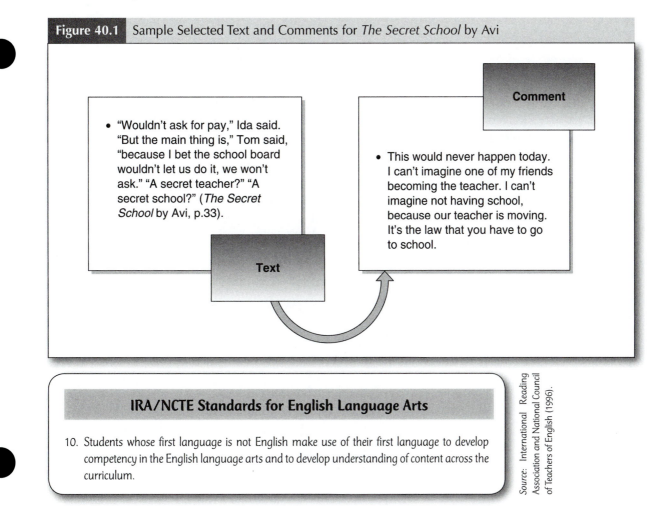

- "Wouldn't ask for pay," Ida said. "But the main thing is," Tom said, "because I bet the school board wouldn't let us do it, we won't ask." "A secret teacher?" "A secret school?" (*The Secret School* by Avi, p.33).

**Text**

**Comment**

- This would never happen today. I can't imagine one of my friends becoming the teacher. I can't imagine not having school, because our teacher is moving. It's the law that you have to go to school.

**IRA/NCTE Standards for English Language Arts**

10. Students whose first language is not English make use of their first language to develop competency in the English language arts and to develop understanding of content across the curriculum.

*Source:* International Reading Association and National Council of Teachers of English (1996).

## Differentiating Instruction for English Language Learners

Gallagher (2004) emphasizes that the power of collaboration leads to deep comprehension of text. To make it work, teachers must select students who will work together. This is true for all students, but it is essential for English language learners. Frequently, students who are linguistically different are hesitant to participate. Therefore, placing English language learners in small sheltered groups will promote higher levels of participation. Emphasize to all students that there are no "right" or "wrong" comments or responses. Ensure that the group has a leader who will be able to elicit responses from students and pace the discussion. For some groups, it may be necessary for the teacher to become a group member and demonstrate the process of sharing responses and comments.

## Differentiating Instruction for Students With Special Needs

For students who have special needs and are not fluent in reading or writing, the teacher should modify the strategy by (1) demonstrating the procedure of selecting text, (2) engaging students in responding to the text, and (3) having the student dictate his/her "last word" as the teacher writes it on the wall chart.

## References

Buehl, D. (2009). *Classroom strategies for interactive learning* (3rd ed.). Newark, DE: International Reading Association.

Fish, S. (1980). *Is there a text in this class? The authority of interpretative communities.* Cambridge, MA: Harvard University Press.

Gallagher, K. (2004). *Deeper reading: Comprehending challenging texts, 4–12.* Portland, ME: Stenhouse.

International Reading Association and National Council of Teachers of English. (1996). *Standards for the English language arts.* Newark, DE: International Reading Association and Urbana, IL: National Council of Teachers of English.

Short, K. G., Harste, J., & Burke, C. (1996). *Creating classrooms for authors and inquirers* (2nd ed.). Portsmouth, NH: Heinemann.

Short, K. G., & Kauffman, G. (1995). "So what do I do?" The role of the teacher in literature circles. In N. L. Roser & M. G. Martinez (Eds.), *Book talk and beyond: Children and teachers respond to literature* (pp. 140–149). Newark, DE: International Reading Association.

## Children's Literature Cited

Avi. (2001). *The secret school.* New York: Harcourt.

# SECTION IX

# Essential Strategies for Teaching Narrative Writing

**W**riting is a complex process that enables students to express ideas and demonstrate understanding. This chapter presents the research on best practices for teaching writing and explores how technology has impacted the process.

## A BRIEF OVERVIEW OF NARRATIVE WRITING

Today's youth are daily engaged in the art of writing as they text, blog, or instant message their peers (Barack, 2009). This digital form of writing is very different from printed versions, yet it still reflects the purpose of writing, which is to communicate (Yancey, 2009). Recent reports suggest that as the world transforms toward digital literacies, the need for skilled writing will become critical (Graham & Perin, 2007). For much of the past decade, the focus of curriculum and instruction has been on reading, to the neglect of writing (Yancey, 2009). As new literacies gain prominence in schools, educators are revisiting the integration of reading and writing as related processes (Headley, 2008).

Despite their many similarities, reading and writing are not completely parallel processes (Graham & Perin, 2007). Readers and writers draw on background knowledge to construct meaning. Yet writing is an act of discovery as students create their own thoughts, critique complex ideas, and reflect on their own understanding (National Commission on Writing, 2003). Research indicates that when students are engaged in the process of writing within a supportive environment, the quality of their work significantly improves (Bromley, 2007).

Effective writing instruction is collaborative, supportive, and focuses on the strategies of skilled writers (Graham & Perin, 2007). Expert writers engage in the writing process as they plan, draft, revise, edit, and publish (Graves, 1983). Instruction that uses the writing workshop approach engages students in these phases of composition and embeds direct teaching in the mechanics of writing, such as grammar and spelling, in the context of use (Bromley, 2007). Best practices in writing instruction also facilitate development of the strategies used by skilled writers:

- *Audience:* Skilled writers keep their audience in mind while writing.

- *Knowledge:* Expert writers are knowledgeable about the genre they are using, its style, and conventions.

- *Research:* Skilled writers use their content knowledge about the topic to compose, or they conduct research to explore it (Graham, MacArthur, & Fitzgerald, 2007).

Recent research has explored the impact of technology on writing instruction (Leu & Kinzer, 2000). Writing process software has been shown to improve young students' fine motor skills and understanding of the revision process (Baker, 2000). Today's students publish their stories on the Internet for a global audience, thereby increasing their motivation and engagement in the task (Leu & Kinzer, 2000). As students use technology to research and read different genres, their knowledge of text structure improves (Leu & Kinzer, 2000).

## GENRE STUDY

When students are engaged in genre studies, they learn the complex structures and text elements that distinguish one type of text from another (Calkins, 1994). Research indicates that even young children are capable of understanding the complex differences between text structures (Read, 2005). In order to write narrative text, students need immersion in story elements such as setting, problem, solution, and consequence (McCormack & Pasquarelli, 2010). One way to immerse students in the study of the narrative genre is by exposing them to rich, quality children's literature (Jarvey, McKeough, & Pyryt, 2008). As students listen to and discuss story elements, they internalize the vocabulary, sentence structure, and voices of great writers.

Effective writing instruction of narrative text engages students in discourse communities where they read and discuss great literature and respond through writing (Rosenblatt, 2004). One effective method for engaging students in narrative text is through oral retelling and summarizing (McCormack & Pasquarelli, 2010). When students engage in discussion, they are given the opportunity to explore differing viewpoints and construct new ideas (Rosenblatt, 2004). Strategies for reader response, such as summarization or personal response journals, allow students to extend their thinking and fully engage in the discourse of the genre (Calkins, 1994). This chapter presents several instructional strategies that use guidelines formed from research on best practice to instruct students in writing narrative text.

## GUIDELINES FOR TEACHING NARRATIVE WRITING

Research indicates that effective writing instruction occurs within a collaborative writing community (Bromley, 2007). The following guidelines provide the framework for instruction in developing composition of narrative text:

1. Effective instruction in the writing process includes explicit modeling and demonstration of genre-specific features (Jarvey et al., 2008).

2. Supportive environments embed instruction for writing across the curriculum and in every lesson (Pressley, Mohan, Fingeret, Reffit, & Raphael-Bogaert, 2007).

3. Expert teachers of writing model and share their own compositions with students in order to foster a community of writers (Pritchard & Honeycutt, 2007).

4. Self-evaluation of writing encourages ownership of the writing process and focuses on development of skills and strategies (Bromley, 2007).

5. Effective instruction in teaching composition of narrative text immerses students in the study of its features and story elements (Calkins, 1994).

## A Strategy for Assessing Narrative Writing

Best practices in writing instruction emphasize "interactive assessments" that occur during the writing conference (Glasswell, Parr, & McNaughton, 2003). In these teachable moments, teachers use an assessment conversation to dialogue with students about their writing strengths and areas that are in need of improvement. During these critical conversations, teachers use "on-the-spot" interventions to explicitly demonstrate a solution to a writing problem or skill area. Teachers also use the Interactive Assessment for Narrative Writing, shown in Figure IX.1, to document students' progress in writing narratives over time. As teachers engage students in their use of voice, word choice, and organization, notes are documented on the chart. This focus on assessment for learning provides students with targeted instruction to develop their skills and explicit strategies to improve.

| **Figure IX.1** Interactive Assessment for Narrative Writing | | |
|---|---|---|
| **Directions:** *Engage student in conversation regarding elements listed. Note date and record skills/strategies needed to improve.* | DATE | NOTES |
| **Name of student:** | | |
| ***Content:*** Student uses content to engage the reader and is knowledgeable of narrative genre. | | |
| ***Organization:*** Student effectively organizes story plot and uses transitions to move the reader to next event or segment. | | |
| ***Voice:*** Student's writing has a definite style and voice is unique. | | |
| ***Word choice:*** Student uses interesting words to construct his or her story, and word choice fits the narrative genre. | | |

*(Continued)*

(Continued)

| |
|---|
| **Monthly progress:** |
| **Targeted instruction needed:** |
| **Summary report:** |

## A GUIDE FOR USING RESPONSE TO INTERVENTION FOR NARRATIVE WRITING

The Interactive Assessment for Narrative Writing (Figure IX.1) may be used to gather progress-monitoring data. After data analysis, teachers may select students who need further intervention in targeted areas, such as organization or improvement in word choice. The Collaborative Writing instructional strategy in this section may be modified for a small-group intervention. Using progress-monitoring data, teachers use the shared pen process to demonstrate how to organize text or select vocabulary for sentence construction. Students at risk may need individualized sessions or dyads for maximized support.

In this section, "Essential Strategies for Teaching Narrative Writing," five instructional strategies are presented for use in facilitating the writing process. The strategies are presented as guides for teachers to use based on their ongoing assessment data.

## PROFESSIONAL RESOURCES

Graham, S. (2007). *Best practices in teaching writing.* New York: Guilford.

Herrington, A., Hodgson, K., & Moran, C. (2009). *Teaching the new writing: Technology, change, and assessment in 21st-century classrooms.* New York: Teachers College Press.

National Writing Project & Nagin, C. (2006). *Because writing matters: Improving student writing in our schools.* San Francisco: Jossey-Bass.

Troia, G. (2008). *Instruction and assessment for struggling writers: Evidence-based practices.* New York: Guilford.

# References

Baker, E. A. (2000). *Instructional approaches used to integrate literacy and technology*. Retrieved February 15, 2010, from http://www.readingonline.org/articles/baker/

Barack, L. (2009). Twittering Dante. *School Library Journal, 55,* 14–15.

Bromley, K. (2007). Best practices in teaching writing. In L. Gambrell, L. M. Morrow, & M. Pressley (Eds.), *Best practices in literacy instruction* (pp. 243–264). New York: Guilford.

Calkins, L. (1994). *The art of teaching writing.* Portsmouth, NH: Heinemann.

Glasswell, K., Parr, J., & McNaughton, S. (2003). Working with William: Teaching, learning, and the joint construction of a struggling writer. *The Reading Teacher, 56,* 494–500.

Graham, S., MacArthur, C., & Fitzgerald, J. (2007). *Best practices in writing instruction.* New York: Guilford.

Graham, S., & Perin, D. (2007). *Writing next: Effective strategies to improve writing of adolescents in middle and high schools.* Retrieved January 30, 2010, from http://www.a114ed.org/files/WritingNext.pdf

Graves, D. (1983). *Writing: Teachers and children at work.* Portsmouth, NH: Heinemann.

Headley, K. (2008). Improving reading comprehension through writing. In C. Collins-Block, L. M. Morrow, & S. R. Paris (Eds.), *Comprehension instruction: Research-based practices* (pp. 214–220). New York: Guilford.

Jarvey, M., McKeough, A., & Pyryt, M. (2008). Teaching trickster tales: A comparison of instructional approaches. *Research in the Teaching of English, 43,* 42–74.

Leu, D., & Kinzer, C. (2000). The convergence of literacy instruction with networked technologies for information and communication. *Reading Research Quarterly, 35,* 108–127.

McCormack, R., & Pasquarelli, S. (2010). *Teaching reading: Strategies and resources for grades 1–6.* New York: Guilford.

National Commission on Writing. (2003). *The neglected 'R': The need for a writing revolution.* Retrieved January 15, 2010, from http://www.writingcommission.org/prod_downloads/writingcom/neglectedr.pdf

Pressley, M., Mohan, L., Fingeret, L., Reffitt, K., & Raphael-Bogaert, L. (2007). Writing instruction in engaging and effective elementary settings. In S. Graham, C. MacArthur, & J. Fitzgerald (Eds.), *Best practices in writing instruction* (pp. 11–27). New York: Guilford.

Pritchard, R., & Honeycutt, R. (2007). Best practices in implementing the process approach in teaching writing. In S. Graham, C. MacArthur, & J. Fitzgerald (Eds.), *Best practices in writing instruction* (pp. 28–50). New York: Guilford.

Read, S. (2005). First- and second-graders writing informational text. *The Reading Teacher, 59,* 36–44.

Rosenblatt, L. (2004). The transactional theory of reading and writing. In R. B. Ruddell & N. J. Unrau (Eds.), *Theoretical models and processes of reading* (5th ed., pp. 1363–1398). Mahwah, NJ: Erlbaum.

Yancey, K. (2009). *Writing in the 21st century: A report from the National Council of Teachers of English.* Retrieved February 1, 2010, from http://www.ncte.org/library/NCTEFiles/Press/Yancey_final.pdf

# Strategy
# 41
# Digital Storytelling

## SPEAKING BRIEFLY: AN OVERVIEW OF THE LITERACY STRATEGY

*Digital Storytelling* enables all learners to explore the power of narrative to express ideas and knowledge of the world (Leu et al., 2005). A digital story is a multimedia text consisting of video clips, photos, artwork with voiced narration, music, or other animation (Slyvester & Greenidge, 2009/2010). The integration of technology, language, and literacy enables all but especially reluctant readers and writers to find their voice and identity as readers and writers (Fallon, 2010).

As technology continues to adapt and change our world, Digital Storytelling is already undergoing rapid transformation. Avatars, or online virtual selves that interact in a virtual space, are increasingly being used for Digital Storytelling and other educational purposes (Antonacci & Modaress, 2005). Multisensory stories that simulate the video-game world of today's students are especially effective in engaging struggling readers/writers to develop a story (Fallon, 2010).

*Source:* International Reading Association and National Council of Teachers of English (1996).

---

### IRA/NCTE Standards for English Language Arts

5. Students employ a wide range of strategies as they write and use different writing process elements appropriately to communicate with different audiences for a variety of purposes.

8. Students use a variety of technological and information resources (e.g., libraries, databases, computer networks, video) to gather and synthesize information and to create and communicate knowledge.

---

## USING DIGITAL STORYTELLING

*When to use the strategy:* Digital Storytelling is designed as a whole-class activity. Many teachers are reluctant to implement Digital Storytelling out of concern that it requires expensive equipment. However, the majority of computers in today's schools are already equipped with software such as iMovie or Photo Story 3 for Windows to create a digital story. The creation of a digital story will take a minimum of three class sessions for students to plan, create, and present the finished product to their peers.

*Strategy modifications for grade levels:* Teachers may adopt this strategy for primary-grade students by partnering them with intermediate-grade students on a cross-grade project.

## IMPLEMENTING THE DIGITAL STORYTELLING STRATEGY: STEP BY STEP

1. **Identify traits of narratives.** Teachers ask students to list their favorite stories and explain why they are so fascinating to them. After discussing their choices, teachers list their reasons, such as good characters or exciting plots, on chart paper for future reference.

2. **Provide writing prompt.** Teachers may jump-start the writing process by displaying the writing prompt, "One morning, I was on my way to school when. . . ." Students discuss possible plots and story titles based on the prompt. Dyads are created to continue the process.

3. **Create storyboards.** Teachers provide students with the graphic organizer illustrated in Figure 41.1. Working collaboratively, students illustrate their ideas for the story on the board with the accompanying text. After completing their storyboard, they share it with the teacher and another dyad for feedback and edits before moving to the production stage.

4. **Provide photographs.** Provide digital cameras or access to the computer for students to create visual images to implement in their storyboards. Students use either iMovie or Photo Story 3 to produce their digital story. They take turns providing the narration for the digital story and decide about special effects such as music or animation.

5. **Edit the digital story.** After production, dyads upload their digital story to the class webpage for the teacher to view. Once the teacher has approved the draft and cited areas for revision, other students are allowed to view it for additional suggestions.

6. **Present products.** Teachers may organize a storytelling festival for other classes to attend or for parents to enjoy. At the festival, students present their digital stories and take questions from the audience. Students may also choose to upload their stories to the class Internet site for permanent display and to elicit feedback from a global audience.

| Figure 41.1 | Storyboard | | | |
|---|---|---|---|---|
| *Scene 1* | *Scene 2* | *Scene 3* | *Scene 4* | *Scene 5* |
| | | | | |
| *Text:* | *Text:* | *Text:* | *Text* | *Text:* |

## Applying the Digital Storytelling Strategy: Second-Grade Lesson

The second-grade teacher gathers students together and displays a chart titled "Our Favorite Stories." The teacher asks students to list their favorite stories and identify what makes them so special. After five or six have been identified, the teacher asks students to identify the patterns across titles, such as interesting characters, exciting plots, or use of humor. After discussing narrative texts, the teacher guides students to write digital stories with the following steps:

- Begin the session with this writing prompt: "One day in the cafeteria, I was so surprised to see . . . ." As students voice their ideas, various characters and plots are recorded on chart paper. Students are placed in dyads and outline their characters and draft a plot for their story.

- Direct students to create a storyboard that illustrates six scenes from their story. The text for each scene is written below the illustrations and will be narrated by the students.

- Distribute digital cameras and take students on a tour of the school building so they can capture scenes from their storyboard illustrations. Students may supplement their digital photos with clip art or other images from the web. When they have finished storing digital images, they use iMovie or Photo Story 3 to create their stories.

- Guide students as they edit their digital stories, and edit text before it is read by the narrators.

When students have completed the editing and narration process, the teacher checks each story before it is uploaded to the class webpage. Students also celebrate their creations with a "film festival" and invite peers from other classes to watch their digital stories.

*Source:* International Reading Association and National Council of Teachers of English (1996).

### IRA/NCTE Standards for English Language Arts

10. Students whose first language is not English make use of their first language to develop competency in the English language arts and to develop understanding of content across the curriculum.

## Differentiating Instruction for English Language Learners

Digital Storytelling is the perfect strategy for multilingual learners (Leu et al., 2005). As English language learners work with a native speaker, they are fully engaged in the writing process. In addition, the second-language learner is given the opportunity to share his or her native language in the narration of the story so that it is bilingual. This opportunity to display proficiency in another language boosts self-esteem and confidence.

## Differentiating Instruction for Students With Special Needs

Similarly to English language learners, research has indicated that digital storytelling is a powerful medium for engaging students with special needs (Kajder, 2006). In order to support students with special needs in the construction of story elements, they may choose to create their own version of a favorite story. Writing an alternate version to a favorite tale or fable will provide them with the basic plot, setting, and characters to complete the task.

## References

Antonacci, D., & Modaress, N. (2005). *Second life! The educational possibilities of a massively multiplayer virtual world (MMVW)*. In the proceedings of EDUCASE Southwest Regional Conference, Austin, TX.

Fallon, G. (2010). Using avatars and virtual environments in learning: What do they have to offer? *British Journal of Educational Technology, 41,* 108–122.

International Reading Association and National Council of Teachers of English. (1996). *Standards for the English language arts.* Newark, DE: International Reading Association and Urbana, IL: National Council of Teachers of English.

Kajder, S. (2006). *Bringing the outside in: Visual ways to engage reluctant readers.* Portland, ME: Stenhouse.

Leu, D., Castek, J., Coiro, J., Gort, M., Henry, L., & Lima, C. (2005). *Developing new literacies among multilingual learners in the elementary grades.* Retrieved January 9, 2010, from http://www.newliteracies.uconn.edu/pub_files/Developing_new_literacies_among_multicultural.pdf

Slyvester, R., & Greenidge, W. (2009/2010). Digital storytelling: Extending the potential for struggling writers. *The Reading Teacher, 63,* 284–296.

# Strategy
# 42

# Dictogloss

## SPEAKING BRIEFLY: AN OVERVIEW OF THE LITERACY STRATEGY

*Dictogloss* is an integrative strategy that was originally used for second-language learners. The purpose of Dictogloss is to improve students' knowledge of text structure and grammar within an authentic context (Van Patten, Inclezan, Salazar, & Farley, 2009). As research indicates, effective writing instruction focuses on grammar and text structure within context of use (Bromley, 2007). In this instructional strategy, students listen to a model of narrative text structure and deconstruct it collaboratively before it is recreated.

The collaborative nature of Dictogloss allows all learners, but especially second-language learners and striving readers, to examine an exemplary narrative passage and discover how the author created it. When students are explicitly instructed in the study of genres and their textual differences, the quality of their writing improves (Calkins, 1994).

*Source:* International Reading Association and National Council of Teachers of English (1996).

---

### IRA/NCTE Standards for English Language Arts

3. Students apply a wide range of strategies to comprehend, interpret, evaluate, and appreciate texts. They draw on their prior experience, their interactions with other readers and writers, their knowledge of word meaning and of other texts, their word identification strategies, and their understanding of textual features (e.g., sound-letter correspondence, sentence structure, context, graphics).

5. Students employ a wide range of strategies as they write and use different writing process elements appropriately to communicate with different audiences for a variety of purposes.

---

## USING DICTOGLOSS

*When to use the strategy:* Dictogloss is designed for whole-class instruction. However, it is easily adaptable for small guided-reading groups or for intervention sessions.

*Strategy modifications for grade levels:* Teachers must use their assessment data in selecting a model passage for the strategy. It may be a picture book, poem, song, basal reader story, or magazine article.

## Implementing the Dictogloss Strategy: Step by Step

1. **Brainstorm about the topic.** Teachers display pictures from the book or photos on the topic and ask students to predict what the passage will be about. Teachers also record vocabulary words that students expect to hear based on their discussion of the illustrations.

2. **Read the text aloud.** Teachers read the model passage aloud to the students. Teachers direct students to think about the main idea during the first read-aloud.

3. **Repeat the process.** For the second reading, teachers instruct students to jot down key vocabulary words and phrases, but not whole sentences, using Figure 42.1.

4. **Discuss text structure.** Students are placed in groups of three to share their notes on the passage. Teachers lead a debriefing to focus on key vocabulary words and phrases. Students compare their predictions regarding the passage with the actual text. The discussion should also focus on how the author's style differs from other narrative texts they have read or written.

5. **Reconstruct the text.** After the discussion, groups collaboratively reconstruct the passage they heard. The text is an approximation of what they heard rather than an exact copy.

6. **Compare versions of text.** When groups have completed their versions, teachers present the actual text on the SMART Board or overhead projector. Students note differences in sentence structure, style, and vocabulary.

7. **Reflect on process.** Teachers instruct students to complete a 2-minute quick-write to jot down how their thinking changed as a result of the activity. A few students share their reflections with the class.

## Applying the Dictogloss Strategy: Fifth-Grade Lesson on Paul Revere

The teacher informs students that they will be using a new strategy to sharpen their writing and listening skills. Using the Dictogloss Strategy Guide (see Figure 42.1), the teacher demonstrates how to use the guide to focus their listening skills and improve their writing:

- *Take a look at the title of the poem, "The Midnight Ride of Paul Revere" (Longfellow, 2010). Based on the title, what can we predict this will be about?* The teacher records students' responses on a descriptive web about the American Revolution. Students also generate vocabulary words they would expect to hear in the poem based on their knowledge of the topic, such as *Britain* or *colonies.*

- *Now I am going to read the poem aloud, and as I read, just listen for the main idea.* After the first read-aloud, students share their responses regarding the main idea.

- *For the second reading, you will jot down key vocabulary words and also key phrases from the poem.* After students report out their vocabulary words and

| Figure 42.1 | Dictogloss Strategy Guide |
|---|---|

| SECOND READING | |
|---|---|
| **KEY VOCABULARY WORDS** | **KEY PHRASES** |
| | |

| RECONSTRUCTION |
|---|
| |

| REFLECTION: |
|---|
| |

phrases, the teacher directs their attention to Longfellow's writing style and how he captured the scene for them. They also discuss how the poem differs from others they have read or heard before.

- Students are placed in groups of three to reconstruct the poem based on their notes and recollections.

- When groups complete their reconstruction, the teacher displays the poem on the SMART Board and asks students to compare it with their versions. Teachers focus the discussion on why key phrases and images stayed in their memory more than others and how they can mimic Longfellow's technique in their own writing.

As groups complete the activity, the teacher asks students to do a 2-minute quick-write to record how their thinking changed as a result of the activity.

*Source:* International Reading Association and National Council of Teachers of English (1996).

> ## IRA/NCTE Standards for English Language Arts
>
> 10. Students whose first language is not English make use of their first language to develop competency in the English language arts and to develop understanding of content across the curriculum.

## DIFFERENTIATING INSTRUCTION FOR ENGLISH LANGUAGE LEARNERS

Research indicates that Dictogloss is an effective strategy for English language learners due to its supportive context and explicit modeling (Van Patten et al., 2009). One adaptation for second-language learners is to prepare a cloze passage for them to use during the activity. Working with a native speaker, the English language learner may use the cloze passage to recreate the original text to focus on vocabulary and text features.

## DIFFERENTIATING INSTRUCTION FOR STUDENTS WITH SPECIAL NEEDS

Students with special needs are often reluctant to engage in the writing process (Graham & Perin, 2007). Yet when they write about a topic they are interested in, students with special needs are more likely to be motivated and engaged. One adaptation of Dictogloss for this population is to select a passage from a favorite story, topic, or author. In addition to gaining their attention, prior knowledge about the passage will also increase self-confidence and motivation as they reconstruct the passage.

## REFERENCES

Bromley, K. (2007). Best practices in teaching writing. In L. Gambrell, L. M. Morrow, & M. Pressley (Eds.), *Best practices in literacy instruction* (pp. 243–264). New York: Guilford.

Calkins, L. (1994). *The art of teaching writing.* Portsmouth, NH: Heinemann.

Graham, S., & Perin, D. (2007). *Writing next: Effective strategies to improve writing of adolescents in middle and high schools.* Retrieved January 30, 2010, from http://www.a114ed.org/files/WritingNext.pdf

International Reading Association and National Council of Teachers of English. (1996). *Standards for the English language arts.* Newark, DE: International Reading Association and Urbana, IL: National Council of Teachers of English.

Van Patten, B., Inclezan, D., Salazar, H., & Farley, A. (2009). Processing instruction and Dictogloss: A study on object pronouns and word order in Spanish. *Foreign Language Annals, 42,* 557–576.

## CHILDREN'S LITERATURE CITED

Longfellow, H. W. (2010). *The midnight ride of Paul Revere.* Retrieved January 31, 2010, from http://poetry.eserver .org/paul-revere.html

# Strategy
# 43 Collaborative Writing

## SPEAKING BRIEFLY: AN OVERVIEW OF THE LITERACY STRATEGY

*Collaborative Writing* provides striving writers with targeted instruction based on assessment data. In today's classroom, there are many students disengaged during the writing process despite their teacher's best efforts to model and demonstrate strategic writing (Glasswell, Parr, & McNaughton, 2003). This instructional strategy jump-starts the process through dialogue and "in-the-moment" scaffolding (Gibson, 2008).

Collaborative Writing is designed for small writing groups or individual instruction. Even though it was designed for striving writers, it may be adapted as an enrichment activity for students who are ready for more complex work.

Source: International Reading Association and National Council of Teachers of English (1996).

---

### IRA/NCTE Standards for English Language Arts

5. Students employ a wide range of strategies as they write and use different writing process elements appropriately to communicate with different audiences for a variety of purposes.

11. Students participate as knowledgeable, reflective, creative, and critical members of a variety of literacy communities.

---

## USING COLLABORATIVE WRITING

*When to use the strategy:* Collaborative Writing is targeted instruction based on assessment data. Therefore, teachers use anecdotal observations or writing samples to discern students' learning needs before planning the session. It is designed for writing conferences or shared-writing sessions.

*Strategy modifications for grade levels:* Teachers modify this strategy based on their assessment data.

## Implementing the Collaborative Writing Strategy: Step by Step

1. **Select strategic writing behavior.** Using assessment data, teachers select a strategic writing behavior such as "Write about what you know."

2. **Discuss strategic behavior.** Teachers discuss the purpose for the session and record the strategic writing behavior on a chart. Lead students in a discussion of a possible topic to write about.

3. **Write collaboratively.** Teachers jump-start the process of constructing text by writing the first sentence. Jointly, teachers and students discuss sentences, word choice, connecting ideas, and genre features.

4. **Query choices.** Teachers use "in-the-moment" scaffolding to prompt students with questions such as, "What would the reader need to know here? How can we make them feel for the character? What would be a more interesting way to say that?" Teachers may need to give targeted instruction on a particular skill, such as word order, during the session.

5. **Review text.** After the text is completed, teachers direct students to read it together. Students are instructed to ask themselves, "Did it make sense?"

6. **Reflect on the process.** When the session is over, students report out what they learned from the session and how they can apply it during their next writing task.

## Applying the Collaborative Writing Strategy: First-Grade Lesson

After analyzing assessment data from previous writing samples, the teacher decides to conduct a guided-writing lesson on using descriptive words. The teacher begins with the following:

- *Today, we are going to write about our recent snowstorm. What would be interesting for the reader to know about it?* After discussing the topic and possible story ideas, the teacher informs students that today they will work on using more descriptive words. The teacher explicitly defines the term and gives some examples, such as "crunchy snow" or "delicious food."

- *Let's begin the story with the following sentence: I awoke on Sunday to lots of snow outside.* Using a whiteboard, the teacher records students' sentences and scaffolds their responses with prompts such as, "What words can we use so the reader sees a picture in their head?"

- Collaboratively, the group reads their story when it is completed and edits the text to see if it "makes sense." The teacher uses a highlighter to focus attention on the descriptive words they used in the story.

At the conclusion of the session, students are asked to comment on what they learned and how they can use descriptive words in their writing.

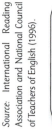

*Source:* International Reading Association and National Council of Teachers of English (1996).

> ### IRA/NCTE Standards for English Language Arts
>
> 10. Students whose first language is not English make use of their first language to develop competency in the English language arts and to develop understanding of content across the curriculum.

## DIFFERENTIATING INSTRUCTION FOR ENGLISH LANGUAGE LEARNERS

One of the most effective ways to instruct English language learners during collaborative writing is to improve their vocabulary (Wilhelm, 2004). One way to adapt this lesson for second-language learners is to provide a word list as a reference tool. Students collaborate with the teacher to generate words related to the story topic. The list or word book becomes a reference tool for the group to use during the session.

## DIFFERENTIATING INSTRUCTION FOR STUDENTS WITH SPECIAL NEEDS

A familiar sight in many classrooms is the student with special needs staring at a blank page, trying to generate text. One way to modify this instructional strategy for students with special needs is to use pictures from a favorite video game to engage and motivate (Compton-Lily, 2009). Teachers should carefully select pictures from video games that emphasize respect and do not promote violence. Using these visuals, teachers can focus the session on students' ideas to reconstruct a narrative.

## REFERENCES

Compton-Lily, C. (2009). What can new literacy studies offer to the teaching of struggling readers? *The Reading Teacher, 63,* 88–90.

Gibson, S. (2008). Guided writing lessons: Second-grade students' development of strategic behavior. *Reading Horizons, 48,* 111–133.

Glasswell, K., Parr, J., & McNaughton, S. (2003). Working with William: Teaching, learning, and the joint construction of a struggling writer. *The Reading Teacher, 56,* 494–500.

International Reading Association and National Council of Teachers of English. (1996). *Standards for the English language arts.* Newark, DE: International Reading Association and Urbana, IL: National Council of Teachers of English.

Wilhelm, J. (2004). Learning from ELL kids: How to teach writing. *Voices From the Middle, 11,* 43–44.

# Attribute Webs

## Speaking Briefly: An Overview of the Literacy Strategy

*Attribute Webs* is an instructional strategy that engages students in character study. The purpose of the activity is to encourage students to delve into why characters behave in a certain way (O'Sullivan, 2004). As students explore character traits or attributes while they read, they apply this knowledge while writing narrative stories. Effective writing instruction uses quality children's literature to immerse students in the genre and its style elements (Rosenblatt, 2004).

This activity is best suited as a component of an author study or literature discussion group. It may also be modified for use during writer's workshop to dissect an author's portrayal of a character and how his or her technique may be imitated.

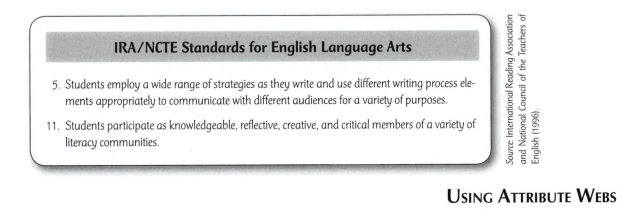

### IRA/NCTE Standards for English Language Arts

5. Students employ a wide range of strategies as they write and use different writing process elements appropriately to communicate with different audiences for a variety of purposes.

11. Students participate as knowledgeable, reflective, creative, and critical members of a variety of literacy communities.

*Source: International Reading Association and National Council of the Teachers of English (1996).*

## Using Attribute Webs

*When to use the strategy:* Attribute Webs may be used as a whole-class or guided-reading lesson. This activity is effective when all students have access to the same book for the activity. As students engage in book discussions and apply their knowledge to a writing task, their sharing of character interpretations improves the quality of their compositions. This activity will also take a minimum of three sessions to implement, depending on the length of the text.

*Strategy modifications for grade levels:* Teachers may adopt this strategy for specific grades by selecting texts that are on students' instructional reading levels.

## IMPLEMENTING THE ATTRIBUTE WEB STRATEGY: STEP BY STEP

1. **Select a quality text.** Teachers select a picture or chapter book for the activity based on students' reading level. Teachers should select books with clearly drawn characters for rich discussions and for models of writing character attributes.

2. **Guided reading of text.** Teachers conduct a picture or chapter walk of the text with the students. Students make predictions about the plot and characters from the picture walk. After reading a passage from the text, teachers lead a discussion of the main idea.

3. **Conduct a character study.** Teachers distribute the Character Pyramid (see Figure 44.1) to students. Working in small groups, students begin to complete their notes on the main character, his or her physical appearance, family background, and experiences. For older or more proficient students, teachers may assign different characters to each group. Groups discuss their notes with the class when they have completed the graphic organizer.

4. **Complete reading of text.** In the next session, teachers lead students in a summary of the text and guide their predictions for the next passage. After students complete the text, teachers prompt discussion with questions such as, "How did the author surprise you? Did the character act the way you thought he/she would? Were your predictions accurate? Was there a special passage that gripped/excited you?" Teachers record students' comments on chart paper to use as a reference tool.

5. **Identify character attributes.** Teachers ask students to summarize their notes on the main character and discuss ways he/she surprised them after completing the text. Teachers explicitly define attributes and model how to complete the first component of the graphic organizer. Teachers distribute Figure 44.2, Character Attribute Web, to groups for discussion of character attributes and actions. Students must provide evidence from the text to back up their answers on the graphic organizer. After groups have completed their task, students report out on the attributes they identified for the main character. Their peers discuss the evidence provided and ascertain whether the character acted appropriately.

6. **Apply to writing workshop.** In the next session, teachers lead students in a review of how the author crafted the character. Students use their two graphic organizers, Character Pyramid and Character Attribute Web, as reference tools during the discussion. Working in dyads, students use the graphic organizers again to develop a character of their own creation. Students discuss the character's physical appearance, family background, experiences, and challenges. After completing the graphic organizers, they draft a plot for their narrative. When students have completed the task, teachers meet with students to debrief and develop their characters further.

7. **Compose narrative.** In the next few sessions, students complete their narrative using the writing process. Teachers meet individually with each dyad to guide them in applying their knowledge of crafting characters to their own stories. Students revise and edit their text before it is published for their peers.

**Figure 44.1**    Character Pyramid

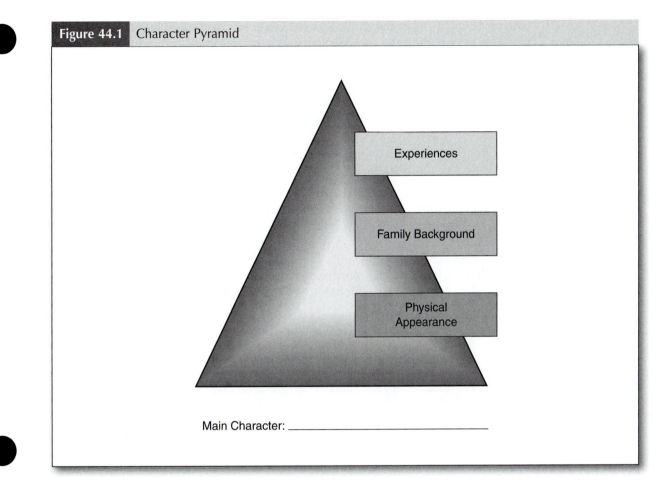

Experiences

Family Background

Physical Appearance

Main Character: _____

## APPLYING THE ATTRIBUTE WEB STRATEGY:
## FOURTH-GRADE LESSON ON *TEAMMATES*

Students gather for a read-aloud of *Teammates* by Peter Golenbock (1992), a book about Jackie Robinson and Peewee Reece from the Brooklyn Dodgers baseball team. The teacher conducts a picture walk and asks students to use the title and pictures to make predictions. The teacher conducts a read-aloud of the first section of the text. Using the Character Pyramid (see Figure 44.1), the teacher directs students to do the following:

- Use the graphic organizer to jot down information about Jackie Robinson or Peewee Reece as to who they were and their experiences. After students complete their responses, they discuss how they would describe both main characters in the story.

- In the next session, after completing the text, students use Figure 44.2, Character Attribute Web, to identify four main attributes of either Jackie Robinson or Peewee Reece. Students record evidence from the story to validate their responses on the graphic organizer. When students complete their activity, they discuss how the author depicted the main characters through their actions. The teacher focuses students' attention on the author's style of characterization and how they can imitate it in their own writing.

- In the third session, the teacher reviews the story *Teammates* and focuses the discussion on the Character Pyramid and Character Attribute Web. The teacher distributes these forms again for students to use as writing tools to brainstorm main characters. Working in dyads, students generate attributes and actions to use in their narratives. They draft a plot for their story and begin to write it collaboratively.

- During the next sessions, the teacher acts as facilitator as dyads complete their drafts and edit work. In writing conferences, the teacher directs students' attention to their development of main characters and how they can use characters' actions to drive the plot.

After they have completed their stories, they are illustrated and printed for the classroom library. Teachers may also choose to hold a storytelling session for students to read aloud their work.

**Figure 44.2** Character Attribute Web

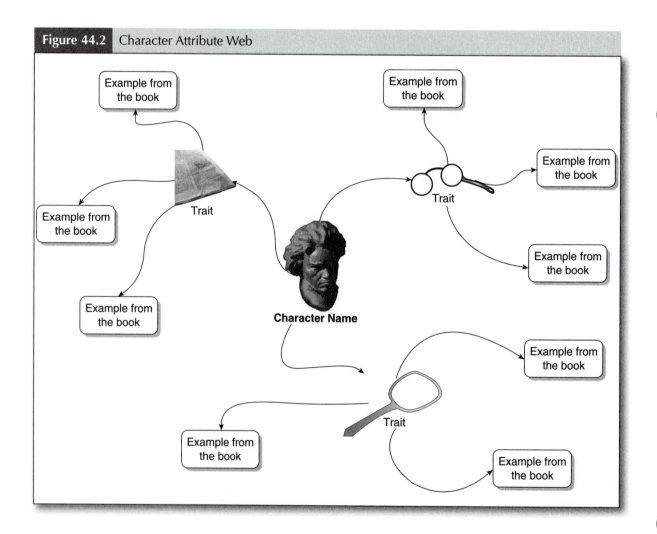

*Source:* International Reading Association and National Council of Teachers of English (1996).

> ## IRA/NCTE Standards for English Language Arts
>
> 10. Students whose first language is not English make use of their first language to develop competency in the English language arts and to develop understanding of content across the curriculum.

## DIFFERENTIATING INSTRUCTION FOR ENGLISH LANGUAGE LEARNERS

When English language learners have a shared experience, their ability to write more complex narratives improves (Schleppegrell & Go, 2007). One modification of this activity for second-language learners is to give them the option of creating a narrative focusing on a class trip or event. Each second-language student would be the main character in the narrative and would complete the graphic organizers based on his or her own experiences. This modification would enable English learners to focus on the process of developing characters in their writing rather than struggling to generate ideas.

## DIFFERENTIATING INSTRUCTION FOR STUDENTS WITH SPECIAL NEEDS

Cinderella tales are excellent vehicles for students with special needs to comprehend character attributes and actions (O'Sullivan, 2004). An adaptation for students with special needs and struggling writers is to use a text such as the *Rough-Faced Girl* (Martin, 1998) to discuss the clear delineation of characters working positively as opposed to other, selfish characters. Since the majority of students are also familiar with the Cinderella tale, they are more likely to engage in the discussion and to feel confident as they approach the writing task.

## REFERENCES

International Reading Association and National Council of Teachers of English. (1996). *Standards for the English language arts.* Newark, DE: International Reading Association and Urbana, IL: National Council of Teachers of English.

O'Sullivan, S. (2004). Using children's literature for character education. *The Reading Teacher, 57,* 640–646.

Rosenblatt, L. (2004). The transactional theory of reading and writing. In R. B. Ruddell & N. J. Unrau (Eds.),

*Theoretical models and processes of reading* (5th ed., pp. 1363–1398). Mahwah, NJ: Erlbaum.

Schleppegrell, M., & Go, A. (2007). Analyzing the writing of English learners: A functional approach. *Language Arts, 84,* 529–539.

## CHILDREN'S LITERATURE CITED

Golenbock, P. (1992). *Teammates.* P. Bacon (Illus.). Orlando, FL: Sandpiper.

Martin, R. (1998). *Rough-faced girl.* New York: Putnam.

# Strategy 45

# Thinking Boxes

## SPEAKING BRIEFLY: AN OVERVIEW OF THE LITERACY STRATEGY

*Thinking Boxes* uses visual imagery to generate ideas and to jump-start the writing process. Today's students are visual learners, as they have grown up playing video games and surfing the net (Leu et al., 2005). This instructional strategy harnesses their strength in focusing on photographs or paintings and illustrates how to use the images to compose.

The purpose of the Thinking Boxes strategy is to integrate visual literacy with writing instruction. As students are taught how to "read a photo or picture," they develop the skills to navigate the digital world. It also facilitates the writing process as students use a common document to brainstorm ideas for plots, characters, and settings.

*Source:* International Reading Association and National Council of Teachers of English (1996).

### IRA/NCTE Standards for English Language Arts

5. Students employ a wide range of strategies as they write and use different writing process elements appropriately to communicate with different audiences for a variety of purposes.

12. Students use spoken, written, and visual language to accomplish their own purpose.

## USING THINKING BOXES

*When to use the strategy:* Thinking Boxes is designed as a whole-class activity. However, it is easily adaptable as an intervention activity or for small guided-writing sessions. Teachers may choose to use photographs, prints, or paintings to implement this activity. It will take approximately three sessions to implement this instructional strategy.

*Strategy modifications for grade levels:* Teachers may adapt this strategy for primary-grade students by using wordless picture books.

## Implementing the Thinking Boxes Strategy: Step by Step

1. **Select the visual image.** Teachers select the photograph, painting, or other visuals based on their students' interests and background knowledge. If students need contextual information to interpret the image, teachers should provide it in a prior lesson.

2. **Introduce "reading an image."** Teachers present the photo or image to students. Teachers discuss the phrase "reading a photo" and what they think it means. Teachers record students' comments on a whiteboard or chart paper for later reference.

3. **Model the process.** Teachers demonstrate the process by directing students' attention to the objects/figures, setting, and colors used in the image. They also raise the following questions:
   - What is the setting of the photo/painting?
   - What just happened or will happen?
   - How does the photographer/artist use color, light, and positioning to create a message?
   - What does the figures' clothing say about their status, culture, and personality?
   - What do you think they are feeling or saying?

4. **Discuss images.** Students use the teachers' prompts to discuss the images and to generate ideas for possible narratives to write.

5. **Construct their thoughts.** Teachers distribute Figure 45.1, Thinking Boxes, to dyads. Students work collaboratively on writing what they think the figures are thinking in the photos or images. After students have completed the sheet, they share their ideas and generate a list of possibilities and how they might construct a story based on them.

6. **Draft a narrative.** In the next session, students use their Thinking Boxes sheet to draft a narrative focusing on the images and figures' thoughts. Teachers lead students through the writing process to bring their ideas to a published text to be uploaded to the class website.

## Applying the Thinking Boxes Strategy: Sixth-Grade Lesson on Afghanistan

The sixth-grade teacher projects the photo of Kabul Market in Afghanistan on the SMART Board (National Geographic Society, 2010). The teacher asks students to examine the photo and describe what is going on and where the scene may be located. Students' comments are discussed and recorded on the SMART Board. The teacher directs students to do the following:

- Work with your partner to discuss the following questions:
   o What is the setting of the photo/painting?
   o What just happened or will happen?
   o How does the photographer/artist use color, light, and positioning to create a message?
   o What does the figures' clothing say about their status, culture, and personality?
   o What do you think they are feeling or saying?

- Dyads report out their responses to the prompts and begin to brainstorm ideas for possible stories based on the photo.

- The teacher distributes Figure 45.1, Thinking Boxes, and directs students to use the graphic organizer to focus on selected figures in the photo and generate a narrative around them.

In the next few sessions, students use the writing process to draft a narrative, edit, and publish it on the class webpage. Students may also choose to create a digital story using the photo or image to project their story.

**Figure 45.1**   Thinking Boxes

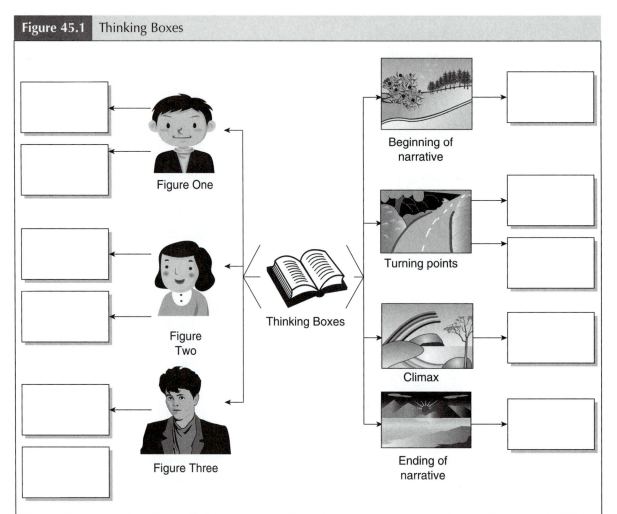

To turn the events of one's own life into a narrative, the author must impose a structure on those events. Think about the parts of the narrative. Why do you think the author made these structural decisions?

**I. Beginning of narrative**

Describe the opening scene. Why did the narrator begin with this scene?

  **A.**

Use the Word Guide to help you find the best vocabulary to express your ideas.

**II. Turning points**

Describe turning points in the story. How does the protagonist's life change as a result of these scenes?

   **A.**

   **B.**

**III. Climax**

Describe the climax. What is the effect on the narrator?

   **A.**

**IV. Ending of narrative**

Describe the closing scene. Why did the narrator choose to end the narrative with this scene?

   **A.**

**V. Figure Three**

Describe the symbols in the narrative. What do they represent to the narrator? To the reader?

   **A.**

**VI. Figure Two**

How does the narrator's point of view affect conflict?

   **A.**

   **B.**

**VII. Figure One**

How does first-person narration affect character development?

   **A.**

When you are ready to finalize your ideas, use the Transfer tool to send your notes to a word processor.

   **B.**

---

## IRA/NCTE Standards for English Language Arts

10. Students whose first language is not English make use of their first language to develop competency in the English language arts and to develop understanding of content across the curriculum.

*Source:* International Reading Association and National Council of Teachers of English (1996).

## DIFFERENTIATING INSTRUCTION FOR ENGLISH LANGUAGE LEARNERS

Visual images are effective tools for aiding English language learners (Strickland, Ganske, & Monroe, 2002). They also benefit when reading and writing are integrated within an authentic context. One adaptation of this instructional strategy for second-language learners is to choose a favorite picture book and use its illustrations to implement the activity. Since English learners would be familiar with the text, they can focus their attention on the illustrations and the meaning behind them. Students would then write their own variation of the plot for the narrative.

## Differentiating Instruction for Students With Special Needs

Similarly to second-language learners, students with special needs also benefit from visual imagery (Compton-Lily, 2009). One adaptation for students with special needs is to use graphic novels or comic books to focus on visual literacy. Teachers may use their assessment of students' interests in selecting a text that will engage them. Teachers use Post-it notes to cover up the dialogue bubbles in these types of texts so students are able to generate their own thoughts for the activity.

## References

Compton-Lily, C. (2009). What can new literacy studies offer to the teaching of struggling readers? *The Reading Teacher, 63,* 88–90.

International Reading Association and National Council of Teachers of English. (1996). *Standards for the English language arts.* Newark, DE: International Reading Association and Urbana, IL: National Council of Teachers of English.

Leu, D., Castek, J., Coiro, J., Gort, M., Henry, L., & Lima, C. (2005). *Developing new literacies among multilingual learners in the elementary grades.* Retrieved January 9, 2010, from http://www.newliteracies.uconn.edu/pub_files/Developing_new_literacies_among_multicultural.pdf

National Geographic Society. (2010). *Photo of Kabul Market.* Retrieved January 31, 2010, from http://travel.nationalgeographic.com/travel/countries/afghanistan-photos/#31210_ 600x450.jpg

Strickland, D., Ganske, K., & Monroe, J. (2002). *Supporting struggling readers and writers.* Portland, ME: Stenhouse.

# SECTION X

# Essential Strategies for Teaching Writing Across the Curriculum

## A BRIEF OVERVIEW OF WRITING ACROSS THE CURRICULUM

The more students are exposed to writing instruction and practice, the better writers they become. Although teachers are aware of the importance of developing proficient writers, this goal is not being realized for too many students. As reported by the National Assessment of Educational Progress on the National Center for Educational Statistics (2007) website, for eighth-grade students, the "average writing scores were higher in 2007 than in previous assessments in 2002 and 1998." However, such increases described the percentages of students performing at or above the "Basic" achievement level, not at or above "Proficient." For students to use writing as an effective tool for learning, they need to write at a level of proficiency.

Duke (2010) reviewed the Progress in International Reading Literacy study that found "U.S. students are relatively poor at reading to acquire and use world information" (p. 68). She explained that in early years of schooling, children have little experience in reading and writing informational text. However, when students in elementary school are given more experience reading and writing informational text, studies show that their growth in comprehension and writing expository text improves (Purcell-Gates, Duke, & Martineau, 2007).

The landscape of literacy is changing rapidly, caused by the day-to-day changes in technology. Although multimedia plays a major role in how students write to represent their ideas (Gee, 2002), the goals for writing and its influence on learning remain the same. For example, as teachers and students are becoming more proficient in using electronic media, incorporating technology for completing required literacy tasks becomes commonplace (Ruddell, 2005). Their purpose for engaging in writing is to learn, regardless of the tools that are used to represent their ideas. Further, when writing is used effectively across the curriculum, it has an enormous influence on restructuring the writer's knowledge. For example, in all content areas as well as in science, "writing to learn activities are designed to use writing as a process in which students generate and clarify understanding of scientific concepts for themselves" (McDermott, 2010, p. 32). Further, writing across the curriculum facilitates students as they engage in assessing different points of view, evaluating ideas and products, and viewing a range of scenarios. In other words, students become critical thinkers (Baker et al., 2008). Educators are calling for use of writing as a primary tool for learning within and across the disciplines. For example, Barone and Youngs (2007) demonstrated the effectiveness of using multi-genre writing for learning in content-area classrooms. Students read a range of texts to learn about content and represented their understanding of the concepts and ideas through writing in various genres, such as postcards, brochures, and letters. The potential benefits of recreating various writing formats and genres to represent ideas from the disciplines that result in student learning are endless.

## Guidelines for Teaching Writing Across the Curriculum

Who are the teachers who support writing to learn? Teachers who integrate writing within the curriculum begin with the fundamental belief that writing is a supporting tool for knowledge construction and restructuring. Their instructional frameworks include strategies and activities that encourage students to inquire, explore, and restructure knowledge. Such teachers are diligent about connecting reading and writing as well as discussion and dialogue to support understanding (Knipper & Duggan, 2006). Their classroom environments are similar to those described by Wells and Chang-Wells (1992) where writing across the curriculum is the tool used for inquiry and learning and students are part of the community of learners receiving the necessary support and respect for their work.

The following are some basic guidelines for integrating writing within the curriculum and using it as a tool for learning:

- Provide students with authentic writing tasks that are rooted in the content learning and that students find engaging.

- Clarify the task for the students by setting clear expectations.

- Have students write frequently, offering the necessary support to sustain their "writing to learn."

- Select strategies that are designed for the literacy levels of the students and are supported by research that represents "best practice."

- Model for the whole class, small groups, and individual students how to write for learning from text.

- Design writing activities that connect reading and writing.

- Assess students' writing and engage students in a self-assessment of their work.

## Assessing Writing Across the Curriculum

When teachers assess students' writing to learn or writing across the curriculum, they will use a holistic scoring guide or rubric that evaluates the students' writing as a whole rather than targeting each of the components of writing. Rubrics are often used to determine the overall quality of the students' writing. However, teachers often use the results of assessments to determine those areas in need of improvement, where students would benefit from additional instruction. Figure X.1 is a sample scoring guide that may be used to assess students' progress in informational writing.

| **Figure X.1** Rubric for Assessing Informational Writing | | | |
|---|---|---|---|
| **Criterion** | **Advanced (3 Points)** | **Proficient (2 Points)** | **Developing (1–0 Points)** |
| **Purpose** | The writing demonstrates the student has a well-developed awareness of the purpose for writing. | The writing demonstrates the student has sufficient awareness of the purpose for writing. | The writing demonstrates the student has a limited or no awareness of the purpose for writing. |
| **Task** | The writing demonstrates the student has incorporated each of the elements of the required task at an accomplished level. | The writing demonstrates the student has incorporated most of the elements of the required task at a competent level. | The writing demonstrates the student has incorporated some or none of the elements of the required task. |
| **Content knowledge** | The writing demonstrates the student understands the topic at an advanced level of accuracy in content knowledge. | The writing demonstrates the student understands the topic at a proficient level of accuracy in content knowledge. | The writing demonstrates the student understands the topic at a minimal level of accuracy in content knowledge. |
| **Organization and coherence** | The writing demonstrates an advanced level with a superior degree of organization and coherence for representing the content knowledge. | The writing demonstrates a proficient level with a high degree of organization and coherence for representing the content knowledge. | The writing demonstrates a developing level with little or no organization and coherence for representing content knowledge. |
| **Academic vocabulary** | The writing demonstrates the student uses academic vocabulary at an advanced level of understanding. | The writing demonstrates the student uses academic vocabulary at a proficient level of understanding. | The writing demonstrates the student uses academic vocabulary at a minimal level of understanding. |
| **Text structure** | | | |
| **Visual** | The writing shows an excellent use of visuals (pictures and illustrations, diagrams, graphs, etc.) that further contributes to the meaning of the topic and indicates an advanced level of understanding. | The writing shows an appropriate use of visuals (pictures and illustrations, diagrams, graphs, etc.) that further contributes to the meaning of the topic and indicates a proficient level of understanding. | The writing shows no or little use of visuals (pictures and illustrations, diagrams, graphs, etc.) that do not contribute to the meaning of the topic and indicate a developing level of understanding. |
| **Sentence structure** | The writing demonstrates an advanced level of writing with no errors in sentence structure. | The writing demonstrates a proficient level of writing with few errors in sentence structure. | The writing demonstrates a developing level of writing with many errors in sentence structure. |

*(Continued)*

(Continued)

| Mechanics of language | The writing demonstrates an advanced level of writing with no errors in the mechanics of language. | The writing demonstrates a proficient level of writing with few errors in the mechanics of language. | The writing demonstrates a developing level of writing with many errors in the mechanics of language. |
|---|---|---|---|
| Word choice | The writing demonstrates an advanced level, having an excellent choice of words at all times that are appropriate for the content. | The writing demonstrates a proficient level, having a good choice of words at most times that are appropriate for the content. | The writing demonstrates a developing level, having a few good choices of words that are appropriate for the content. |

**Scoring Guide**
<u>Directions:</u> Assign a score of [1] for each [+] assessment. If you recorded a [–] mark,
assign a score of [0].
Advanced: 27–19 points
Proficient: 18–10 points
Developing: 9–0 points

# A Guide for Using Response to Intervention for Writing Across the Curriculum

As students progress through the grades, greater demands are made for writing in content areas. It is important that they are afforded the opportunities in all grades to receive instruction in writing across the curriculum. In addition to teaching writing across the curriculum, teachers need to provide constructive feedback and intervention for students who do not reach the required standard. Providing opportunities for writing in all content areas and systematically evaluating students' performance in writing informational text, teachers will be able to target specific areas that need improvement. Using a rubric such as the one in Figure X.1 will allow the teacher to identify students and their instructional needs. Students are then grouped by skill areas for instruction using an intervention strategy.

# Professional Resources

Calkins, L., & Pessah, L. (2008). *A principal's guide to leadership in the teaching of writing.* Portsmouth, NH: Heinemann.

Duke, N. K., & Bennett-Armistead, V. S. (with Huxley, A., Johnson, M. K, McLurkin, D., Roberts, E., Rosen, C., & Vogel, E.). (2003). *Reading and writing informational text in the primary grades: Research-based practices.* New York: Scholastic Teaching Resources.

Fisher, D., & Frey, N. (2007). *Scaffolded writing instruction: Teaching with a gradual release framework.* New York: Scholastic.

Kendall, J., & Khuon, O. (2006). *Writing sense: Integrated reading and writing lessons for English language learners.* Portland, ME: Stenhouse.

# REFERENCES

Baker, W. P., Barstack, R., Clark, D., Hull, E., Goodman, B., Kook, J., et al. (2008). Writing-to-learn in the inquiry-science classroom: Effective strategies from middle school science and writing teachers. *Clearing House: A Journal of Educational Strategies, Issues, and Ideas, 81*, 105–108.

Barone, D., & Youngs, S. (2007). *Writing without boundaries*. Portsmouth, NH: Heinemann.

Duke, N. K. (2010). The real world and writing U.S. children need. *Phi Delta Kappan, 91*(5), 68–71.

Gee, J. P. (2002). Millennials and Bobos, *Blue's Clues* and *Sesame Street*: A story for our times. In D. E. Alvermann (Ed.), *Adolescents and literacies in a digital world* (pp. 51–67). New York: Peter Lang.

Knipper, K. J., & Duggan, T. J. (2006). Writing to learn across the curriculum: Tools for comprehension in content-area classes. *The Reading Teacher, 59*(5), 462–470.

McDermott, M. (2010). More than writing to learn. *The Science Teacher, 77*(1), 32–37.

National Center for Educational Statistics. (2007). *NAEP reports: The nation's report card*. Retrieved February 7, 2010, from http://nces.ed.gov/nationsreportcard

Purcell-Gates, V., Duke, N. K., & Martineau, J. (2007). Learning to read and write genre-specific text roles of authentic experience and explicit instruction. *Reading Research Quarterly, 42*(1), 8–45.

Ruddell, M. R. (2005). *Teaching content reading and writing* (4th ed.). Hoboken, NJ: Wiley.

Wells, G., & Chang-Wells, G. L. (1992). *Constructing knowledge together: Classrooms as centers of inquiry and literacy*. Portsmouth, NH: Heinemann.

# Strategy
# 46

# All-About Books

## SPEAKING BRIEFLY: AN OVERVIEW OF THE LITERACY STRATEGY

The *All-About Books* strategy provides children with the opportunity to publish books about a content-area topic they are learning. As students read and discuss topics across the curriculum, they focus on aspects of a topic that they are learning and have a special interest in and write and publish their own books on that topic. To present the ideas on their topic, students are encouraged to read to acquire a breadth of knowledge and select the appropriate information for their books. Students are connecting and integrating their reading with their writing as they use the publishing process to construct knowledge. Reutzel and Cooter (2008) state that "of the many ways to help readers succeed with content materials, teaching them to become authors of expository texts may be the most powerful" (p. 504). In addition to discovering, expanding, refining, and deepening meanings of ideas, students are also learning about authoring informational texts, a genre that is not familiar to all students.

Although writing All-About Books has frequently been used by teachers in the primary grades, we suggest that students in the intermediate and middle grades continue to engage in informational writing through authoring books. Teachers in kindergarten or first grade may first introduce this strategy through interactive writing of an All-About Book. Using chart paper, the teacher models writing the book with the class, limiting the length of the book to five to seven pages. The book is short, with each page including an illustration and a sentence. For students in the intermediate and middle grades, the teacher reviews the parts of a book and explains the process, showing examples of All-About Books.

## USING ALL-ABOUT BOOKS

*When to use the strategy:* All-About Books are appropriate for reading and writing across the curriculum. After students learn about a topic of study through reading and discussion, they write their books. Oftentimes, as they are writing, they will stop to search for more information in related books or on websites.

*Source:* International Reading Association and National Council of Teachers of English (1996).

## IRA/NCTE Standards for English Language Arts

1. Students read a wide range of print and nonprint texts to build an understanding of texts, of themselves, and of the cultures of the United States and the world; to acquire new information; to respond to the needs and demands of society and the workplace; and for personal fulfillment. Among these texts are fiction and nonfiction, classic and contemporary works.

3. Students apply a wide range of strategies to comprehend, interpret, evaluate, and appreciate texts. They draw on their prior experience, their interactions with other readers and writers, their knowledge of word meaning and of other texts, their word identification strategies, and their understanding of textual features (e.g., sound-letter correspondence, sentence structure, context, graphics).

5. Students employ a wide range of strategies as they write and use different writing process elements appropriately to communicate with different audiences for a variety of purposes.

7. Students conduct research on issues and interests by generating ideas and questions, and by posing problems. They gather, evaluate, and synthesize data from a variety of sources (e.g., print and nonprint texts, artifacts, people) to communicate their discoveries in ways that suit their purpose and audience.

11. Students participate as knowledgeable, reflective, creative, and critical members of a variety of literacy communities.

12. Students use spoken, written, and visual language to accomplish their own purposes (e.g., for learning, enjoyment, persuasion, and the exchange of information).

*Strategy modifications for grade levels:* For young students, All-About Books are short, often limited to five to seven pages. As students advance through the grades, the books become longer and the illustrations more elaborate, providing additional information. With longer books, students need time to read and learn about the topic as well as develop a plan for organizing the information. Students in the intermediate and middle grades may work in small groups to coauthor longer books, each developing an aspect of the topic that is being studied.

## IMPLEMENTING THE ALL-ABOUT BOOKS STRATEGY: STEP BY STEP

The length and depth of information within an All-About Book is dependent on the students' grade level and literacy development. As students become fluent readers and writers and as their understanding of content knowledge deepens, their books become longer, filled with more information on the topic of study.

1. **Prepare students for writing.** The teacher prepares students for writing through reading and discussing the topic. For young students, the teacher may use dialogic reading of informational children's literature; for older students, the teacher may use text sets to be read by students. A text set consists of a set of children's literature choices that are closely related to the topic.

2. **Engage students in a guided discussion on the information from their readings.** The teacher guides the discussion of the students' readings, focusing the essential

questions on the information that they have read about the topic of study. During the discussion, the teacher helps students deepen their understanding of the concepts and ideas along with the vocabulary from their readings.

3. **Select and organize ideas for writing.** The teacher guides students in determining the information that they will include in their books and facilitates them in organizing the specific ideas that they will write about.

4. **Demonstrate and discuss the page format.** For younger children, their books include a picture and a sentence. For older students, the books are longer and each page may include illustrations, pictures, diagrams, or graphs with a paragraph or more to explain the central ideas. The teacher shows students how the illustration provides further information than is given in the text.

5. **Assist students in completing their books.** Help students determine a title page and cover illustration by thinking about the ideas they included in their books. Older students may include additional features of a book, such as a table of contents, page numbers, references, a list of further readings, a glossary, and even a book jacket.

6. **Decide on how students will share their books.** Before students share their books with other students, they read them to the teacher. Take this opportunity to provide feedback to help students read and correct any misconceptions or errors. Choose a way for students to share their books with others, such as through a class read-aloud or paired reading. Display the students' books for others to read during independent reading.

## APPLYING THE ALL-ABOUT BOOKS STRATEGY: FIRST-GRADE LESSON ON INSECTS

First-graders were learning about insects during science. They listened to a read-aloud of *Spiders* by Seymour Simon (2003). After a book discussion, the teacher and students reviewed the important facts and interesting information that they learned from the readings. The teacher used the All-About Books strategy to integrate students' reading and writing across the curriculum. Each student wrote and illustrated one page for their book, titled *All About Spiders*. Figure 46.1 shows a sample page written by one student for her *All About Spiders* book.

*Source:* International Reading Association and National Council of Teachers of English (1996).

> ### IRA/NCTE Standards for the English Language Arts
>
> 10. Students whose first language is not English make use of their first language to develop competency in the English language arts and to develop understanding of content across the curriculum.

## DIFFERENTIATING INSTRUCTION FOR ENGLISH LANGUAGE LEARNERS

For English language learners, writing longer All-About Books may be overwhelming. Although they may understand the content that is being studied, writing about it in their

| Figure 46.1 | A Sample Page from *All About Spiders* |

SPIDERS MAKE SILK. THEY USE THE SILK TO MAKE WEBS. THEY CATCH THEIR FOOD IN THE WEB. WAIT WAIT WAIT. THEN THE INSECT IS TRAPPED IN THE WEB. THEY EAT THEIR FOOD.

MISTY 1B

second language poses a challenge. Teachers may differentiate instruction for this strategy by having the students create All-About Posters that contain a combination of pictures, diagrams, maps, graphs, and webs that illustrate the content. When they have completed most of the visuals, they work with the teacher to explain their meanings. Together, they "talk through" the text that will become part of the poster. To ensure that students are learning the academic vocabulary that conveys the content, the teacher will provide mini-lessons when they jointly decide on the content of the text. The students then return to their posters to add the text under the appropriate visual.

## DIFFERENTIATING INSTRUCTION FOR STUDENTS WITH SPECIAL NEEDS

Teachers may differentiate instruction for students with special needs who are experiencing reading and writing problems by using the All-About Books strategy within a collaborative environment. Students work together in publishing a class book. The following approach may be used for writing a class All-About Book: (1) Under the direction of the teacher, the group chooses a topic to write about and brainstorms different aspects of the topic to be included in the book. (2) The teacher reviews the parts of a book. (3) Each member of the group selects an area to write about. (4) The teacher models how to write and illustrate their content on one page. (5) As the students work on their pages, the teacher assists them in writing the content. (6) Each member of the group contributes a page to the class book, which may be published as a wall book or put together as a traditional book and placed on display. (7) Members of the group read and discuss their book with the class.

## References

International Reading Association and National Council of Teachers of English. (1996). *Standards for the English language arts*. Newark, DE: International Reading Association and Urbana, IL: National Council of Teachers of English.

Reutzel, D. R., & Cooter, R. B. (2008). Teaching children to read: The teacher makes the difference (5th ed.). Upper Saddle River, NJ: Merrill Prentice Hall.

## Children's Literature Cited

Simon, S. (2003). *Spiders*. New York: HarperCollins.

# Frames for Writing Biographies

## Strategy 47

---

The purpose for the *Frames for Writing Biographies* strategy is to provide students with a scaffold for gathering and organizing information for writing a biography. The increased requirements placed on students to read and write informational text has been documented. Yet the kind of literacy experiences in primary grades focus on reading and writing stories. Most young children learn about reading and writing through numerous experiences with fiction. When primary-grade students learn to write, they receive large doses of experience in story writing. As a result, they develop positive attitudes toward reading and writing stories as well as a schema for supporting this type of literacy development. It is understandable that Daniels (1990) declared the existence of an "expository gap" for students as they receive increased requirements for writing informational text. One way to facilitate students' informational literacy is to begin to widen their range of reading and writing to include biographies, a start that promises to advance students' academic knowledge and its use across the curriculum.

A strategy that facilitates students as they write biographies should help them "collect and synthesize information for informative writing" (Tompkins, 2007, p. 293). Vacca (2002) explains that when students read and learn about the life of a historical figure and then are asked to write about that person, they are required to "think on paper." This type of thinking promotes students' exploration of ideas encountered in text.

When students begin to write a biographical sketch of someone they have read about, they are required to gather facts and information from that person's life and organize them in a coherent manner. Good writers use a process of critical inquiry that is based on creating questions and then searching for answers. Therefore, as students write biographies, they start with questions that will facilitate their research in gathering ideas and facts. When teachers understand that reading and writing are reciprocal processes (Shanahan, 2006), they assist students' informational literacy development by providing them with outstanding children's literature and other print materials to answer their questions. As students read biographies, they will identify those aspects of a person's life to write about, find answers to their questions and sometimes raise new questions to research, explore different ways to organize and present their information, and build background knowledge that may be used across the curriculum.

*Source:* International Reading Association and National Council of Teachers of English (1996).

---

### IRA/NCTE Standards for English Language Arts

1. Students read a wide range of print and nonprint texts to build an understanding of texts, of themselves, and of the cultures of the United States and the world; to acquire new information; to respond to the needs and demands of society and the workplace; and for personal fulfillment. Among these texts are fiction and nonfiction, classic and contemporary works.

11. Students participate as knowledgeable, reflective, creative, and critical members of a variety of literacy communities.

12. Students use spoken, written, and visual language to accomplish their own purposes (e.g., for learning, enjoyment, persuasion, and the exchange of information).

---

## Using Frames for Writing Biographies

*When to use the strategy:* The strategy is a tool to help students prepare for writing. It should be used before they write to prepare them for writing a biography as well as before, during, and after reading. The teacher uses the strategy before students read to help them establish a purpose for reading and develop their initial questions in their search for information. During reading, students use the frames to collect and record information for writing, and after reading, they will use the frames to organize and synthesize the material for writing.

*Strategy modifications for grade levels:* The graphics or frames that are used to prepare students to write should be modified for grade levels as well as reading and writing levels. For the primary grades, a simplified graphic that helps students think about the beginning, middle, and end of the person's life may be developed. As students move into the intermediate and middle grades, the graphic should be more complex and help students think about the accomplishments, character traits, values, and so forth of the person they are writing about.

### Implementing the Frames for Writing Biographies Strategy: Step by Step

Depending on the grade level and the students' reading and writing levels, this strategy will take students more than one day. They need to learn about biographies, how to use the frames for collecting and synthesizing information from literature, and writing a biographical report.

1. **Read aloud a short biography.** The teacher begins by selecting a short biography to read aloud, one that is motivating and within students' comprehension

level. After a brief book discussion, the teacher asks students to name the most important events about the subject of the book that they would like to remember. The teacher records them and shows students how to change the events into questions for further inquiry.

2. **Demonstrate how to use the frames for writing biographies.** Using the biography that was read aloud, model for students how the frames are used to guide their collection of information from the text. The teacher refers to three or four essential questions that will help students search for information and then encourages them to ask their own questions.

3. **Provide students with biographies to choose from.** Offer students a selection of biographies from outstanding children's literature and have them choose a person they wish to read about.

4. **Review the frames before reading.** Prior to reading, review the frames that will guide them in collecting and synthesizing information during and after reading. One example is shown in Figure 47.1. However, the teacher may redesign the graphic for the appropriate grade level and to fit the biography that they are reading.

5. **Monitor students' use of the frames during reading.** Have students read their books. While students are rereading for information, monitor their use of the frames for collecting information.

6. **Demonstrate how to use the information for writing.** After students have completed their frames, they will use their information for writing a brief biographical report. Monitor students' writing by showing them how to select the important information from their frames to write a paragraph on the person that they chose.

## APPLYING THE FRAMES FOR WRITING BIOGRAPHIES STRATEGY: SECOND-GRADE LESSON ON PRESIDENTS

During Presidents' Day, the students in the second grade were listening to biographies of some of the great presidents. The teacher conducted a read-aloud of *Young Abe Lincoln: The Frontier Days, 1809–1837* by Cheryl Harness (2008). She then demonstrated how to use the graphic organizer to gather important information from what was read. She explained that after they collect and organize the information about a person's life, they may use it to write a short biography about the person. Figure 47.2 shows how the class took notes from the biography and recorded them on the graphic organizer.

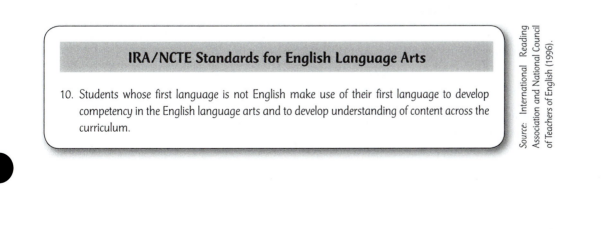

### IRA/NCTE Standards for English Language Arts

10. Students whose first language is not English make use of their first language to develop competency in the English language arts and to develop understanding of content across the curriculum.

*Source:* International Reading Association and National Council of Teachers of English (1996).

**Figure 47.1**   Sample Frame for Writing Biographies

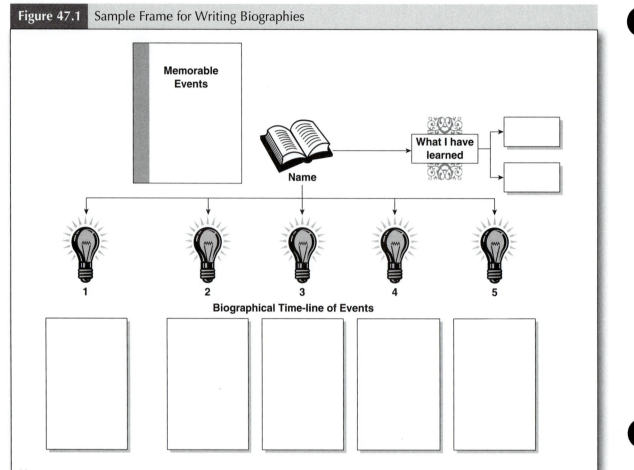

Biographical Time-line of Events

**Name**

Choose an important or memorable person in your life to write about.

**I. 1**

Name

Date/place of birth

Profession

**II. 2**

What are your most important memories of this person? Type key words into the search field on the Symbol palette to find the best images to express your ideas.

**III. 3**

What is this person like? Write adjectives that describe him or her, and back them up with examples. Use the Word Guide to help find the right word.

**IV. 4**

What kinds of things does this person do? Consider his or her work, recreation, leisure time, etc.

**V. 5**

What does this person believe about life, the world, society, etc.?

**VI. What I have learned**

What have you learned from this person?

**A.**

**B.**

**Memorable Events**

**Figure 47.2**    Frame for Writing Abraham Lincoln's Biography

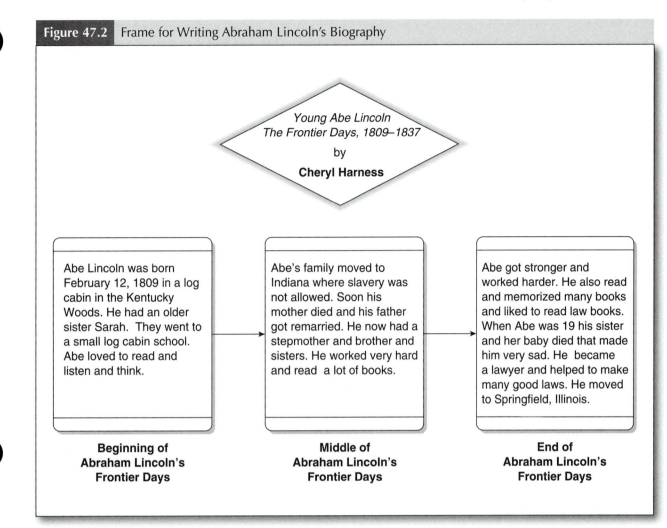

## DIFFERENTIATING INSTRUCTION FOR ENGLISH LANGUAGE LEARNERS

For English language learners, the graphic should be fashioned for the students' language and literacy levels. One teacher who worked with English language learners having little experience in writing informational text and just learning English simplified the graphic to include three parts of the person's life—the beginning, middle, and end. Each box was clearly labeled, along with a picture of the person as a child, teenager, and adult. After reading and discussing the book together, the teacher worked with the children to write one sentence about each of the three parts of the person's life.

## DIFFERENTIATING INSTRUCTION FOR STUDENTS WITH SPECIAL NEEDS

Students with special needs who are disabled readers and writers will need direct instruction and continuous monitoring when using the strategy. Such support may be given to the students using a collaborative approach and working in small groups. The teacher prepares by redesigning the graphic to prompt students for explicit information that may be found easily within the text. Using a guided reading approach, the students read and discuss the biography with the teacher. Next, the teacher distributes and explains the graphic to the students. Finally, the teacher guides the students in rereading the biography for the purpose of searching for information marked on the graphic. Together, they record it on the appropriate frame. After reviewing and selecting the appropriate information, the teacher and students use a "shared-pen" approach to write a short biography. This approach to writing allows the students to work with the teacher in writing together. As the teacher begins to write the biography on the chart, she shares the pen with a student who may write a word or complete the sentence.

## REFERENCES

Daniels, H. A. (1990). Developing a sense of audience. In T. Shanahan (Ed.), *Reading and writing together: New perspectives for the classroom* (pp. 99–125). Norwood, MA: Christopher-Gordon.

International Reading Association and National Council of Teachers of English. (1996). *Standards for the English language arts.* Newark, DE: International Reading Association and Urbana, IL: National Council of Teachers of English.

Shanahan, T. (2006). Relations among oral language, reading, and writing development. In C. A. MacArthur, S. Graham, & J. Fitzgerald (Eds.), *Handbook of writing research* (pp. 171–186). New York: Guilford.

Tompkins, G. (2007). *Literacy for the 21st century: Teaching reading and writing in prekindergarten through grade 4.* Upper Saddle River, NJ: Merrill Prentice Hall.

Vacca, R. T. (2002). Making a difference in adolescents' school lives: Visible and invisible aspects of content-area reading. In A. E. Farstrup & S. J. Samuels (Eds.), *What research has to say about reading instruction* (pp. 184–204). Newark, DE: International Reading Association.

## CHILDREN'S LITERATURE CITED

Harness, C. (2008). *Young Abe Lincoln: The frontier days, 1809–1837.* Washington, DC: National Geographic Children's Books.

# Entrance and Exit Slips

# Strategy 48

*Entrance Slips* are used prior to instruction when students are asked to write what they know about the topic, while *Exit Slips* are used on completion of the lesson and readings when students summarize what they have learned, areas they need to learn more about, or whether they thought the lesson was helpful in learning about the topic. The strategy is another excellent approach to help students engage in writing to learn. When teachers use Entrance Slips, students write what they know prior to the lesson, requiring them to tap their prior knowledge as they begin to think about the topic. Zwiers (2008) explains that such strategies help students prepare themselves "with content, thinking, and language that they will encounter in the text" (p. 229). Students' completed Entrance Slips may be used by teachers to determine whether their instructional plans need to be amended.

When using Exit Slips at the completion of the lesson and readings, Fisher and Frey (2004) suggest the following three categories be used by teachers for writing prompts to focus students' writing: (1) prompts that document learning, (2) prompts that emphasize the process of learning, and (3) prompts that evaluate the effectiveness of instruction. Exit Slips offer students an opportunity to write to learn content. When students are given activities that incorporate writing across the curriculum, they recall information that they learned, clarify ideas and facts, integrate the new ideas that they know, and query about what they need to learn. Teachers may use students' writing as a diagnostic tool to clarify information or correct misconceptions (Daniels & Bizar, 2005) or to assess their teaching and modify it when needed.

## USING ENTRANCE AND EXIT SLIPS

*When to use the strategy:* The purpose for using Entrance Slips is to activate prior knowledge and encourage students to begin to think about the topic of study. Therefore, they should be used before reading. After students complete the lesson, readings, and discussions, the teacher uses Exit Slips to help students recall what they learned, clarify meanings, and think about what they need to learn.

*Source:* International Reading Association and National Council of Teachers of English (1996).

---

### IRA/NCTE Standards for English Language Arts

3. Students apply a wide range of strategies to comprehend, interpret, evaluate, and appreciate texts. They draw on their prior experience, their interactions with other readers and writers, their knowledge of word meaning and of other texts, their word identification strategies, and their understanding of textual features (e.g., sound-letter correspondence, sentence structure, context, graphics).

5. Students employ a wide range of strategies as they write and use different writing process elements appropriately to communicate with different audiences for a variety of purposes.

12. Students use spoken, written, and visual language to accomplish their own purposes (e.g., for learning, enjoyment, persuasion, and the exchange of information).

---

*Strategy modifications for grade levels:* The strategy may be modified for use with primary-grade students. For very young students, the teacher may act as a scribe as she or he writes on large chart paper students' responses to prompts that will elicit what they know about the topic and what they learned. In the intermediate and middle grades, students work independently to write their responses on the Entrance and Exit Slips.

## IMPLEMENTING THE ENTRANCE AND EXIT SLIPS STRATEGY: STEP BY STEP

Entrance Slips are used as an introduction to the lesson and readings for the purpose of activating students' prior knowledge and establishing a purpose for learning. Exit Slips are used at the completion of the lesson and readings to assist students in recalling, interpreting, and reflecting on their learning. Teachers may use both Entrance and Exit Slips, or they may decide to use only one.

Entrance Slips are used before the lesson and readings as a way to help students think about what they will be learning.

1. **Introduce the lesson and readings.** Begin the lesson with a motivating discussion on the topic that will help students focus on that topic. Provide a brief introduction to the book and the lesson for the purpose of getting students ready for the lesson.

2. **Distribute Entrance Slips.** Figure 48.1 is an example of an Entrance Slip where the teacher used prompts or questions to focus students on the topic to be studied. Ask students to use the Entrance Slips to write as much information on the topic as they know.

3. **Provide students with time to write what they know on the slip.** After students receive their Entrance Slips, provide them with no more than 5 minutes for writing what they know about the topic.

4. **Collect the students' Entrance Slips.** After 5 minutes, collect the slips, quickly skim students' responses, and continue with the lesson. The students' writings will help teachers determine how to proceed with the lesson.

**Figure 48.1**   Sample Entrance and Exit Slips

---

### ENTRANCE SLIP

**Tell what you already know about . . .**

**What would you like to learn about . . . today?**

**Name:**                    **Date:**          **Grade:**

---

### EXIT SLIP

**Tell what you learned about . . . from your readings and discussions.**

**What do you need to learn about . . . ?**

**What would have made this activity more enjoyable?**

**Name:**                    **Date:**          **Grade:**

---

Exit Slips are used when the lesson and readings are completed. Students summarize what they have learned and areas related to the topic that they wish to learn more about and evaluate the instructional activities that were used in the lesson.

1. **Bring the lesson and readings to a close with a discussion.** Engage students in a brief discussion that summarizes the readings and related topics. The teacher may decide to have a large-group or small-group discussion.

2. **Distribute the Exit Slips.** The teacher distributes the Exit Slips, similar to Figure 48.1, which were prepared in advance with appropriate prompts that require students to write about the content they learned, areas for further learning, and how the instructional activities have facilitated their learning.

3. **Provide a brief explanation of the task.** The teacher may decide to demonstrate how to use the Exit Slip. Students should understand that the purpose of "writing to learn" is to help them recall and clarify the information they have learned. Therefore, their focus should be on representing content they have learned rather than on the writing process.

4. **Allow approximately 5 to 7 minutes for writing.** Tell students to complete the prompts within the given time. When students have finished writing, collect the Exit Slips.

The teacher may use the students' responses on their Entrance and Exit Slips as a diagnostic tool to help determine what they have learned and need to learn, as well as using their responses to examine their perceptions of the process of learning. At the beginning of the next lesson, the students' responses may be shared with the class to initiate a discussion that will segue into the next lesson. When necessary, the teachers may modify instruction to further develop students' ideas and content knowledge or clarify any of their misconceptions.

## Applying the Entrance and Exit Slips Strategy: Eighth-Grade Lesson on Cells

Eighth-grade students completed a study of cells in science class and were beginning a lesson on stem cells and their value in research. Before the teacher introduced the lesson, she distributed the Entrance Slips and asked students to complete the prompts. When students finished writing to the prompts, the teacher collected and skimmed the slips to discern how to proceed with the lesson. A sample of a completed Entrance Slip is shown in Figure 48.2.

After an introduction to the lesson, the students read two chapters on stem cells and their use in research from *Great Medical Discoveries: Stem Cells* by Toney Allman (2006). That was followed by a guided discussion of the readings. At the end of the discussion, the teacher distributed the Exit Slips and students were given 5 minutes to answer the prompts. The teacher collected the slips and used them to assess student learning and prepare for the next lesson. A sample of a student's Exit Slip is shown in Figure 48.2.

*Source:* International Reading Association and National Council of Teachers of English (1996).

### IRA/NCTE Standards for English Language Arts

10. Students whose first language is not English make use of their first language to develop competency in the English language arts and to develop understanding of content across the curriculum.

| **Figure 48.2** | Sample Entrance and Exit Slips |
|---|---|

### ENTRANCE SLIP

**Tell what you know about Stem Cell Research. What would you like to learn about the topic?**

*Stem cells are cells and are mostly like all other cells. But they are different in a way. I know that there are some people for stem cell research. There are a group of people that think that stem cell research should not be allowed by law.*
*I would like to know why scientists believe that stem cells can be used to cure diseases.*

**Name:** Joel                    **Date:** February 9                    **Grade:** 8

### EXIT SLIP

**Tell what you learned about Stem Cell Research from your readings and discussions.**

*Stem cells are different than most cells. They are not specialized. That means that they do not have the function of a special organ like the heart or the lungs. Stem cells can change into specialized cells. So scientists believe that stem cell research can help to find cures for many diseases. Not everyone believes that stem cell research should be used in fighting diseases. They believe that when scientists use embryonic stem cells they break God's law. What is the difference in stem cells?*

**Name:** Joel                    **Date:** February 9                    **Grade:** 8

## DIFFERENTIATING INSTRUCTION FOR ENGLISH LANGUAGE LEARNERS

As English language learners begin to write on their Entrance and Exit Slips, work with them to put their ideas in a simple coherent sentence. Students should begin by using illustrations and diagrams to represent one or two ideas or concepts they have learned. Teachers should encourage students to talk about their illustrations and support them by using academic vocabulary that accurately represents their ideas. After students retell what they have learned, teachers should assist them in writing it down on their slips.

## DIFFERENTIATING INSTRUCTION FOR STUDENTS WITH SPECIAL NEEDS

Frequently, students with special needs have low literacy levels and will find it difficult to activate prior knowledge related to a lesson. Before students use Entrance Slips, the teacher should engage them in a brief discussion that will help them make connections between the topic and their personal lives and experiences. This will assist them in drawing on their background knowledge related to the topic of study. For Exit Slips, the teacher should ask students what they have learned and encourage them to tell all they know. As they begin their summaries, the teacher guides them through each sentence.

Many teachers find it beneficial to model the process before using the slips with students. Through a guided discussion, the teachers elicit the students' responses and record them on a group chart. When students understand the process, they use their own Entrance and Exit Slips.

## REFERENCES

Daniels, H., & Bizar, M. (2005). *Teaching the best practice way: Methods that matter, K–12*. Portland, ME: Stenhouse.

Fisher, D., & Frey, N. (2004). *Improving adolescent literacy: Strategies that work*. Upper Saddle River, NJ: Merrill Prentice Hall.

International Reading Association and National Council of Teachers of English. (1996). *Standards for the English language arts*. Newark, DE: International Reading Association and Urbana, IL: National Council of Teachers of English.

Zwiers, J. (2008). *Building academic language: Essential practices for content classrooms, Grades 5–12*. San Francisco: Jossey-Bass.

## CHILDREN'S LITERATURE CITED

Allman, T. (2006). *Great medical discoveries: Stem cells*. Farmington Hills, MI: Lucent.

# Strategy 49

# Data Charts

## Speaking Briefly: An Overview of the Literacy Strategy

The purpose for using *Data Charts* is to present a structured approach for collecting, organizing, and synthesizing information. Data Charts are graphic organizers that provide students with a method to organize information from varied sources of data around conceptual categories or essential questions. Similar to Inquiry Charts, or I-Charts, the Data Charts offer students a procedure for assembling information from several sources. Tompkins (2009) describes how the grid is used to gather information from a number of texts around four or more subtopics; whereas, in the I-Chart, the students use questions to guide their research and organize their information (Tierney & Readence, 2000).

The Data Charts benefit students in multiple ways. Students learn a strategy for organizing and using information from multiple sources. Herrell and Jordan (2006) explain that the use of the Data Charts supports students' comprehension. As students begin to look for information from multiple texts, they will survey texts by using the table of contents, chapter headings, as well as illustrations and graphics. The categories or questions encourage students to focus their reading and writing on the required topics of information.

Another significant advantage of using the charts is to assist students in organizing information around categories or essential questions for writing informational text. Antonacci and O'Callaghan (2006) explain the problems students face in writing about information garnered from multiple texts. One major challenge they face is how to organize so much information for use in their writing. The Data Chart offers a visual display of information that is arranged around conceptual categories or essential questions, affording students a sense of organization for writing. When writing to learn, students may use the organized information on the chart to compare, analyze, evaluate, and summarize (Wood & Taylor, 2006).

## Using Data Charts

*When to use the strategy:* Data Charts should be used before, during, and after reading and writing. In preparing students to read, the chart will help students establish a purpose for reading. During reading, students will record information gathered from their

*Source:* International Reading Association and National Council of Teachers of English (1996).

### IRA/NCTE Standards for English Language Arts

1. Students read a wide range of print and nonprint texts to build an understanding of texts, of them-selves, and of the cultures of the United States and the world; to acquire new information; to respond to the needs and demands of society and the workplace; and for personal fulfillment. Among these texts are fiction and nonfiction, classic and contemporary works.

3. Students apply a wide range of strategies to comprehend, interpret, evaluate, and appreciate texts. They draw on their prior experience, their interactions with other readers and writers, their knowledge of word meaning and of other texts, their word identification strategies, and their understanding of textual features (e.g., sound-letter correspondence, sentence structure, context, graphics).

5. Students employ a wide range of strategies as they write and use different writing process elements appropriately to communicate with different audiences for a variety of purposes.

7. Students conduct research on issues and interests by generating ideas and questions, and by posing problems. They gather, evaluate, and synthesize data from a variety of sources (e.g., print and non-print texts, artifacts, people) to communicate their discoveries in ways that suit their purpose and audience.

12. Students use spoken, written, and visual language to accomplish their own purposes (e.g., for learn-ing, enjoyment, persuasion, and the exchange of information).

data sources, and after reading, they will decide on the information they will include in their writing.

*Strategy modifications for grade levels:* Teachers in the primary grades may use fewer sources of data and have students focus on three or four categories for collecting infor-mation. Teachers in the intermediate and middle grades may expand the number of texts for gathering information and use questions that are prepared by the teacher and the students.

## IMPLEMENTING THE DATA CHARTS STRATEGY: STEP BY STEP

To support and extend writing to learn, the teacher considers the students' literacy levels, their experience with the strategy, and the topic when designing their Data Charts.

1. **Select the appropriate data sources.** When selecting the texts, consider the topic of study, the type of book, as well as the grade and literacy levels of the students. For primary grades, limit the number of texts to two or three and choose books that contain explicit information. For intermediate and middle grades, several books, including the textbook, may be used along with Internet sites and information from multimedia sources.

2. **Develop the Data Chart.** Using the data sources, decide on categories or essential questions that students may use to guide their search of information. A sample Data Chart is shown in Figure 49.1.

3. **Introduce the topic.** Engage students in a motivating discussion on the topic of study, tapping their prior knowledge and related experiences. At this time, the

teacher may conduct a book introduction to provide students with an overview of the readings, showing students how each reading relates to the topic of study. When other sources of data are used, provide a similar introduction that will assist students in finding information.

4. **Demonstrate how to use Data Charts.** Display the chart and explain how it is developed with categories of information or questions recorded at the top and sources of data at the side. Clarify the purpose for using Data Charts, showing how information is recorded and organized around a specific subtopic or question. Ask students if any other category needs to be included, and make necessary revisions to the chart when needed. Model how to record information from the readings when it relates to a category or answers a question.

5. **Assist students as they use the Data Charts.** The teacher may decide to implement the Data Chart strategy with the whole class and then gradually release the responsibility to small groups of students. Within the small-group approach, each group may be responsible for one reading to search for information. When students learn the strategy, they may work independently and use several data sources to locate information. In any case, when the students are reading and using the chart to collect information, the teacher assists and guides them at each step.

6. **Provide a time to share information.** When students have completed the Data Charts, the teacher provides a time for sharing. The teacher may use a large class chart for sharing information. As the students contribute their findings, the teacher records the information on the wall chart. At this time, the teacher and students synthesize the information, decide if more is needed, and consider what they learned.

7. **Demonstrate how to use information in writing a summary paragraph.** The teacher shows students how to use the information in writing a summary paragraph. The categories or questions are used to help them organize the information into a coherent paragraph. As students write their summaries, the teacher assists them when needed.

## APPLYING THE DATA CHARTS STRATEGY: THIRD-GRADE LESSON ON MAMMALS

For students in third grade, the science curriculum included the study of mammals. After the class learned the characteristics of mammals, the teacher focused on polar bears, known as sea mammals, to further their study. The teacher introduced the Data Chart strategy by explaining how it was used to collect and organize information from a number of different books. The teacher motivated the students to learn about polar bears by conducting a read-aloud of *A Pair of Polar Bears: Twin Cubs Find a Home at the San Diego Zoo* by Joanne Ryder (2006). The teacher and students worked together to develop questions that they would then use to guide them in their search for information in their books. Using the Internet, the teacher projected a website about polar bears (http://www.seaworld.org/animal-info/info-books/polar-bear/index.htm), which they read and used to answer the questions. The students worked in small groups, reading one piece of literature, discussing the questions on the chart, and finding information in their texts to support their responses. After they finished reading and discussing their books, they shared their information and recorded it on the class Data Chart, as shown in Figure 49.2. The students then used the Data Chart to write a summary paragraph about polar bears.

| Figure 49.1 | Data Chart |
| --- | --- |

Name: _____ Date: _____

Topic of Study: _____

| Data Source | Question #1 | Question #2 | Question #3 | Question #4 | Interesting Facts |
| --- | --- | --- | --- | --- | --- |
|  |  |  |  |  |  |
|  |  |  |  |  |  |
|  |  |  |  |  |  |
|  |  |  |  |  |  |
|  |  |  |  |  |  |
|  |  |  |  |  |  |

**Figure 49.2**    Class Data Chart for a Unit on Polar Bears

**Name:** *Third-Grade Unit of Study on Polar Bears*
**Date:** *January 11 to January 15*

Topic: **POLAR BEARS**

| Data Source | What do polar bears look like? | Where do polar bears live? | How do polar bears keep warm? | What do polar bears eat? | Interesting Facts |
|---|---|---|---|---|---|
| *Face to Face with Polar Bears*<br><br>*Norbert Rosing*<br>*(2007)* | *Polar bears are the largest animals. Their paws are 12 inches and they weigh about 1,700 pounds.* | *They live in the Arctic. Manitoba, Canada is called the "polar bear capital of the world" because there are so many.* | *The polar bears love to stay near the icy Arctic Ocean. Polar bears need to keep their fur coats clean because a clean coat keeps them warm.* | *They eat mainly fat and meat from other animals. Seals are their favorite food, but they also eat walruses and caribou.* | *Polar bears look like brown and black bears, but they are different. Brown and black bears are land animals and polar bears are marine mammals.* |
| *Polar Bears*<br><br>*Jolyon Goddard*<br>*(2008)* | *Male polar bears (boars) are about 1,700 pounds. They are larger than the females (sows) that are about 750 pounds.* | *The Arctic is the home of the polar bear. They do not live in one place. They follow the ice that expands in the winter and melts in the summer.* | *Polar bears have two layers of fur. The outside layer is long guard hairs and the inside layer is shorter called the under-fur. The fat or blubber under the fur also keeps them warm.* | *In order to survive in the Arctic, polar bears have good senses. They can smell a seal that is about a half a mile away even when it is hidden in its den under the ice.* | *Polar bears are outstanding swimmers. Some take a journey of over 2,000 miles when they swim and float on the ice. Polar bears lie and wait on the ice for seals or they creep up to catch them.* |
| *A Polar Bear Journey*<br><br>*Debbie S. Miller*<br>*(1997)* | *Polar bears have huge paws that help to distribute their weight on the ice so they won't fall in.* | *Polar bears live in the Arctic where it is very cold. They live by the water to get their food.* | *Polar bears have paws insulated with fur. The thick layers of fat help the heat from escaping their bodies.* | *Polar bears hunt for seals. This is the food they mainly eat.* | *Polar bears are true marine mammals because they spend more time on ice and in the sea than on land.* |
| *Polar Bears*<br><br>*Gail Gibbons*<br>*(2001)* | *Most male polar bears are 10 feet tall and weigh 750 to 1,000 pounds. Female polar bears are smaller. They have webbed paws for swimming.* | *They live in the Arctic where it is very cold. Sometimes it can get 50 degrees below 0 degrees.* | *The top layer of fur made up of hollow hairs that keep the bear warm. The blubber and black skin under the fur soaks up the sunlight to help warm the bear.* | *Polar bears eat meat. The ringed seal is their favorite food. They also eat musk oxen, caribous, and seabirds.* | *Polar bears do not have eyelashes because they would collect ice. They have an extra eyelid to protect their eyes from the bright sun.* |
| http://www .seaworld.org/ animal-info/info-books/polar-bear/ index.htm | *Polar bears are the largest land carnivores. Males are three times as large as the females.* | *They live in the Arctic and spend most of their time on ice and in the ocean traveling between ice flows.* | *They keep warm with fur and fat. They need to be careful about overheating so they walk slowly and swim to cool down.* | *They eat mainly ringed and bearded seals. They will also eat parts of beluga whales, walruses, narwhals, and bowhead whales.* | *Polar bears are considered marine mammals because they spend so much time in the ocean traveling between ice flows.* |

*Source:* International Reading Association and National Council of Teachers of English (1996).

## IRA/NCTE Standards for English Language Arts

10. Students whose first language is not English make use of their first language to develop competency in the English language arts and to develop understanding of content across the curriculum.

## DIFFERENTIATING INSTRUCTION FOR ENGLISH LANGUAGE LEARNERS

Data Charts provide categories for students to use in finding information within the text. To differentiate instruction for English language learners, provide explicit instruction in developing students' skills to survey the text prior to using the chart (Herrell & Jordan, 2006). For example, if the book has a table of contents and an index, help students use them to find information. Assist students in developing skills for finding information in charts, graphs, diagrams, and illustrations.

## DIFFERENTIATING INSTRUCTION FOR STUDENTS WITH SPECIAL NEEDS

Students who have reading and writing disabilities will frequently have problems looking for information in the text and organizing it for use, and the Data Chart provides an excellent scaffold for students with special needs. Data Charts will help them focus on the topic of study and organize the information for writing. To modify the strategy, teachers may do the following: (1) Select texts that are appropriate for students' reading level; (2) limit the number of texts; (3) limit the number of categories or essential questions that guide students' search for information; and (4) assist students in understanding the category or question, finding the information in the text, and using the information in writing the summary.

## REFERENCES

Antonacci, P. A., & O'Callaghan, C. M. (2006). *A handbook for literacy instructional and assessment strategies, K–8.* Boston: Allyn & Bacon.

Herrell, A. L., & Jordan, M. (2006). *50 strategies for improving vocabulary, comprehension, and fluency: An active learning approach* (2nd ed.). Upper Saddle River, NJ: Merrill Prentice Hall.

International Reading Association and National Council of Teachers of English. (1996). *Standards for the English language arts.* Newark, DE: International Reading Association and Urbana, IL: National Council of Teachers of English.

Tierney, R. J., & Readence, J. E. (2000). *Reading strategies and practices: A compendium* (5th ed.). Boston: Allyn & Bacon.

Tompkins, G. (2009). *50 literacy strategies: Step by step* (3rd ed.). Boston: Allyn & Bacon.

Wood, K. D., & Taylor, D. B. (2006). *Literacy strategies across the subject areas: Process-oriented blackline masters for the K–12 classroom* (2nd ed.). Boston: Allyn & Bacon.

## Children's Literature Cited

Gibbons, G. (2001). *Polar bears*. New York: Holiday House.

Goddard, J. (2008). *Polar bears*. New York: Scholastic.

Miller, D. S. (1997). *A polar bear journey*. Boston: Little, Brown.

Rosing, N. (with Carney, E.). (2007). *Face to face with polar bears*. Washington, DC: National Geographic Society.

Ryder, J. (2006). *A pair of polar bears: Twin cubs find a home at the San Diego Zoo*. New York: Simon & Schuster.

# Strategy
# 50

# Learning Logs

## SPEAKING BRIEFLY: AN OVERVIEW OF THE LITERACY STRATEGY

*Learning Logs* are an essential tool for learning through writing. Often referred to as learning journals, their wide use in classrooms has spawned a variety of purposes for the simple Learning Log. The Learning Log strategy is used by teachers who encourage students to write and draw their understanding of concepts and ideas that they learn through reading. For most teachers and students, the Learning Log is not a notebook of facts; rather, it is a written record of the students' interpretations of others' words, and it is their way of knowing and working out ideas they heard or read. Students use these logs as a tool for learning; in other words, they are writing to learn.

As students write down ideas they read or heard, they think about them more deeply and are more apt to understand and remember them (Fulwiler, 1987). Writing requires students to organize their ideas in ways that make sense, and when they return to their logs, they frequently revise their entries according to newly acquired or restructured knowledge. Learning Logs may be used across content areas, including English language arts, and are frequently used with thematic units as students record their ideas on a topic they are learning (Tompkins, 2007). Popp (1997, pp. 79–82) explains that although Learning Logs may be used for a variety of purposes and across all content areas, teachers should utilize an approach to help students explore the complexity of the ideas and concepts that they record. The model that she suggests is REACT: (1) *R*ecord ideas from reading, listening, viewing, or experiencing; (2) *E*valuate what was learned; (3) *A*sk questions that occurred during the learning process; (4) *C*onnect the new ideas with those already known; and (5) *T*ransform the ideas learned by expressing them in a visual such as an illustration, chart, graph, web, or diagram.

Learning Logs are not meant to be evaluated for content knowledge or for writing skills. However, the teacher evaluates students' Learning Logs to plan instruction and to monitor students' levels of understanding, misconceptions, or undeveloped concepts and ideas so that additional assistance may be given.

## USING LEARNING LOGS

*When to use the strategy:* The students use Learning Logs during and after reading, participating in a discussion, viewing a DVD, listening to a presentation, or taking a

### IRA/NCTE Standards for English Language Arts

1. Students read a wide range of print and nonprint texts to build an understanding of texts, of themselves, and of the cultures of the United States and the world; to acquire new information; to respond to the needs and demands of society and the workplace; and for personal fulfillment. Among these texts are fiction and nonfiction, classic and contemporary works.

3. Students apply a wide range of strategies to comprehend, interpret, evaluate, and appreciate texts. They draw on their prior experience, their interactions with other readers and writers, their knowledge of word meaning and of other texts, their word identification strategies, and their understanding of textual features (e.g., sound-letter correspondence, sentence structure, context, graphics).

5. Students employ a wide range of strategies as they write and use different writing process elements appropriately to communicate with different audiences for a variety of purposes.

field trip. They write and draw in their logs to enter ideas and thoughts that they have learned and frequently return to their journals to expand or reinterpret the initial ideas they have entered.

*Strategy modifications for grade levels:* Students in the primary grades use Learning Logs to demonstrate what they have learned. The teacher may demonstrate the process through interactive writing sessions with the class after a reading or discussion on a topic that they were learning about. In the intermediate and middle grades, students use Learning Logs independently.

## IMPLEMENTING THE LEARNING LOGS STRATEGY: STEP BY STEP

Students personalize their Learning Logs and may use them as they learn new ideas in various content areas.

1. **Define the purpose for using Learning Logs.** Establishing a purpose for using Learning Logs is especially important if students have no experience using them. Emphasize the role of the log as a tool for learning new ideas.

2. **Assist students in understanding what they will be writing in their logs.** One approach in helping students understand what types of entries are useful is to show them sample entries and explain why students decided to record them in their logs. Another approach is to demonstrate how and when to make entries in the log.

3. **Provide students with a simple structure for making entries in their logs.** Like good researchers, students need to keep track of where they acquired their information and when they recorded their entries. The teacher may offer a template similar to the one shown in Figure 50.1 that will help students organize their entries and responses.

4. **Direct students to use their Learning Logs at the appropriate times during the lesson.** After readings, discussions, hands-on activities, viewing a video, and participating in other learning experiences, have students think about some important ideas they have learned and enter them into their journals.

5. **Monitor students as they record their entries.** The teacher assists students individually, helping them expand and develop their ideas, offering them feedback and clarifying ideas, and providing mini-lessons to help students who may have misconceptions.

6. **Provide an approach that will assist students in reviewing and expanding their ideas.** The teacher may ask students to reflect on their ideas and expand their interpretations or may provide them with a structure to follow. The model suggested by Popp (1997) and discussed in the introduction is REACT:

   • *R*ecord ideas from reading, listening, viewing, or experiencing;

   • *E*valuate what was learned;

   • *A*sk questions that occurred during the learning process;

   • *C*onnect the new ideas with those already known; and

   • *T*ransform the ideas learned by expressing them in a visual such as an illustration, chart, graph, web, or diagram.

When using REACT, the teacher should assist students in following each step. For primary-grade students, the teacher may have students follow along with each step as she or he demonstrates how it is used.

## Applying the Learning Logs Strategy

One school celebrating Women's History Month visited the National Women's History Project at http://www.nwhp.org/whm/index.php. Each grade level participated with a different project. The fourth-graders chose to design a mural named after the theme, "2010 Writing Women Back Into History." The teacher introduced students to Learning Logs to record facts, information, and interesting stories from their readings. Each student was asked to select a book about a historical woman, famous or not-so-famous. Students read and kept notes in their journals about important facts and information that they thought would be of interest. Using their notes, they wrote summaries and drew pictures for their fourth-grade mural. One student wanted to be a reporter and found the book *The Daring Nellie Bly: America's Star Reporter* by Bonnie Christensen (2003). Figure 50.1 is an excerpt of her Learning Log, which she kept while reading and used to write about Nellie Bly.

*Source:* International Reading Association and National Council of Teachers of English (1996).

### IRA/NCTE Standards for English Language Arts

10. Students whose first language is not English make use of their first language to develop competency in the English language arts and to develop understanding of content across the curriculum.

## Differentiating Instruction for English Language Learners

Learning Logs will assist English language learners in developing an understanding of the content that they are learning. Especially important to their progress in literacy and achievement in the content areas is their development of the academic vocabulary. Students' understanding of conceptual knowledge may be emerging, but they may lack

| Figure 50.1 | Sample Page From a Student's Learning Log |

### My Notes on Nellie Bly
#### (Elizabeth Cochran)

Title: The Daring Nellie Bly: America's Star Reporter

Author: Bonnie Christensen

Nellie Bly became a reporter at a time when girls and women stayed home and took care of their kids. Her real name was Elizabeth Cochran and her pen name was Nellie Bly.

When she was young her father died, and her mother married again to a man who abused the family. She knew that she would get a job to take care of herself. The only job that she could get was a teaching job, but she had no money to finish college.

She was angry when women and girls were treated unfair. She stood up for her rights. Finally, she got a job as a reporter in Pittsburg and wrote stories how unfair women were treated.

She then worked for a newspaper called the New York World. She also wrote about the Women's Lunatic Asylum. This made her famous. When she wanted to go around the world, her boss thought it was great. But he did not want her to go he wanted a man to go.

March 8

the academic language to express their ideas. Teachers may differentiate their instruction by having English language learners sketch their ideas through the use of a variety of visuals, including pictures, graphs, diagrams, and webs. Working together and using a group discussion of the illustrations, the teacher will assist students in framing their ideas using accurate academic language.

## DIFFERENTIATING INSTRUCTION FOR STUDENTS WITH SPECIAL NEEDS

There are several ways that teachers may modify the Learning Log strategy for students with special needs who are disabled readers and writers. Before students write in their Learning Logs, the teachers should share the purpose for writing and model the process through an interactive writing session. When students feel confident and are ready to write in their Learning Logs, the teacher should offer support through the following: offering informal conversations about the topic of study; highlighting interesting ideas they have learned; and providing joint interpretations of pictures, graphs, and diagrams. The teacher needs to give students individual assistance as they write, which may be in the form of simple prompts or sharing the pen with them as they write. Monitoring students' Learning Logs will provide an opportunity for the teacher to determine whether further instruction is needed.

## REFERENCES

Fulwiler, T. (1987). *The journal book*. Portsmouth, NH: Boyton/Cook.

International Reading Association and National Council of Teachers of English. (1996). *Standards for the English language arts*. Newark, DE: International Reading Association and Urbana, IL: National Council of Teachers of English.

Popp, M. S. (1997). *Learning journals in the K–8 classroom: Exploring ideas and information in the content areas*. Mahwah, NJ: Erlbaum.

Tompkins, G. E. (2007). *Literacy for the 21st century: Teaching reading and writing in prekindergarten through grade 4*. Upper Saddle River, NJ: Merrill Prentice Hall.

## CHILDREN'S LITERATURE CITED

Christensen, B. (2003). *The daring Nellie Bly: America's star reporter.* New York: Knopf.

# Index

# About the Authors

**Patricia A. Antonacci** is a professor of education and teaches in the literacy education program at Iona College. Antonacci entered the teaching profession as a classroom teacher for the middle and elementary grades and continued as a reading specialist. Her long career in public schools brought her a range of experiences as a teacher at all grade levels, including a number of years working in diverse classroom settings. As a reading specialist for K through 12, she assisted teachers in integrating literacy instruction in content areas. Working in a large urban school district afforded her rich experiences teaching striving readers and English language learners.

Antonacci has taught courses at Fordham University and Iona College, including the following: reading in the content areas for middle and secondary grades, foundations of literacy, literacy across the curriculum, and action research in literacy. She has also mentored doctoral students in conducting research in literacy education. Currently, she is teaching courses in the literacy program at Iona College. She has published numerous journal articles and books, including (as coauthors) Antonacci and O'Callaghan, *Portraits of Literacy Development: Instruction and Assessment in a Well-Balanced Literacy Program, K–3* (2004); Antonacci and O'Callaghan, *A Handbook for Literacy Instructional and Assessment Strategies, K–8* (2006); and Antonacci and O'Callaghan, *Using Children's Literature Across the Curriculum: A Handbook of Instructional Strategies (K–8)* (2010).

**Catherine M. O'Callaghan** is a professor of education and chair of the Education Department at Iona College. She entered the teaching profession as a classroom teacher and continued her career as a literacy specialist with teaching experiences that span across the grades. Teaching in New York City within diverse settings afforded her a wide range of teaching experiences. Her doctoral degree in Language and Literacy from Fordham University initiated her research interests in new literacies, critical literacies, teacher education, and intervention plans for helping striving readers and writers. O'Callaghan began working with pre-service and in-service teachers at St. Joseph's College in the Child Study Department and as an adjunct at Fordham University in the School of Education. She currently teaches courses in literacy education at the graduate and undergraduate levels, including the following: language development, action research in literacy, literacy across the curriculum, and reading in the content areas. She is also involved in supervising in-service teachers who work with struggling readers and writers in the literacy practicum course.

O'Callaghan has published numerous journal articles and books, including (as coauthors) Antonacci and O'Callaghan, *Portraits of Literacy Development: Instruction and Assessment in a Well-Balanced Literacy Program, K–3* (2004); Antonacci and O'Callaghan, *A Handbook for Literacy Instructional and Assessment Strategies, K–8* (2006); and Antonacci and O'Callaghan, *Using Children's Literature Across the Curriculum: A Handbook of Instructional Strategies (K–8)* (2010).

# SAGE Research Methods Online
## The essential tool for researchers

**Sign up now at
www.sagepub.com/srmo
for more information.**

### An expert research tool

- An **expertly designed taxonomy** with more than 1,400 unique terms for social and behavioral science research methods

- **Visual and hierarchical search tools** to help you discover material and link to related methods

- Easy-to-use navigation tools
- Content organized by complexity
- Tools for citing, printing, and downloading content with ease
- Regularly updated content and features

### A wealth of essential content

- The most comprehensive picture of quantitative, qualitative, and mixed methods available today

- More than **100,000 pages of SAGE book and reference material** on research methods as well as editorially selected material from SAGE journals

- More than **600 books** available in their entirety online

**Launching 2011!**

**$SAGE** research methods online